DIY COMMUNITY ACTION

Neighbourhood problems a
community self-help

Liz Richardson

First published in Great Britain in 2008 by

The Policy Press
University of Bristol
Fourth Floor
Beacon House
Queen's Road
Bristol BS8 1QU
UK

Tel +44 (0)117 331 4054
Fax +44 (0)117 331 4093
e-mail tpp-info@bristol.ac.uk
www.policypress.org.uk

British Library Cataloguing in Publication Data
A catalogue record for this book is available from the British Library.

Library of Congress Cataloging-in-Publication Data
A catalog record for this book has been requested.

ISBN 978 1 84742 084 8 paperback
ISBN 978 1 84742 085 5 hardcover

Cover design by Qube design Associates, Bristol.
Front cover: photograph kindly supplied by www.thirdavenue.co.uk
Printed and bound in Great Britain by Henry Ling Ltd, Dorchester.

Contents

List of tables, figures and boxes

Tables

Figures

Boxes

ONE

Introduction

This book is about what people in low-income neighbourhoods are doing to improve the places where they live. It is about why they put themselves forward as volunteers, what they are able to achieve and how. It is about how residents and service providers can work together. Most importantly, it is about how 'Do-It-Yourself' community action fits into the bigger picture of work by local and central government and others on neighbourhood renewal, community building and social inclusion. And it is about how more formal organisations can help support the creation and development of community self-help activity.

The core material on which the book is based is drawn from in-depth group interviews with around 300 community volunteers working in 82 deprived neighbourhoods across England and Wales. Contact was made with these community groups, and hundreds of others, through a five-year experimental national programme, called the Gatsby Training and Small Grant Project, which was designed to stimulate and facilitate community self-help action in low-income neighbourhoods.

DIY community action

In this book the term 'DIY community action' is used interchangeably with 'community self-help activity' and is taken to mean: *informal groups of people, acting on a voluntary basis, working together to solve common problems by taking action themselves, and with others.* While much community self-help is organised around neighbourhoods, it can also be organised around a shared concern across neighbourhoods. It is where people do something themselves to directly tackle problems. The scale of the activity might be modest, and could take the form of, for example, organising a youth disco, digging and planting a communal garden, hiring a coach for a social outing or running a community drop-in house.

Community self-help can (and should) have outside supporters – it may even be initiated by outside agencies such as public sector bodies. But in essence, the groups' members dictate the activity as a response to the needs of the wider community. It often involves residents working with the public sector, for example lobbying a social landlord or local council for better facilities. Community self-help is a form of community engagement – people getting involved in decision making by the police, the planning department, or whoever. But, it involves more than residents commenting on what *someone else* should be doing.

The definition of 'DIY community action' used here is about informal collective activity, although it is often difficult to say definitively where the informal ends and the formal begins. Formality increases by degree, rather than a jump. Some community groups have constitutions, others have legal structures, and some have neither. Some have paid staff, but most have no paid help. The Gatsby Training and Small Grant Project assessed whether community volunteers dominated decision making and did the bulk of the work, which was strongly linked to the size and scale of their operation and their financial turnover.

The importance of neighbourhood conditions

The community groups that were interviewed through the Gatsby Project talked about damaged and delicate neighbourhood conditions, about why community mattered to residents and how public service provision impacted on their lives. Active community volunteers talked about why they bothered and how people in poor areas felt they could help make things better. They talked about what success they had had, how the group related to the wider community, how their members worked together, what barriers they faced and what external support they valued.

Many of the problems, past and present, in the social housing estates where the groups' members live demonstrate the importance of how poor neighbourhoods are managed. The residents gave examples to illustrate what could happen when management organisations performed badly, and their concerns chime strongly with the high political priority given to the ongoing task of improving the effective delivery of core public services. Given the scale of the task of improving public services, the study explored service users' worries and problems, how organisational culture affected how public services were delivered to the residents and what day-to-day ground-level jobs could make a difference to residents on the estates.

Social capital and community engagement

The study focused on geographical neighbourhoods, and the relationships between people within them. 'Community', embracing both the places where people live and the relationships between the people who live in those places, continues to be highly relevant for residents. Despite the many problems that people experience in deprived neighbourhoods, there are also positive signs of resilience, often described by residents as a 'community spirit'. Such signs of community spirit include the existence of supportive friendship networks and community-led activity. These relationships and positive signs of valued social activity within neighbourhoods are forms of what has been called 'social capital', which refers to the shared resources that being able to work together, and get along together, gives to an area or group. Like other forms of capital such as human and financial capital, social capital is an asset for deprived areas, and in academic and policy circles there has been a renewed interest in the role played by social capital in people's quality of life (Aldridge and Halpern, 2002; Babb, 2005). The 2000 Local Government Act gave local authorities a power to do 'anything' that would improve the economic, social and environmental 'well-being' of local communities. But talking about people getting along together in a neighbourhood may sound to some like an old-fashioned ideal or a modern piece of 'fluffy' thinking – is it an outmoded perspective to talk about 'community'? A key motivator for the groups was their desire to see a stronger sense of community, and this study explores what kinds of communities they were trying to build, why community mattered to people and whether an emphasis on community meant that privacy and tolerance of difference were sacrificed.

Community engagement is at the heart of this story. It is also now at the heart of policies across political parties. The New Labour administration promoted a role for citizen engagement in civil renewal, public service improvement, neighbourhood renewal and neighbourhood governance and local government reform (Home Office, 2005a; ODPM and Home Office, 2005; DCLG, 2006). And the Conservative Party has argued for the community and voluntary sectors and social enterprises to play a much bigger role in fighting poverty, educational failure, drug addiction and worklessness (SJPG, 2006). Local authorities, regeneration organisations, health authorities, landlords, the police, schools and others are making efforts to consult and involve communities in decisions that affect service users and local people. There are many challenges facing organisations that are trying to engage with customers and communities, such as, what a community engagement and community building strategy would look like, whether the minority of self-selecting people who shout the loudest – 'the usual suspects' – are a stumbling block to getting genuinely representative feedback and what gives a minority of active participants the right to advocate on behalf of other residents.

New recognition of the role of broad community consultation, together with the growth of partnership working arrangements, has prompted a re-examination of the structures of local democracy. In particular some local councillors now fear that their role is being downgraded, if not displaced, by these newly created partnerships. The weak state of local democracy, as evidenced by low turnouts for local elections in many areas, shows the need for democratic renewal. This study discusses whether a focus on community engagement takes away from locally elected members' roles, how grassroots participatory democracy and representative formal democracy can work together and in what ways they differ or complement each other.

The residents interviewed believed that local councils and service providers carried direct responsibilities for making their areas better places. They placed great emphasis on the need for longer-term strategic plans to tackle difficult-to-manage and difficult-to-live-in neighbourhoods, alongside better coordination of services, partnership working between public, private, voluntary and community sectors and community involvement. Improving mainstream services and tackling neighbourhood problems on a wider scale is part of neighbourhood renewal, and the residents were involved as supportive partners, as consultees and lobbyists for a neighbourhood renewal agenda. They wanted to be round the table and have the opportunity to influence the work. Neighbourhood renewal is very closely linked to tackling social exclusion, because existing residents should be given more opportunities to get on in life; it is not just about making the neighbourhood more attractive. The groups in the study show how difficult it is sometimes to link people into the mainstream, and to bring neighbourhood conditions up to the standard of better-off areas.

Residents showed clearly where problems existed in their neighbourhoods and what those problems were, and much of their anger and motivation to get things put right was about tackling these problems. However, the Gatsby Training and Small Grant Project was not designed to create or build large-scale neighbourhood renewal interventions. The Project did support groups to do 'community engagement' as commonly understood, that is, residents influencing work by other organisations, including helping people make links to key agencies in their estates. But it could not, of itself, stimulate area-wide regeneration, or put communities in the lead role. The programmes were primarily designed to facilitate another less understood and acknowledged aspect of community engagement, that is, communities engaging with themselves. The groups involved with the Project are making their own contribution to solving problems through their community self-help activity.

The groups' community self-help activity was generally in the form of small-scale projects such as youth activities, creating small areas of green space, play schemes and tea bars, and the organisations doing this work were made up of non-professionals, operating at a small scale on a voluntary basis. Their projects were often developed ad hoc and outside either a local- or a national-level coordinated approach to area problems. Even when they were part of strategic interventions led by much larger organisations, much of what they did could seem trivial in the face of more deep-seated area problems and broader exclusionary trends (Richardson and Mumford, 2002). In practice, it is very difficult to assess the value of community self-help. The book explores what contribution the groups made and whether our proposition that small neighbourly actions form a vital web of social life holds up. It examines whether their work contributed to neighbourhood building or social inclusion, and whether it was necessary for people to do this work themselves or if it could have been better delivered by bigger organisations not working on a self-help basis. It also considers how the volunteers saw their work fitting with that of bigger agencies.

Community involvement and self-help rely on people volunteering, and the government has set targets of increasing volunteering, particularly among people at risk of social exclusion. The research explored why some people put themselves forward, why some tried to solve local problems rather than rely on formal channels, and whether it mattered that only a minority were actively involved. The groups offered models of people taking individual and collective responsibility. Could they be seen as exemplars of active citizenship? If the evidence is that the groups do play a valuable role, then we need to understand how they develop and continue playing that role, especially if we want to have more of this type of activity.

The groups could be seen to be doing something of negligible value, or, at the very least, to be engaged in activity to which it is difficult to assign a value, or easily identify significant impacts. Their activity is being organised by people who may never have done such an activity before, and they rely on voluntary contributions. Their organisations are barely funded, mostly unincorporated and informal. In the main, no one asked the groups to do what they do; they took it upon themselves to start projects, and got varying levels of backing from external parties. Community self-help activity can therefore be fragile and often needs nurturing. The Gatsby Project aimed to provide some forms of nurturing for community self-help to assist in groups' attempts to overcome their lack of connection to mainstream activity, their lack of recognition, lack of capacity or confidence. Nearly all the groups that were involved in the project levered in other external support, and while some of this was of good quality and valued by the groups, other community development help was of poorer quality. The renewed emphasis on community engagement has given momentum to the community development world, underlining the need to raise and maintain standards of community development work. This study examines which forms of capacity building were valued by groups, and which were not.

The Gatsby Project piloted its community development approach based on bringing people together using residential training as the starting point for problem solving and community organisation. Pump-priming grants linked into training then underlined the connection between learning and doing. The idea tested was to see whether groups that had never done anything similar before could start something new, if they wanted to. Through this we wanted to test community capacity for renewal through local self-help initiatives. The project itself was a catalyst for change, and the creation of many small grant funds by local authorities and others, such as Community Chests, shows how this approach is gaining support. A question to consider is whether ideas and skills are as important as funding – why not just give people the money?

The structure of the book

In Chapter Two we describe the Gatsby Project, the study areas and the groups. We look at how the information was collected, analyse what people told us, what possible biases we and the groups have, and how these were overcome.

In Chapter Three we look at the neighbourhoods in which the residents live and operate. We explore aspects of community that affect residents, particularly the management of homes and neighbourhoods by social landlords. We explore the following questions: what do services do to tackle, or exacerbate, physical and social disorganisation in disadvantaged neighbourhoods? How do service providers fulfil their responsibilities? How does the way they do this impact on their users? We then examine communities as people. What does 'community' mean to residents? What positive and negative features do communities have for the people in them? What are the tensions within communities between members? How do residents see more difficult, disruptive and vulnerable members?

In Chapter Four we show how the work of the groups contributes to tackling social exclusion and neighbourhood decline. At first sight the things the groups do seem like worthy activities but drops in the ocean compared to the scale of problems. This chapter explores how we understand the value the groups' work has, what the groups actually do in practice, how their work makes small in roads into serious deep-seated neighbourhood problems, whether we can create more social capital and citizenship on the back of community self-help activity, and what the difficulties are in getting credible evidence about the value of small-scale community activity.

In Chapter Five we explore the triggers that generate citizen involvement and community self-help activity. Neighbourhood problems do not automatically mean that people will respond. This chapter considers why some people put their heads above the parapet to take local action, and what motivates community volunteers. It looks at how altruistic their concern is, and whether it is fair to expect those with the least advantages to do the most to compensate for others' failures. Are we letting mainstream providers off the hook? How does community involvement actually work to affect service provision?

In Chapter Six we examine the internal workings of community organisations, how these informal associations organise themselves, how they develop internally in order to deliver activities and services, what leadership models they have, what organisational problems they experience, how they create systems and procedures for their work and what a 'good' community group looks like.

In Chapter Seven we examine whether people's good intentions are enough, what legitimacy the community organisations have to act on behalf of other residents and how they relate to the wider community, and whether that makes the groups 'representative'. We also look at where they sit in the context of other forms of representation and local democracy, and how they link in with wider bodies.

In Chapter Eight we explore the many barriers and obstacles that groups have to contend with, as well as the support they receive. We explore the limits of what groups can, or want to, do, and the potential there is to facilitate groups' work. We also look at whether the groups are financially sustainable. Given the problems of 'apathy', we consider whether it matters that only a minority get involved. We also discuss whether community organisations are geared up to meet new expectations, such as service delivery. The personal costs and downsides for volunteers are explored. We look at the range of external supports the groups receive, what kind of help they get and where it comes from, what forms of support the groups value and what potential there is to facilitate groups to do more.

In Chapter Nine we point to some of the bigger issues connected with these problems, such as whether people still need 'communities', whether we are talking about a golden age that never was, and why a focus on economic renewal is not an alternative. We explore why neighbourhoods matter, whether it is patronising residents to talk of community self-help solutions, what role community self-help plays, what the implications are for strategies to engage and build communities and what all this means for national and local government, social landlords, other service providers and residents in trying to create and maintain thriving neighbourhoods and communities.

Findings

Our conclusion is that residents in difficult-to-live-in and difficult-to-manage neighbourhoods often chose collective solutions to combat communal problems. Active community groups were positive about the idea of community and of the social relationships that this entailed because it helped people to rub along together, and help each other out in times of trouble. They believed that strong community ties added to their ability to tackle difficult conditions and neighbourhood neglect. Active residents in social housing neighbourhoods saw their voluntary contributions positively in the context of work by other agencies to revive difficult areas. They wanted to see 'everybody doing their bit', including residents, the police, the council and landlords. While recognising the limits of their role, they argued that the unique position of residents as insiders in neighbourhoods meant that they could provide a service to other residents in ways that professionals could not. There were many examples, however, where residents felt forced into doing something because of the failure of service providers to take the necessary action. Ultimately, they supported the principle of community self-help as fundamentally more empowering for the 'beneficiaries' of help, even where they saw themselves as the 'givers' and others as the 'receivers', precisely because their fortunes were woven together within the same community. The advantage of community self-help was to create a sense of civic responsibility in places where cynicism about change was high, but where needs were dominating and the urge to solve problems overwhelmingly strong in 'natural' community leaders.

Community-based activities are often undertaken by a minority of self-selected people. Their legitimacy as representatives is based on their ability to engage with their neighbours through the activities they organise, and through informal relationships that appear to support their initiatives. Their mandate to organise activities is based on the usage of the services they provide. The minority create benefits for the majority. We collected over 450 examples of community work that we judged to have improved the delivery of public services, increased levels of citizenship and social inclusion, increased opportunities for the creation and strengthening of social networks and social capital, improved the physical environment and provided ideas for replication.

There are clear links between community building, neighbourhood viability and tackling social exclusion. However, the role of small community organisations should not be seen as a substitute for but as complementary to mainstream institutions. The groups play a liaison and brokering role between residents and services. The worm's-eye view of residents can provide invaluable information for mainstream services on how services impact on the ground – positively and negatively. Their detailed experiences highlight the importance of ground-level supervision on estates, dedicated and approachable staff, good customer care and continual reinvestment in buildings, institutions and environments. And importantly, the groups had positive suggestions for change, many of which have been welcomed and implemented by statutory services, for example different ways to deal with empty houses other than boarding them up, or more flexible ways to allocate social housing to create more stable communities.

TWO

Talking to communities

'You're the only nosey person we've had! No seriously, it's nice to see that someone's interested in everything we've done. It's like a pat on the back.' (resident, Walsall)

The study areas

The study covered groups of community volunteers working in low-income neighbourhoods in the UK. All of the people interviewed and visited had been involved in a five-year experimental national programme to stimulate and facilitate community self-help actions in low-income neighbourhoods – the Gatsby Training and Small Grant Project. The Gatsby Charitable Foundation funded the project for £1.25 million over five years, from 1996 to 2001.

We used the interviews and visits with the community groups in order to better understand how communities operate, how services impact on neighbourhoods, how and why citizens decide to help themselves and how others can support them in doing so.

Despite concern about some deprived communities being over-researched to date, none of the groups chosen for this study had been researched before, and they were not aware of any research having taken place in their neighbourhoods. Other than a handful of examples of national recognition, their work was not known in the public domain, other than some local coverage. The material for the bulk of this book was gathered using face-to-face group interviews during visits on home turf to active members of 82 community groups based in low-income neighbourhoods. The groups were running 90 different community-led and run projects that had been grant-funded in the four years between 1997 and 2000 under the Gatsby Project.

The 82 groups interviewed were drawn from a larger pool of 1,800 people from over 700 groups that participated in 93 residential community training courses organised by the project between March 1996 and February 2001. We used written feedback from over 1,600 training participants, looking at the project's outcomes and at barriers identified by the groups to their work.

The majority of study neighbourhoods were social housing estates made up of less than 1,000 homes. The study groups were mostly small, unincorporated tenants' and residents' associations, youth groups and community associations, with average annual turnovers of under £5,000. Many were newly started groups at the point they got involved with the Project. They were engaged in a wide range of small-scale community activities.

The groups' work, experiences and opinions were that of a selection of relatively unusual people in low-income neighbourhoods, in that they were active volunteers (although many of their views and priorities do reflect those of the national population). The larger pool of 700 groups that attended training courses were already in a minority as active community volunteers. Based on our work, and other sources (for a list of data sources, see Ruston, 2001), discussed more fully in Chapter Eight, we estimate that these community volunteers involved in local neighbourhood issue groups make up somewhere between 1% and 7% of the population in the most deprived wards.

The 82 groups interviewed were all those groups that applied for and were awarded grant funding for 90 projects between 1997 and 2000. The project funded a total of 115 projects over the five years to 2001.

The community volunteers the findings were based on had many different viewpoints, but shared some common features: they were concerned about their neighbourhood enough to have done something about a particular issue; they were organised enough to have joined or formed a local group; and they were networked enough to have accessed support from a national community training organisation. They were in a minority in their neighbourhoods, and had put themselves forward for community work. The people interviewed were well informed about aspects of their neighbourhood[1] precisely because of their active involvement. Groups' members were able to give us an insight into their motivations, and the internal workings of their informal organisations. Additional back-up evidence was used where possible to confirm details about the groups' work, including external 'referees' and photographs.

This chapter describes the Gatsby Project in more detail, the information collected, the grant-funded projects and groups, the study neighbourhoods and research methods.

The Gatsby Project

The Gatsby Project was a five-year experimental national programme to stimulate and facilitate community self-help actions in low-income neighbourhoods, and it ran between 1996 and 2001. It was led by LSE Housing, a research group within the Centre for the Analysis of Social Exclusion at the London School of Economics and Political Science. The Gatsby Charitable Foundation, one of the Sainsbury Family Charitable Trusts, supported the work. The project was organised in partnership with Trafford Hall,[2] home of the National Communities Resource Centre, a charity set up in 1991 to offer training and support to residents in low-income areas.

The Gatsby Training and Small Grant Project started with the 'million-dollar' question: what would you do if you had, say, one million pounds to help combat social exclusion in needy communities? The aim was to test out whether it was possible to unlock people's desire and potential to solve community problems, how residents' desire to see their neighbourhoods improve could develop into practical

The Gatsby Project was delivered in partnership with Trafford Hall, home of the National Communities Resource Centre

action – from 'something must be done' to 'we can do this'. It was premised on the notion that self-help is intrinsic to human survival, is an instinctive form of self-preservation, but also links with social organisation and a 'sense of community'. A programme was proposed to generate many small ground-level projects through capacity building for groups. This approach was then tested out, with the support of the Gatsby Charitable Foundation (Power and Richardson, 2001).

The model used in the project combined intensive residential training for community organisations on community organising and action planning, with a small grant fund to help participants put ideas into practice back in their own areas. The residential training courses covered practical 'how-to' subjects, such as how to work with young people, how to improve environments and how to run community facilities. The small grant fund supported projects such as community centres, youth activities, community gardens, cafes, parents and toddlers groups, after-school clubs, fishing trips and advice sessions.

The majority of participants in the project came from social housing areas. The project offered 20 grant awards a year of up to £5,000 and awarded a total of 115 grants in total over five years to the end of 2001 – an average of 23 per year. We visited all of the projects that received awards from the small grant fund until 2000 and interviewed the people involved.

Researchers from the London School of Economics and Political Science (including the current author) designed the shape of the project, and outlined specifications for the training and small grant programmes. Alterations and adaptations to the training programme were negotiated, and the researchers helped make grant award decisions. Follow-up action by groups that attended the training

Over 1,800 community volunteers came on Gatsby training courses

programme and the grant-funded projects was tracked, and developmental work done, for example to see if the groups' expansion could be accelerated.

Further detail on the training projects and small grant funds is included in the Appendix.

Types of community group

The groups that received grant funding from the Gatsby Project that were interviewed were mostly small, unincorporated tenants' and residents' associations, youth groups and community associations, with average annual turnovers of under £5,000. Most were not registered charities, and therefore represented a handful of 'the thousands of small community-based groups that are under the radar beam of regulators' (NCVO, 2006a, p 3). Even so, the groups were typical of just over half (56%) of the voluntary sector (that is, registered general charities) that had an annual income per small charity of less than £10,000 in 2003/04. New groups starting out ran just under half of the projects. The grant was the first grant, or grant of that size, for two thirds of the groups, including groups that had been in existence for a number of years. The Gatsby Project had aimed to reach embryonic or start-up groups and activity. In total a quarter of the groups were made up of people in work. Most of those in employment, however, were in low-paid jobs. In total, half the 82 groups were predominately made up of people who were not working, mostly under retirement age. Seven of the 82 group leaders were from minority ethnic groups and 14 of the groups had ethnically mixed memberships among the core of the groups' active volunteers. Of the groups working in ethnically mixed neighbourhoods, only one group did not have any minority members. The remainder had either minority leaders, committee members or volunteers, as well as users.

More information on the community groups involved in the project is given in the Appendix.

Types of community project

Geographical spread and area size of the interview groups

The community projects covered a relatively wide geographical area and had a strong neighbourhood focus, particularly on small neighbourhoods of under 2,000 homes. This is in line with other definitions of neighbourhood scale, for example, it has been argued that areas of between roughly 500 and 2,000 homes form 'natural' or 'home' neighbourhoods (The Young Foundation, 2005), and:

> Recognisable urban neighbourhood for social and management purposes [are] rarely more than 5,000 households. (Power, 2004, p 2)

The 90 projects were spread across England, Wales and Scotland, as shown by Figure 2.1.

Table 2.1 shows the regional breakdown of projects using the government's regional boundaries.

The 82 groups running the projects were based in 76 different places. Twelve of the groups were based in the same neighbourhood. Twenty covered a broader area than the neighbourhood itself, for example a group for Chinese women across Leeds. The study areas were therefore made up of 56 neighbourhoods, plus 20 broader areas covering several neighbourhoods.

The 20 wider area groups had a neighbourhood focus, but across several neighbourhoods. Thirteen were town or city centre-based or town and city centre-wide for particular communities of interest. Most of the groups' members

Figure 2.1: Map showing the Gatsby Project study areas and grant projects

Table 2.1: Regional spread of community projects in the study

Region	Number of projects	% of total projects	Rank
North West	28	31	1
Wales	14	15.5	2
West Midlands	11	12	3
Yorkshire and Humberside	10	11	4
East Midlands	9	10	5
London	6	7	6
South East	4	4	7
North/North East	3	3	8
East	2	2	9
South West	2	2	10
Scotland	1	1	11
Total	**90**	**98.5**	

and users were drawn from low-income neighbourhoods. The other seven were town- or area-wide groups providing particular services for all client groups, for example a community newspaper covering ex-mining villages and council estates across three wards and an environmental recycling organisation focusing on deprived, predominantly Asian neighbourhoods in Birmingham.

The 56 neighbourhoods in which the majority of the groups were based were areas you could walk across. Two thirds (38) consisted of fewer than 1,000 homes; 16 of these small neighbourhoods were actually areas with 500 units or less. In total, four fifths (45) were made up of less than 2,000 homes.

We do not have the precise figures for six of the 56 neighbourhoods because of the nature of those places, which, at the time we visited, were undergoing major physical change such as demolition and rebuilding of homes at different densities. These neighbourhoods were all around 2,000 units.

Types of neighbourhoods and areas

The groups were working in low-income areas and with disadvantaged people. They were working in some of the most difficult and disadvantaged areas. Twenty-two of the 76 neighbourhoods and wider areas the groups covered were ethnically mixed, and just over two thirds (54) had a predominately white British population. This reflects the breakdown of social housing tenants more broadly.

There were 20 groups that covered an area wider than a single neighbourhood, and 12 of these focused on:

- struggling black and minority ethnic communities
- young people at risk

- people with physical disabilities or mental health problems
- families under stress
- adult learners
- social housing tenants across a borough.

In total, eight of the 20 wider area groups worked with people from client groups that lived in specific social housing or low-income areas. For example, the two groups providing support for families under stress drew their members and users from a range of social housing estates in those towns.

Fifty-six groups covered a specific neighbourhood. We used the ACORN classification of neighbourhoods to look further at the nature of these. (ACORN is a commercial tool used to classify neighbourhoods, based on linking a combination of Census data, market research and other lifestyle databases.) The 2001 classification clustered areas into six 'types', within which there were 17 groups, containing a total of 54 sub-categories of area. We used the 2001 classifications to classify the areas[3] (CACI Ltd, 2001).

In total, three quarters (43 out of the 56) of the study neighbourhoods fell into the lowest socio-economic type of the six 'types', the 'striving' type of area. By comparison nationally, 22% of the UK population lived in that type of area (CACI Ltd, 2001).

Within the 'striving' type, a third of the 56 neighbourhoods (19) were in the 'council estates with better-off homes' group. This included the sub-categories of:

- council areas, residents with health problems
- council areas with young families, some home owners
- low-rise council housing, less well-off families.

Another third (18) were 'council estates' in the 'greatest hardship' or 'high unemployment' groups. These included the sub-categories of:

- council flats, very high unemployment, singles
- council flats, elderly people, health problems
- council areas, high unemployment, lone parents
- council flats, greatest hardship, many lone parents.

Also within the 'striving' type, four groups were in neighbourhoods classified as 'people in multi-ethnic low-income areas' and two of the community groups were in the 'older people, less prosperous areas' category.

Another nine neighbourhoods (16%) were a mix of the following groups:

- skilled workers, home-owning areas
- new home owners, mature communities (including the category of 'local authority areas, some new home owners').

Nationally 38% of the UK population lived in those types of areas (CACI Ltd, 2001).We were unable to get classifications for the remaining four groups, either because the group covered too small an area (for example, 'single sheltered housing block in otherwise aspiring/affluent area', or because of lack of availability of a classification on ACORN).

None of the groups worked in neighbourhoods in the top three ACORN 'types', which were 'thriving' affluent suburban and rural areas where 19.6% of the UK population lived, 'expanding' affluent family areas where 11.6% of the population lived, or 'rising' affluent urban areas where 8.6% of the population lived (CACI Ltd, 2001).

Two thirds of the neighbourhoods were predominantly social housing areas. Across the UK, in the period we did the research, just over a fifth of all households lived in social housing (23% in 1996 falling slightly to 21% in 2001) (ODPM, 2002). Three quarters of the 56 neighbourhoods had been subject to special regeneration initiatives and spending, such as the Single Regeneration Budget, Estate Action, City Challenge, Housing Action Trusts, Objective 1 and 2, European Social Fund, European Regional Development Fund, Health Action Zones and New Deal for Communities, as well as schemes developed locally by local authorities and landlords.

We now describe the research in more detail – what information was collected and how this was done, and the structure of the neighbourhood visits.

Methods

Basic monitoring information was collected throughout the project, including how many people went on courses, where they were from, how old they were and if they were tenants or owner-occupiers. We collected basic information about the throughputs of the grant programme, such as the number of grants awarded, what courses the applicants had attended, when the applications were made, how much and what the application was for.

Information on training

Everyone who attended a training course was asked to complete a two-page written feedback form at the end of the last day of training. This form asked about how satisfied people had been with the course, if the training had given participants new ideas, what they felt they had learnt from and got out of the experience, what they liked about the training and any suggestions for changes: 90% of participants completed a form, a total of over 1,600 responses.

We attended 20 of the training courses to gather observations and to talk to participants. This helped us to develop and adapt the courses and was an important quality check that complemented the written feedback from participants. While we sat in on the courses, we met and chatted to around 100 groups on training courses, listening to their experiences of their neighbourhood and their work.

Information about groups' activity

After a training course had finished, people went back to their neighbourhoods. We waited three to four weeks to give people a chance to talk to the rest of their groups, and hopefully start putting their plans into action. We then wrote to everyone, asking about what had happened since the course. We gave people three to four weeks to reply, so most of the responses were received six to eight weeks after the training. Using a simple two-page form and SAE, we asked about the groups' follow-up work, if the training had helped them, what support they had and what barriers they faced. Fifty-two per cent of individual participants sent forms back and gave their opinions, for example how useful they as an individual had found the course. The courses were designed to encourage action by groups (rather than individuals). Sometimes we received forms from several members of the same group. We counted some outcomes by group, for example if they had taken action following the course. We got information back from 66% of the groups (around 460 groups), which was a very high response rate for a postal survey, where expected response rates are usually nearer 10-30%.

The information from the larger pool of 460 groups was on a self-report basis. In Chapter Eight we use this information from the training participants to look at the outcomes of the Gatsby Project: if it was a successful way of stimulating and supporting community activity, what kind of support groups value and the barriers faced by these groups.

Visits and interviews with groups that got grants

The material for the other parts of the book was gathered through more in-depth discussion with a number of the groups that had participated in the training. We talked in-depth to all 82 groups that received grant funding for 90 different projects between 1997 and 2000 under the Gatsby Project. We interviewed and visited the groups that had been grant-funded by the project in this period. We visited the groups at around six to nine months after they had been awarded grant funding, over a period of four years. We saw groups of between two and ten people, but typically three or four of the core group members, plus any workers or external 'referees' for the groups' work.

We interviewed workers and sympathetic external commentators alongside the groups for 19 of the 82 groups.

In the interviews, we asked about the following topics:

- the area and general background
- the neighbourhood: what size; how old; history of neighbourhood; built type; people living there; facilities; popularity; neighbourhood problems and positives

- services in the neighbourhood: how services performed; how homes were managed; what the problems and successes were; what relationships residents had with service providers
- the community groups and their work: their history; previous activity; current work and progress; problems and successes; barriers; funding and fundraising; structures and internal relationships, memberships and relationship with the wider community
- groups' external links: community development supports; membership of partnerships and other links; relationship to Trafford Hall training and small grant programmes.

Structure of the visits

We spent a total of around four hours on each visit to the groups in the neighbourhoods, often in people's own homes, or in community meeting places. We typically saw three or four residents per visit, but group numbers varied between two to eight in total including residents and supporters. As well as the semi-structured interview, we did an estate walkabout to clarify neighbourhood issues and visually check information on things like disrepair, empty homes, vandalism etc. We tried to observe activities in operation whenever possible, such as sitting in on youth sessions, or eating in community cafes. We always visited facilities developed by the group such as community gardens, play areas or community buildings. We also saw back-up documentary evidence where available, such as sign-in attendance lists, surveys, photographs and newsletters.

Our primary focus was on work that had been grant-funded by the Gatsby Project. However, the groups were also engaged in other projects and pieces of work, not grant-funded by the project. Examples of the full spread of groups' work have been included in this book.

Following the interviews, extensive written notes of the interviews were typed up in full. We then analysed the material under the different issues people raised, and the common themes that emerged. For each topic, we counted the number of separate comments referring to different points, or stand-alone examples for that point. The direction the interviews took was guided by the semi-structured interview schedule, and by the groups' areas of interest.

We went back to see a selection of four of the groups to establish a more structured and systematic assessment of their quality. We selected four groups that we had previously visited and judged to be performing at different levels, from poor to excellent, and that represented a range of organisational styles (stronger or weaker team, closed or open leadership, more or less experienced). We tried to define what we meant by a 'good' community group, and we used exercises to explore further the groups' internal relationships, their common goals, their relationships to the wider community and their external links. The results of this work are documented in Chapter Six.

Issues in the research interviews and analysis

The interviews were partly basic monitoring of grant-funded work, partly developmental evaluation of grant-funded work and partly research into communities and community groups. This presented a potential conflict of interest for the groups, in that their ability to be open and honest was potentially constrained by their desire to put on a good performance for the grant monitor. This tension had to be managed through the relationship developed between the researcher and the interviewees. We emphasised that we were there to learn from the interviewees. We feel the results of the interviews indicate that the groups did share problems as well as achievements, and that they were forthright in their comments.

Informal evidence

While we did collect back-up documentary evidence, this was often informal in style. The groups did not have much formal written material on themselves or their work, such as an annual report or other performance reports. This meant that other sorts of documentary evidence were very important. We were shown press cuttings of both local bad episodes as well as successes. In particular, photographs were extremely useful as corroboration of before-and-after transformations, or of attendance at events. This was an important way for the groups to evidence their work, given the difficultly for small community organisations of collecting and presenting evidence in more formal ways.

Outsiders' opinions

Another way we tried to confirm what the group told us was to talk to a referee, that is, someone outside the group in a position of authority who knew of the group's work. The referees were identified by the group on their grant application, or in discussion with the group when preparing for the visit. This was not ideal as a way of getting a wholly neutral opinion as the groups naturally tried to invite someone external who could give them a positive report. However, this was a way of them showing that they had managed to win local backing from people or organisations of standing in their local communities, an important measure of their credibility in itself. External stakeholders we spoke to included headteachers, local clergy, community development workers, housing managers, police officers and local councillors.

Our biases

As all the interviews and analysis of the material was carried out by the author of this work, this has the advantage of giving a relatively consistent interpretation of the material, and the opportunity for detailed comparisons. However, it also has the disadvantage of giving the work unavoidable biases. The project was a piece of action research, and the author was directly involved in creating and overseeing it. The research was not intended to be an experimental evaluation of the impact of the project (for a longer discussion about using experimental or economic evaluation methods, see Sefton et al, 2002). The work was used to try to understand how the groups operated, what they did, what happened as a result of particular interventions and people's explanations.

The starting point for the research was that, in principle, community organising has many potential benefits and pitfalls. The sympathetic relationships that were developed with the subject and subjects of the investigation enabled the interviewees to talk to us with a degree of honesty that may not have been possible otherwise. What was up for grabs was the effectiveness of particular individual groups or projects. The Gatsby Project team waited to be convinced on the detail of the groups' work, representativeness and quality of their organisation. In the Project we struggled to find good measures and comparators to back up the validity of the findings, because of the nature of the activities we were investigating – mostly undocumented, not captured by existing data and unregulated in the main. The face-to-face visit and use of innovative forms of evidence such as photographs were ways we used to overcome this.

The groups' biases

The groups and people interviewed had some obvious biases. They had already jumped several hoops to qualify for a grant award. They therefore represented the possibilities for community organising by stronger community groups. The examples given in this book are of groups that had achieved some success – they engaged in community activity out of choice, and it is likely that they would want to present their work in a positive light. To counter this bias, we used specific examples of their work and relationship to the wider community, about which we collected as much detail as possible, down to the actual dates that events were held, the names and backgrounds of helpers, numbers attending, what refreshments were served and how much they cost. This was to try and unpick exaggeration and unsupported positive statements. Their self-critical insights, fears and doubts have been presented to give as balanced a picture as possible of community self-help.

More significantly, the perceptions of the community representatives of the importance of community are open to question. It may initially seem self-serving to suggest that residents who are directly involved in defending communities are in any way evidence for the value of community to residents, but it must be remembered that part of the volunteers' initial motivations for becoming involved in residents' groups or neighbourhood-focused groups, rather than volunteering elsewhere for the many other possible worthy causes there are, was their pre-existing interest, as ordinary individuals, in the places where they live, the welfare of their neighbours and the things that they saw directly affecting them.

The other issue is how well placed residents were to judge their own situations and that of their areas. The people we spoke to were well informed about their neighbourhoods. Some of this was based on their direct personal experience, and some of their information came through their active involvement in neighbourhood decision making and problem solving with public bodies. The groups' work, experiences and opinions gave them an overview of what was happening locally. Many stories of local events become distorted in the retelling, or are based from the start on misinformation – the same set of facts can be interpreted or presented in so many different ways. As we have described we attempted to verify information wherever possible, and collect back-up documentation, but the immense volume of detailed information offered throughout this book adds up to a bigger picture of valuable local knowledge held by the active residents.

In Chapter Five we look at how two-way information flows worked, and in Chapter Seven at how 'representative' the residents' views were. National figures are used across all the chapters to illustrate how well the Gatsby residents' situations and opinions compared to the views of the majority.

Ordering and ranking the comments

In the analysis the number of examples and comments that particular experiences, practices and opinions received have been used to rank the relative importance of a point. This method was used to order and make sense of the type and level of responses to the open questions. There were some interesting insights raised by particular interviewees, which were noted and explored in more detail. Conversations with the groups, when at their best, were relaxed and free flowing. Some subjects were touched on, returned to later in the visit or reflected and expanded on through the course of the discussion. Continuous quotes on a single topic were used as far as possible for ease of reading, even when there was a series of related statements on the same topic made at different times throughout the interview.

Summary

This study is based on a piece of action research that set out to stimulate and develop community self-help activity – the Gatsby Training and Small Grant Project. The five-year pilot ran between 1996 and 2001. The model used in the project combined intensive residential training for community organisations on community organising and action planning, with a small grant fund to help participants put ideas into practice back in their own areas.

The Gatsby Project started with the 'million-dollar' question: what would you do if you had, say, one million pounds to help combat problems in disadvantaged communities? The aim of the experiment was to test out whether it was possible to unlock people's desire and potential to solve community problems; how residents' desire to see their neighbourhoods improve could develop into practical action – from 'something must be done' to 'we can do this'. It was successful in attracting 1,800 community volunteers from over 700 community groups over five years to 'How-To' training courses, and awarded small grants of £50–£5,000 to 115 of those groups to put their ideas into practice. The groups were small community groups, based in low-income neighbourhoods. Two thirds of the neighbourhoods were made up predominantly of social housing, and three quarters of the neighbourhoods had special regeneration initiatives. The study neighbourhoods were disadvantaged areas.

The community groups were small-scale informal associations, typical of over half of the voluntary sector as a whole. They were nearly all composed solely of volunteers, who were a mix of ages including younger residents; most were not in paid work.

A rich range of feedback, information and comments from the community volunteers was gathered about their neighbourhoods, about their work and about perceptions of the project's value.

Residents were well placed to judge their own situations and that of their areas. The groups' work, experiences and opinions gave them an overview of what was happening locally – active residents held vast stores of valuable local knowledge.

The primary aim of the project was to help people who wanted to do things to better their neighbourhoods, to explore how the groups operated, what they did, what happened as a result of particular interventions, and people's explanations of why. Before we look at what the groups did, we look in the next chapter at some of the neighbourhood issues that drove them to want to tackle problems themselves.

Notes

[1] Including details of numbers of homes, tenure breakdown, service performance and current local issues.

[2] Following the successful operation of the first five years, Trafford Hall is continuing to run a community self-help training and grant programme. Trafford Hall has used the model to develop and run a capacity-building programme for social housing tenants who want to be more involved in decisions about their areas. The programme was supported by central government through the Office of the Deputy Prime Minister (now Communities and Local Government). Trafford Hall used the model in its 'Barefoot Basic Skills Workers' package, developed with the help of the Adult and Community Learning Fund, and accredited by the Open College Network, in its Active Family Learning Breaks and Young Movers Programme. The Glass-House, a national service to support communities' involvement in urban design and the built environment, have set up a training and small grant programme directly based on the Gatsby Project, supported by the Glass-House Trust.

[3] Categories have now been expanded and amended based on updated data available from the 2001 Census; for more information see CACI Ltd (2004).

THREE

Why neighbourhoods and communities matter to residents

'Estates have such a terrible image. All the language, "social exclusion".
We're not socially excluded from each other, and there are things we're
not deprived of. The problem on estates like this is that we're so badly
served by mainstream service providers. It's slapdash and indifferent at
best, and hostile at worst.' (resident, south London)

The groups in the study were all community groups with links to their
neighbourhoods. They were led and run by people from a particular community,
were created as a result of neighbourhood problems and aimed to deliver
community benefits through their work. Neighbourhoods, or geographical
communities, are places where local services and facilities are provided and
consumed, and where people live and relate to each other, and these were the
focus of the groups' work. This chapter explores the problems and issues that the
groups were tackling; the residents provided detailed examples of the things that
had upset them, both small and large.

The study neighbourhoods were typical of deprived neighbourhoods in the
range of problems that they faced (SEU, 2001). Their dissatisfaction with public
services was representative of a significant minority of unhappy customers across
social housing nationally. Their priorities for service delivery largely mirrored those
of social housing residents nationally in the same period. This chapter describes
the profound distress and dissatisfaction felt by residents about neighbourhood
problems, and provides detailed illustrations of the causes of their distress, which
include both public services and the behaviour of other residents in their areas, as
well as the impacts of public services on relationships between people, particularly
those caused by housing allocations. The stories and illustrations are occasionally
darkly humorous, but more frequently puzzling or upsetting, and they help to
explain what was underlying and partly driving the groups' motivation to take it
upon themselves to tackle neighbourhood problems.

The residents interviewed had privileged access to information from
service providers. They were therefore aware of and praised emerging service
improvements, which is in contrast to normal 'consumer' perspectives on service
change that do not follow actual changes closely, or lag behind.

This chapter also explores the meaning and value of community to the residents.
In contrast to trends towards increasing societal fragmentation, the neighbourhoods
stubbornly remained tight-knit closely bonded communities, as did other low-
income neighbourhoods in the UK. The neighbourhoods represented what to

many is a dead or dying 'golden age' of British working-class community openness. However, far from being a form of nostalgia for lost patterns of relations, residents described an ongoing reality for those neighbourhoods. The high value that residents placed on 'community spirit' is discussed, and, contrary to the many debates about 'community' as an outmoded idea, this chapter shows that this actually reflected a wider longing for cooperation and shared understanding across areas and incomes. The groups' advocacy of 'community' was not wholly based on a simplified and idealised notion of the purely positive aspects of communities, and they were able to articulate many arguments found in the academic literature about the downsides of community ties and place-based social networks.

The study neighbourhoods were heavily dependent on public services for the management and maintenance of their homes and areas. This chapter also explores what happens when services fail or are provided badly, and what kind of management approaches residents wanted to see. One crucial issue in areas of social housing is the landlord's gatekeeping role in deciding who would live there. The chapter looks at why people felt strongly about the way homes were allocated to tenants, and on what basis some residents criticised their neighbours for the way they lived, as well as why people might want to defend and rebuild their community, despite the many tensions, downsides and potential for division, including what people thought about their neighbours.

Background to area problems

The residents and staff were dealing with the multiple interlinked problems that fragile low-income neighbourhoods present. This study was not a detailed analysis of area problems or their roots (for an exploration of the dynamics of neighbourhood decline and renewal, see Lupton, 2003), but the examples below of three different estates illustrate some of the issues that people described, which closely echo the problems of neighbourhood decline and deprivation in the government's national strategy for neighbourhood renewal (SEU, 2001):

- stigma or a poor reputation
- lack of demand for homes in the neighbourhood
- physical or psychological isolation
- lack of a thriving local economy, unemployment, high benefit dependency
- poor facilities
- high crime, anti-social behaviour and youth nuisance
- poor or heavy-handed policing
- health, literacy and family problems.

The three neighbourhoods described below are all physically unremarkable, medium-sized inter- or postwar estates, made up of semi-detached or terraced houses with gardens, typical of many UK social housing estates. These descriptions are summaries based on interviews with residents and frontline workers.

Many of the study neighbourhoods were physically unremarkable, inter-war and post-war estates, made up of mainly semi-detached or terraced houses with gardens, typical of many UK social housing estates

After the steelworks closed

This estate in Derbyshire is an ex-iron and steel village. The forge/steelworks closed in 1961/62, and the council bought the stock in 1970. The local authority then added another 400 units to the old village which doubled the size of the village, at a point immediately after the local economy had collapsed. "You only used to get houses here if you worked in the steelworks." When the council bought the old village they moved the tenants out "closer to town" while they rebuilt, and many people "stayed there". The council put up the new properties "where there was no work or transport. The council has done just about everything to make sure it isn't sustainable". The estate does not have a waiting list, and transfer requests are high. "You can get a house on [the estate] quick, if you're desperate, you can get a place here. It is a problem when the only people coming in are desperate." The estate has high levels of deprivation even compared to the rest of the ward. The estate had a meningitis outbreak a couple of years ago that further blighted the area.

Source: Residents and paid staff from a range of agencies, Derbyshire

A 'dead end'

This estate, in Kent, feels very cut off. It is on an island off the mainland, and the estate is tucked away with an industrial estate on one edge, and the sea on another. There is a car breakers and a sewage plant beside the estate. Some people have not travelled very far out of the area or been off the island much. There is a disused concrete social club building nearby, but "no facilities". There is a chip shop, and a paper shop but the shop is "scruffy and depressing, everything just piled up, it's not clean and the family look at you suspiciously when you go in".

> 'The mums have to walk 1½ miles to school, past all this, it's terrible. There's no school, or hall, or church, it's just an empty shell. There are a couple of pocket parks. The estate is a dumping ground. No one comes here unless they live here. It's a dead end. People are nervous about coming here because they've heard so many stories.' (community worker, Kent)

These are about problems with graffiti, drugs and "kids beating people up". "Puff is rife, I used to walk into people's houses and you could smell it." There have been several incidents, for example: "They sealed [one road] off with armed police". The police came with guns to arrest "one particular person" who had guns in the house.

Source: Residents and community worker, Kent

The 'untouchables'

Twenty years ago "you couldn't get onto this estate, it was one of the best in the county, people scrubbed their steps on a Monday morning, that kind of thing". Two members of the group moved to this estate in County Durham in 1992 by their own request, and had "a full year no bother" until 1997 when it was "hell from the beginning". The single-person flats have become the site for a lot of trouble. Some younger residents and "druggies" who have been allocated there allow their homes to be used for drugs, and let younger children come round. The council is demolishing some of these flats and demolished some a year ago. The residents also described a nucleus of five young boys who cause the bulk of the more serious offences, aged between 14 and 19. Theirs is the "drug house". They have been charged with arson with a view to endanger life, all five have been charged with grievous bodily harm (GBH) and they have 27 motoring offences between them. Some have "never seen outside [the estate]". The estate has loan sharks and debt collectors: "They take turns on a Friday – you see them knocking on the same doors."

Source: Residents, County Durham

The residents in the study saw neighbourhood problems in the context of wider socio-economic processes and pressures that affected their small areas, such as the economic weaknesses of peripheral areas, the decline of manufacturing, gaps in political power for particular communities, the development of large out-of-town supermarkets and the decline of the high street, or the decline of traditional British seaside resorts. These wider processes affecting neighbourhoods have been well documented in the literature (see, for example, Lupton, 2003), and it was interesting to see how aware the residents were of this wider context.

Economic weakness of peripheral areas

"Houses are cheap because it's an island." The council is trying to get a new static bridge built across to the island. "The island has lost contracts because lorries can't get on and off." "If we get a new bridge we will get 600 new houses and contracts and house prices will rise. The economic prospects for the island are looking good if we get the bridge." The chair of the group is on the Strategic Group for the economic development of the island. The place is "insular" because of the geography.

Source: Residents and community worker, Kent

The decline of manufacturing

In the late 1970s and early 1980s the local economy, dependent on engineering, disappeared. A local factory that made nuts, bolts and screws went, as did the place that made gas fires, and a firm who made tubes. This caused problems for the estate as people were made redundant.

Source: Residents, Birmingham

Gaps in political power for minority ethnic communities

Oldham is "the king of textiles", but now the textiles have largely gone. It is changing into a "retail development" place and has shifted to service industries. The minority ethnic population came over in the 1950s to work in the textile factories. "There has been an African Caribbean community here since 1954, but we've never had an African Caribbean councillor." "As a community we don't have any particular swing because we're not concentrated, and we've not been very political." Oldham as a whole is "a very political place".

Source: Residents and community worker, Oldham

The decline of the high street

"We're near to the country and we've got the river." But the town is suffering. "The High Street is like a ghost town. [X large supermarket] is moving out from the town centre. Shops are shutting." Businesses are being attracted out to places like Milton Keynes (30 minutes' drive away) so Bedford is losing shops and firms.

Source: Residents, Bedford

The decline of traditional British seaside resorts

When tourism in Rhyl declined the B&Bs in west Rhyl started to turn into holiday flatlets, then became "permanents". The area is now a privately rented area, mostly for people on benefit in houses of multiple occupation. "Cheap holidays – package holidays killed Rhyl." The primary industry of the area was tourism and it has been hit hard. The secondary industries were utility services like the gasworks, water board and electricity boards for the whole area, and "hundreds" worked there. As these industries have become "more mechanised and less people intensive" jobs have been lost.:

> 'The original purpose has gone. With the decline of tourism you're just left with the housing stock. There are lots of small individual units, with social needs but it's a big problem, it needs radical solutions.' (community worker, Rhyl)

The economy in Rhyl itself is mainly the remaining service/retail sector jobs. Informal wages on the sea front are as low as £1–£1.50 an hour, "but you can have Thursday mornings to sign on". Many of the jobs available are unskilled temporary work on short-term contracts with no holiday pay and unsocial hours.

Fifteen months after visiting this group, this newspaper piece appeared with an almost identical description of the same area:

> '[Rhyl] is a ... seaside resort whose candyfloss glory days faded when holidaymakers discovered that Spain was cheap and warm.... As Rhyl's allure has declined, many guest houses on the west side of town where the posh people once lived have been converted into cheap bedsits, homes for locals and incomers united by poverty and sometimes drugs.' (*The Guardian*, 16 March 2002)

Poor management of neighbourhoods

Within this wider context, the groups' focus was on examples of neighbourhood problems that directly affected the lives of the people who lived there. This included problems that were the consequence of the anti-social behaviour of some individuals, and problems caused by system failures. The interviewees felt that people who acted outside of the normal rules were partly responsible for their own behaviour, and they were concerned about the effect of the disruptive actions of some of their neighbours on their areas.

But there was also a strong focus on the failures of the services and organisations responsible for the public management of their areas. The residents' explanations of service delivery failures also combined an understanding of things that had gone wrong because of policy gaps, and things that had gone wrong because of the poor performance of individual members of staff. In areas of publicly built, financed, owned and managed housing, the negative consequences of the design, upkeep, gatekeeping and overseeing functions performed by public authorities or landlords were a clear target for criticisms where poor, and praise where good.

Housing management and maintenance is a bread-and-butter task that is at the core of any landlord's work. It involves keeping properties and communal areas in good repair, collecting rents and chasing rent arrears, allocating properties and dealing with re-lets when people move on, and managing any breaches of tenancy. It was these basic tasks, and the attitude with which they were performed, that rankled most with the residents interviewed. Research on social housing tenants' attitudes in the same period also shows that this was a common opinion. For example, 53% of council tenants felt that carrying out good quality repairs was the most important priority for the local housing service, and 44% said that the council dealing with repairs quickly was a priority (Taper, 2001).

National surveys of residents in deprived areas show that overall in this period there were relatively low levels of satisfaction with public services and relatively high levels of dissatisfaction. For example, in 1998 fewer than half (47%) of adults in deprived areas were satisfied with council housing (Duffy, 2000; Taper, 2001). This compares badly to satisfaction ratings among people in the same deprived areas for other services such as the Post Office – 90% satisfaction – and even 85% satisfaction with high street banks and building societies.

Likewise, the ratings that social housing tenants nationally gave for social landlords' performance were also not very impressive, at 64% of council tenants and 76% of housing association tenants fairly or very satisfied with their landlord overall (ODPM, 2002b). Furthermore, The Housing Corporation evidence shows that 22% of housing association tenants were actively dissatisfied with landlord performance on repairs, and 20% of council tenants were fairly or very dissatisfied with council housing, leaving a significant minority of unhappy customers (Taper, 2001), which is reflected in the interviews.

Poor households were also one-and-a-half times as likely to be dissatisfied with their local area generally as households on average incomes, and nearly three times as likely as high-income households to be very dissatisfied (Howarth et al, 1998).

The interviewees represented the most disgruntled of these households, and the most vocal of those dissatisfied people in deprived areas. Because for some landlords, the majority of their staff's time, and repairs budget, are consumed by tenants in rent arrears or those causing trouble in the neighbourhood, this leaves those tenants who do pay rent dissatisfied at the levels of service they receive, particularly where households who do not fulfil their responsibilities still receive the same level of service (Manion, 2002).

A total of 222 comments were collected about poor service delivery, shown in Table 3.1. The top six issues were all primarily related to social landlords' responsibilities:

- poor repairs, arrears and voids management
- poor tenancy enforcement and ineffective action against anti-social behaviour
- poor customer care
- poor management of public and communal space or facilities
- inappropriate allocations
- poor quality housing refurbishment.

Ineffective housing management and maintenance

Ranked first (36 comments) were comments about poor housing management and maintenance, particularly in relation to the management of repairs, arrears and voids (empty homes). Good practice in prompt and sensitive rent arrears management is in the clear interests of the landlord organisation, which needs to maximise rental income in order to pay for services. The residents pointed out that this is also in the interests of tenants, as debts accrued by tenants that are allowed to accumulate are more difficult to pay back, and serious rent arrears are grounds for eviction.

Table 3.1: Criticisms of service delivery

Comment	No. of comments	Rank
Poor housing management and maintenance	36	1
Lack of action on anti-social behaviour	26	2
Poor customer care	24	3
Poor management of communal areas	20	=4
Inappropriate housing allocations and lettings	20	=4
Poor refurbishment	17	6
Not doing job	14	7
Lack of consultation/information	12	8
Badly designed neighbourhood	11	=9
Services not tailored	11	=9
Other	(31)	n/a
Total	**222**	

Managing empty homes

Dealing quickly with empty or unlet properties (known in housing management as 'voids') is another housing management task that benefits both landlords and tenants. Empty properties not only represent lost rental income, they are unattractive and signal the undesirability of the neighbourhood, and attract vandalism which also increases costs:

> 'The borough is only prepared to put in £35,000 a week on voids across the borough. It's taking so long because something else is more priority. Voids have increased in the last 12 months across the borough because they've been put in abeyance because of the transfer. But you start off with £2,000 needed, leave it six months and it's £10,000 because of vandalism. You save a penny and waste a pound.' (resident, Walsall)

One particular approach to temporarily dealing with empty or unlet homes that residents felt had negative consequences was to board up void properties with wood or metal shutters. While this was done out of concern for the security of the property and to prevent it being stripped of copper piping, boilers and other fixtures, it also made the status of the unit visible, and could make a property a more obvious target for vandalism. Here the residents were ahead of 'good practice' in the housing management field, and it was a number of years after residents identified this issue that many social landlords changed their approach.

Residents' concern about empty properties was in the context of the broader consequences for the neighbourhood of low demand for housing and signs of the incipient abandonment of neighbourhoods at the time. In this period there was growing recognition of the issue of low demand for housing, and oversupply of social housing in some northern cities (Power and Mumford, 1999), since translated into a government-funded housing market renewal programme (ODPM, 2004a).

According to a housing officer and residents from one estate in Liverpool, there were over 100 such voids and high levels of turnover: "One street has 13 houses empty now; it was full last year"; "This used to be a really desirable place ... there used to be a waiting list":

> 'People are moving off the estate, there are houses boarded up. It really blights the estate. The kids commit vandalism; they set fire to the empty houses and watch. There are burnt-out houses and pulled-down fences. People dump rubbish. People here have been evicted from other homes. People on the estate feel it's a dumping ground. They're giving the homes away in lucky bags – they advertise them in the paper. Because people are leaving the estate in [droves], so it's easier to get in.' (resident, Liverpool)

Repairs and maintenance

Landlords' failures to keep up with day-to-day repairs and planned maintenance were a bugbear for residents. Groups pointed out the additional costs incurred through deterioration due to a lack of preventative or day-to-day maintenance:

> 'The place got done up 15 years ago. Sinks, bathrooms and put pitch roofs on, and they've never touched them since. It's not the repairs; it's the maintenance. They've mithered them to death, then let them deteriorate, and the money that's been allocated in the past has been spent elsewhere. It's the same as the council. They don't maintain as they should and a £10 job ends up costing £500.' (resident, Manchester)

Other complaints were about long response times to repairs requests, small maintenance jobs neglected due to inadequate estate inspection or a reduction in eligible repairs by the landlord. In two local authorities in particular, there had been a history of serious inefficiency and alleged corruption. According to some residents and housing officers, the city council had a "long reputation of disgraceful management". Examples included: windows being delivered when the glaziers were not there, so the delivery people left them in the garden and they were stolen three weeks later. Another example was:

> 'An old lady needed new gates. So, three wagons rolled up. The first one dropped the gates. The second one dropped some bits and pieces. The last one dropped 41 bags of nails. But you don't use nails in gates, you use screws. So, we said to her, they're going to come back and ask for the nails so they can sell them on. When they do, you tell him, What nails? And we gave a bag of nails to every house on the street.'

In the other authority one resident said: "We call it the 'Republic of [X]'!" The residents said that the council had the fifth lowest rents in the country and some of the highest salaries – it had been a political decision to set rents low, but now the housing department was effectively "bankrupt". The council were only doing emergency repairs, and were looking at transferring as much of the stock to a new social landlord as possible to sort things out. The DLO (Direct Labour Organisation, the council in-house repairs team) was "expensive", and "inflexible", and sometimes invoiced twice for the same job.

Bad design

Repairs problems were referred to separately from the poor original design of the homes, which was more about bad urban design. But poor design in terms of the built quality of the homes was a linked problem to poor maintenance (11 examples, ranked joint 9th; see Table 3.1). For example, in one case some blocks of flats had not had any maintenance for 25 years. The new landlord did a structural survey, and "half the bits were missing!", for example wall ties. "Basically they were thrown up quickly" between 1959 and 1965. The blocks had had security doors put on since the new landlord took over. "With the corporation, you got the key to the door and your rent book and that's that." The chair of the group had only had two repairs completed in 28 years: "all they're interested in is the rent paid and they're not bothered with you" (resident, Liverpool).

Badly done refurbishment

However, refurbishment and housing improvement works did not necessarily alleviate design and repair problems. There were 17 examples (ranked 6th) of badly managed or executed physical improvement programmes.

In one example from London a change of political control midway through a refurbishment programme caused uneven standards between properties, and more serious social consequences. In the 1980s the then Conservative-controlled borough sold half the estate to a private developer. The developer decanted the people and started doing repairs and upgrading. Then Labour won back political control, and they brought people back onto the estate who wanted to return, but this left the estate with half of the flats empty. So, the council found 150 new residents, mostly vulnerable families from the homeless waiting list. The new more vulnerable residents got the poorer quality, unmodernised homes. The borough then had to bring the unmodernised flats up to the same standard as the others but their improvements were not of such a high quality and they were already starting to disintegrate, for example the double-glazing was "rubbish" and fell out. The privately modernised flats had soundproofing/noise insulation done, but noise was still a problem with the ones the council refurbished.

In other illustrations, the poor quality of the refurbishment caused further repairs problems:

> 'They said because of the refurbishment the repairs bill should go down, but it has actually gone up, because there are no vents in the windows or extractors in the bathrooms so you get damp. And where they took out the old boilers and flattened the wall on the inside they left the pipes and gully open at the top so they fill with water. They spent £22,000 per house but they were ruddy cowboys. They're paying £300 for £40 doors.'

The way refurbishment programmes were run sometimes had negative unintended consequences, such as encouraging movement of criminals around the estate, or reducing positive street-level activity in the area. Throughout the interviews the residents pointed to the unintended consequences for people in neighbourhoods of how services are managed:

'There's been a shift in the population. They spent £100,000 10 years ago on the flats then knocked them down. They've got the best security doors on the estate, so all the drug dealers have gone there – the police know they're running it, but they're stuffed.' (resident, Wrexham)

In another example, a neighbourhood in Oldham was made up of terraces and used to be "vibrant" and teaming with life, but then the local authority put in traffic calming which stopped the throughput of people and "killed off the area" (resident, Oldham).

Tenancy enforcement and anti-social behaviour

Another central housing management task is managing tenancies once people have moved in. The tenancy agreement that a tenant signs when they move into a property details the rights and responsibilities of both sides. These include conditions that govern tenants not disturbing neighbours, and the landlord can take action if a tenant breaches the conditions of their tenancy agreement. The lack of enforcement of tenancy agreements is the problem that ranked 2nd in the discussions on service failures and area problems (26 comments; see Table 3.1).

Landlords' approaches to the question of rights and responsibilities have been the subject of controversy, particularly over the past decade. There has been a shift in policy by individual landlords, alongside a general move in government policy, towards a more proactive, interventionist position emphasising the responsibilities of tenants and the willingness of landlords to take action if people do not fulfil these responsibilities. Examples of this shift are the introduction of measures such as probationary tenancies, anti-social behaviour orders and new legal precedents with local authorities using criminal actions to gain legal grounds for eviction. The tenants in the study supported these new approaches. They saw it as the landlord's responsibility to manage disruptive behaviour by tenants because of the way that individuals' behaviour impacted on the wider neighbourhood, coupled with the overseeing role of the landlord in the neighbourhood, as well as the ability of the landlord to act. They were critical where landlords and other authorities failed to manage anti-social behaviour:

'[One family] stole and damaged cars, attacked OAPs. If you approached the mum to say, Do something about your 15-year-old son, she said, My son don't do wrong. So we helped others to put a petition together, not saying we want them out but asking her to control her son. She realised that it wasn't just the odd one but the whole community. [The housing officer] wouldn't move her. The pensioners are intimidated so they're moving out, so there are more voids. Now there's three.' (resident, Walsall)

Problems with one family in a neighbourhood in Keighley have been going on for two-and-a-half years and the issue has been passed on to the Tenancy Enforcement Team, but:

> '… they don't do owt as yet but they do respond. We're determined to get them out. Everyone's had stuff done, except me, you'd think I'd be the first…. Social services, the goodie goodie people put a stop on Tenancy Enforcement. They've got a lot to answer for.' (resident, Keighley)

Anti-social behaviour, new tenants and allocations to social housing

Ranked joint 4th (20 comments) were inappropriate allocation policies in social housing. The allocation of housing to vulnerable or disruptive tenants is one precursor to high levels of anti-social behaviour. Comments about allocations and anti-social behaviour partly reflect some of the wider trends of increased tenure polarisation, and the residualisation of the social housing sector (Burrows, 1997), a process that was greatly accelerated from the 1980s (Lee and Murie, 1997). Social housing has become the tenure of last resort, and people coming into social housing have become increasingly more disadvantaged (Lupton and Power, 2002).

Blaming outsiders

The residents felt that inappropriate and insensitive allocations by social landlords of new or 'bad' tenants to homes in the area created damaging pressures on their neighbourhoods. In their comments about the negative aspects of relations with neighbours, the negative consequences of allocations policies ranked top (17 comments, ranked first; see Table 3.4). These opinions are sometimes seen as a simple dislike of new groups. It has been argued that people create an 'in-group' identity by pathologising other groups of people as the 'out-group' (Sherif, 1970). The idea is that dislike of people not in your in-group is based primarily on the fact of difference, rather than anything more substantial (Elias and Scotson, 1965).

Some of the ways that residents expressed the debate may initially seem to back up this view, for example, appearing to blame an influx of people from a different geographical area for area decline:

> 'It was okay until they modernised it in 1979/80, then we got all the scum from Crocky [Croxteth].' (resident, Liverpool)

Another estate was made up of around 350 terraced coal board and railway houses, with only 32 people still living there: "This is what community was, you know bowls of broth and that sort of thing, and look at it now, it's a dead thing". There was a spiral of decline when a local train station closed, and some tenants from another neighbourhood were moved there who had previously been evicted:

> '... all undesirables from Darlington. There were numbers coming in, but it disrupted the community. The council thought they were filling homes and housing people, but they actually devastated a community.' (resident, County Durham)

Some of the emotive and pejorative descriptions of the issues related to severely disadvantaged individuals and neighbourhoods could also be seen as part of 'out-group' denigration by the residents in the study. For example, in one of the study areas, we were told that there were a couple of families who were still causing problems for other residents on the estate: "There are, how shall we say, undesirables on X Road" (resident, Walsall). There had been two deliberately started fires. However, we were later told that some of the families in the area had a lot to cope with. One young girl came from a family of nine children, one who had a disability: "Her mother uses them as babysitters" (youth worker, Walsall).

In other areas the group's main concerns were "the crap the council are putting into the houses" (resident, Derby). There were waiting lists for social housing in all areas except this area, and one other. One of the group's member's husbands came from the other undesirable area and "he thought moving [here] was a step up!". The "crap" residents the interviewees referred to were drug dealers who sold both hard and soft drugs, and nuisance neighbours who had already caused problems in other social housing areas.

Residents' anger with people who disrupted the neighbourhood

Residents' anger was not about newcomers or difference per se. This was an entirely separate discussion to that around wariness or hostility to incomers or new residents more generally – some of the vulnerable families at issue had actually been on the estate for some time. The groups made it clear that it was the lifestyle clashes and additional stresses that vulnerable or anti-social tenants placed on their neighbourhoods that was at the root of their anger, rather than the mere fact of newness or difference, for example behaviour that exacerbated the poor quality of the physical environment; criminal behaviour that added to neighbourhood disorder; intimidating behaviour by people involved in crime that increased population turnover and threatened area stability and viability even further; families with disruptive children; nuisance behaviour by young people; or behaviour related to substance misuse.

For example in one neighbourhood, residents described a partially sighted woman and her two daughters aged 16 and 18 who had been attracting a lot of male company. Their visitors were "queuing round the block, throwing bottles in the garden, pissing in the garden. We can't say, because we don't know for sure [but we suspect] it must have been business" (resident, County Durham). In another area:

> 'There's meetings today [about the homes] we can't let them, can't sell them. The drug situation has a lot to do with it. The flats are run down. There are anti-social types in there. They intimidate their neighbours so the neighbours move out. Half of [the block of flats] has been torn down.' (resident, Wrexham)

Social engineering

The interviewees felt that the residents causing these negative effects were ultimately responsible for their own behaviour. At the same time, the groups criticised the role that the urban design and lettings and allocations policies of social landlords had played. They described how vulnerable families had been "dumped", and how their estates were "dumping grounds", that is, places where disadvantaged people were concentrated with adverse effects.

The wider socio-economic trends of polarisation and falling demand for social housing that contribute to these problems are out of the control of social landlords, who are dealing with these external pressures. However, the focus of residents was on those things at the margin that social landlords did have control over. As illustrated in the examples below, in order to mitigate some of the worst consequences of the inevitable social engineering that allocation of housing involves, the interviewees contrasted policies contributing to polarisation and concentration with allocations policies and procedures that used a more careful approach:

> 'The old corporation policy was to put decent families next to bad ones and hope it rubs off, not now though. But it's like you put a rotten apple in the barrel, they all go bad. [When it was built this] was a prime estate, because we had gardens. People were being decanted from high-rises and the inner city. You needed a letter from the queen to get here before.' (resident, Liverpool)

In Wrexham in the early 1970s tenants needed "two references and a job, it was for the working poor, and key workers for industry". Then the estate became:

> '... dilapidated, very run down. There was no sense of ownership or community. They used it as a dumping ground for problem tenants from [a neighbouring estate]. It was just a bunch of people stuck here. It got run down very badly. It got stigmatised, if you were desperate you'd come here.' (resident, Wrexham)

We were told:

> 'I love my house and it annoys me when the council puts people in who ruin it. They're three bedroom with ... gardens. [X council] are putting the bad in with the good on the idea that it'll rub off. It don't work. Who knows where the council get their ideas from?' (resident, Walsall)

In one block of flats in a different area in Walsall gangs of young people with disruptive friends tipped the balance: "in a block of flats it only takes one bad apple. Visitors emptied this block" (housing officer, Walsall).

Poor customer care

Residents described how the way services were delivered at frontline level created frustrations for recipients. Criticisms of poor customer care by service providers ranked third in critical comments about service delivery (24 comments; see Table 3.1). They felt that staff in service organisations treated clients in a rude, offhand or unresponsive manner. The quote at the beginning of this chapter sums up how badly served residents felt by services. Other groups commented on the way that staff added to the stigmatisation of the neighbourhood. For example, on one estate in Derbyshire, the exchange board for council properties had notices on with "anywhere but [the estate]". The local councillors also used to say the estate was a bad place to live, and staff at the council would make jokes in front of residents that if you went on to the estate you would not have any wheels left on your car. In Wales:

> 'the housing officers themselves tell people on the waiting list that the estate is rough and not to go there. Officers show surprise when people want to stay. We've heard them say it, and people have told us!' (resident, Rhyl)

Residents felt 'fobbed off' and patronised

The lack of sensitivity or courtesy of service providers further compounded the residents' feelings of lack of status and power to command a response from providers.

At a community conference in Hull people said in the workshops that they were being "fobbed off" by housing officers. The chair of the group tried for years to get action but she did not get a good response from the housing officers or police: "it's the silly old woman syndrome" (resident, Hull). In Rhyl a housing office had put up a partition so officers could no longer be seen from the reception "so they can hide from you" (resident, Rhyl):

'[Professionals] talk over our heads, they kept talking about "Joe Public". I said, I am Joe Public and you're alienating me. One woman from probation says, Did you see that wonderful article [on low-income communities and crime] … we've blown it up and put it in the surgery, and people actually read it! I said to her – you're reading it, but we're living with it. They're 10 years behind – going on in a patronising manner. We don't have the answers, don't get me wrong, but you've got to know what the questions are.' (resident, North Yorkshire)

Residents wanted staff to do their jobs

There were 14 references (ranked 7th) to services not performing their tasks:

'[The housing association are] a very promise-y association, but they don't tend to deliver what they promise. Residents come into us and say is this going on? We say, they say they're doing it, but whether they are doing it is another matter.' (resident, Bedfordshire)

Poor management of communal areas and public spaces

Poor or inadequate management of public and communal spaces was a significant issue for the residents in the neighbourhoods (20 comments, ranked joint 4th; see Table 3.1). The spaces in between homes were as important for quality of life as the condition and management of the homes themselves. Open green spaces and other communal areas not under the direct control of individual households were areas where responsibility and ownership were often unclear, and problems arose because of this. One example of a skate park in a public park illustrated how neglected and badly designed spaces could attract negative behaviours. The skate park was open 24 hours, had no gates, was not locked and was not staffed. It was "a drugs haven". "Amenities and leisure department manage it, or rather don't"; "[It's] dark, enclosed"; it is stuck in a corner because of "NIMBYism"; "The local authority is all style and no substance. They do it to look good" (residents, Stoke).

There were examples of controversial decisions about the management of communal facilities, such as shops, community centres, libraries and schools:

'The tenants' and residents' association came about because of the closure of the library – everything else has grown out of it. [It] was the last straw. We were getting more and more angry about the way the estate was neglected. The ward councillors didn't even go to the meeting about the closure of the library. After the library closure in 1994 we met with [the chief executive of the local authority], we made videos and petitions about the library and nursery. [The council] were going to let it as archive storage facilities, so we went storming down

Uncared for public and communal spaces created a depressing environment in the neighbourhoods

to the environment committee and reminded them that they had the power to give it over to community use.' (resident, South London)

Praise for management of neighbourhoods

The critical comments collected partly reflected the more involved overview position of the resident volunteers and activists. The examples were of issues that often affected whole estates rather than one individual or family. Some of the problems referred to were historical and have since been dealt with. More broadly, there were moves by existing and new social landlords towards changing their practices, for example to improve customer care and provide better quality services, such as more prompt or tailored responses to customers' requests. There were many 'go-ahead' landlords attempting innovative new ways of managing, for example Irwell Valley Housing Association's 'Gold Service' that gives additional service benefits where tenants pay rent promptly. The critical comments above are a reminder of the necessity for reinvention in the social housing field, and the need, recently recognised by many social landlords and regulators of the sector, for continuous improvement (The Housing Corporation, 2001), for example HouseMark, a new internet-based benchmarking service for the housing sector owned by the Chartered Institute of Housing and the National Housing Federation. The critical comments discussed support the government's attempts to put pressure on landlord performance through mechanisms such as inspection and competition, as seen in policies like Best Value in housing, housing stock transfer and arm's length management organisations (ALMOs). More broadly, the reform of local government has been a significant government policy agenda, with more than 20 policies (including Best Value) to modernise local government introduced through the 1998 and 2001 White Papers. These policies were collectively referred to by government as the 'local government modernisation agenda' (Martin and Bovaird, 2005).

The active residents interviewed were not just critical; they also praised emerging service improvements. In this the residents interviewed are not typical of other service users. They had privileged access to information from service providers, and were more aware than the bulk of service users of changes in delivery and policy. Partly as a consequence, they were more positive than the general population about these changes, which is in sharp contrast to the more commonly held views of the bulk of service users on the performance of public services. Resident satisfaction levels are positively correlated with levels of information from councils (Grant et al, 2002). However, people's perceptions of changes in delivery tend to lag behind, or at least not follow closely, actual changes measured in different ways (Dean and Hastings, 2000; Grant et al, 2002; Barber, 2003, 2004; ICM, 2004; Page, 2004).

Proof that public perceptions do not match changes in service outputs can be seen in the evidence. Evaluation of improvements in the performance of local government found that performance was going up. A basket of indicators (Best Value Performance Indicators, Performance Assessment Framework scores and Department for Education and Skills indicators) suggested that, overall, local authority services had improved by 12.5% between 2000/01 and 2003/04 (Martin and Bovaird, 2005). However, in the same period, findings from the same research project suggested that long-term patterns of public confidence in councils had either just been maintained, or deteriorated slightly, between 2001 and 2004 (Cowell et al, 2005). Other research also showed that satisfaction with local government remained low, or fell, in this period, despite performance improvements. For example, just over half of respondents in one survey (55%) were satisfied with the way that their councils ran things in 2001, and 24% were actively dissatisfied (responses to the question 'Which of the following describes how satisfied you are with the way [council name] runs things?') (DTLR, 2001). Another survey, using information that councils are required to collect (local authority Best Value Performance Indicator No. 3 'Taking everything into account, how satisfied or dissatisfied are you with the way the authority runs things?'), showed slightly better results in 2000/01: 65% of residents were satisfied overall with the way that their authorities ran things (ODPM, 2004b). By 2003/04, satisfaction results based on local authority information stood at 55%, a 'significant' decline of 10% in satisfaction (Martin and Bovaird, 2005), and when an increase in dissatisfaction of 3% was added, net change in satisfaction was down 13% compared with the same results three years earlier (ODPM, 2004b; Martin and Bovaird, 2005), or no change compared to the other survey result. Local government is increasingly emphasising the importance of good communication with residents and service users for these reasons (Edomi, 2004), particularly in the face of rising consumer expectations generally (ODPM and Home Office, 2005).

Better service delivery

There is change for the better happening in service delivery, which was recognised by the residents interviewed. While the neighbourhoods generally faced much poor service delivery, the residents noted progress or positive service quality where they could see it. The critical comments were to some extent balanced out by praise for positive aspects of service delivery. Table 3.2 shows a breakdown of the 151 positive comments collected about service provision in the neighbourhoods.

Three themes emerged for praise:

- recognition by service providers of area and service problems, and strategic planning for the future
- practical change and good existing practice in day-to-day management
- increased transparency, accountability, consultation and involvement.

Recognition of problems and long-term planning

The most positive move on the part of service providers was an acknowledgment of residents' priorities and a commitment to tackling problems (34 comments, ranked 1st). This included both signs of financial investment in the neighbourhoods and symbolic investment. One particular tenants' association was set up in 1992, "just after the poverty profile came out", which was an influential report on the estate and the problems it faced. "For once they were saying in black and white what we'd been saying for ages" (resident, Wrexham).

Table 3.2: Praise for service delivery

Comment	No. of comments	Rank
Recognition of issues/investment in area	34	1
Good housing and area management	27	2
Good tenant involvement	20	3
Effective staff	15	4
Socio-economic work	12	5
Action against anti-social behaviour	11	6
Long-term strategy	9	7
Good customer care	8	=8
Good youth work	8	=8
Accountability	7	10
Total	**151**	

Linked to this were positive comments about the development of longer-term strategies to make the work of different agencies more coherent, or to overhaul services, or for the development of the wider area (9 comments, ranked 7th):

'It has been in decline – it had become a deprived area ... in pockets. I'd say it's on the up now. There's been a lot of investment. We are now starting to turn the curve upwards. It's changed. It was a seven-year strategy but I feel personally confident we can have a long-term strategy. It gives you confidence.' (resident, Wrexham)

Practical change and good existing practice in day-to-day management

As well as residents' support for strategic work, they welcomed immediate and practical change or effective existing practice, such as improvements to day-to-day housing management and the management of public spaces (27 comments, ranked 2nd), as well as tackling anti-social behaviour (11 comments, ranked 6th), better youth services (8 comments, ranked joint 8th) and more community-based or socio-economic work (12 comments, ranked 5th):

'We've had a caretaker from the beginning, and two cleaners in the morning – they do all the hallways. [The caretaker] keeps an eye. He's handy on the small jobs, instead of waiting for civic to come, although civic are good for out of hours, like if you're locked out.' (resident, Hull)

On an estate in Derbyshire, they now had an estate caretaker who was a joiner by trade and also did handyman things. He "made a big difference". For example he did the pensioners' window boxes, cleaned up dog mess and did the weeding. "All little things that didn't get done before." They also have their own 'swat' team, made up of a plumber, bricklayer, carpenter and electrician, and are based locally in the resource centre (community centre) and "get repairs done that day" (resident, Derbyshire).

Better customer care, better staff

When talking about poor service delivery, the residents interviewed did differentiate between faults in an organisation's systems or policies and failure to deliver by individual members of staff. This distinction also came through in their praise for services, which highlighted structural and personnel changes as linked but distinct. Residents picked out more responsive and customer care-focused services as having made a positive difference to service delivery (8 comments, ranked joint 8th), as well as officers and structures that created more effective delivery of work (15 comments, ranked 4th). In one example, the area housing office was down the road. The old staff were "rude". A new social landlord was doing the management, and they were "nice and polite". "The plumber rings you direct, and they'll call people sir." The new landlord used small local firms to do jobs. The firms wanted the business and competed on price. When contacting housing management they "are friendly and they do their best". A housing officer came one day a week for a surgery, and you could also make an appointment with her privately. She was "accessible" (resident, Liverpool).

Increased transparency, accountability, consultation and community involvement

The third set of aspects of service delivery praised by residents was increased transparency and accountability of services (7 comments, ranked 10th), linked to better tenant consultation and involvement (20 comments, ranked 3rd). Here, the residents interviewed were very much in line with the views of service users and people more widely. The Gatsby resident volunteers were pushing for more openness from service providers. Forty-two per cent of council tenants nationally in the same period said they knew 'hardly anything at all' about housing department services, and 34% of council tenants felt poorly informed about services (Taper, 2001). Thirty-seven per cent of housing association tenants nationally thought that taking tenants' views into account, and keeping tenants informed, were priorities for the service they would like from their landlord (Taper, 2001). Looking across a range of public services, only 9% applied the word 'openness' to public services (Grant et al, 2002). Around half of the respondents in the 1998 British Social Attitudes Survey's module on local democracy felt that they were not well informed by councils about services provided (Chivite-Matthews and Teal, 2001). Groups significantly more likely to be the most dissatisfied with the council's information provision include people out of work and those in the least well-off socio-economic group (Chivite-Matthews and Teal, 2001).

As with the responses of the residents in the study, nationally people generally want to know more about services, and be consulted more often and on more issues by public authorities (Bromley et al, 2000). Despite many advances in policy and practice on public engagement people still feel that public bodies do not listen to them (Page, 2005; Richardson, 2005a) and they believe that more consultation would result in better decision making (Chivite-Matthews and Teal, 2001). Increasing council attention to accountability has not yet led to the public feeling better informed about council actions (Cowell et al, 2005). There may be low levels of active engagement in decision making, but there is a desire by the public to be more involved, which the residents in the study also promoted.

What community means to residents

The groups were working to make the places where they lived better. Neighbourhood viability is partly about the way that services are delivered, and about how that affects the population of those areas. It is also about how people get along together. In the interviews, residents expressed a series of linked opinions about the nature of the relationships between people in their neighbourhoods. Tables 3.3 and 3.4 summarise the positive and negative comments about what community meant to interviewees.

A desire for strong and stable communities

Overall, despite tensions and divisions, the groups put a high premium on a strong and stable community. They liked to see their neighbourhoods as places where people looked out for each other, they preferred population stability and wanted to see commitment to the neighbourhood from the people that lived there. Nationally, in 2003, 71% said they felt that they belonged to the neighbourhood very or fairly strongly (this question was first asked in the 2003 Home Office Citizenship Survey; see Home Office, 2003). They wanted to increase levels of civic responsibility and integration of ethnic groups.

For example, some residents from Leyland felt that a neighbouring estate was very different to theirs. "They have the same problems and deprivation", but the community was different. "They know everything about everybody there. It's like an extended family, the community stick together there, they've got a community spirit we haven't. They work together as a community, unlike here. [Here] there's pockets with nothing to connect our little bits … there's no middle, no centre or base. Things are too spread out." One of the residents contrasted it to an estate

Table 3.3: Positive aspects of community

Positive aspects	No. of comments	Rank
Long-standing residents add to area stability	18	1
Close-knitted and supportive community	15	2
Need for community	12	3
Existence of mutual aid	11	4
Need for civic responsibility	7	5
Total	**63**	

Table 3.4: Negative aspects of community

Negative aspects	No. of comments	Rank
Community damaged by allocations	17	1
Closed and defensive community	14	2
Racial divisions	9	3
Other tensions	8	4
Total	**48**	

in Milton Keynes where she used to live: "Each estate is like a little village, they work together and have their own community houses – I was surprised when we moved here. [There], you got to know everyone on the estate, here they keep to themselves. I hope for that here".

Residents described neighbourhoods where there was a core of long-standing residents, alongside some newer families moving in. They felt that long-standing residents contributed to neighbourhood stability. Nationally the picture was that 19% of social renters had lived in the same property for over 10 years, and another 15% for 20 years or more (ODPM, 2002b). The interviewees were a mixture of people that had lived in the area all their lives, people who were new to the area and those in between:

> 'I moved in 27 years ago when the estate was just built. We all moved in together, it was nice. There are older people who've moved to the bungalows. There's lots of new families but they have nothing to do with anybody.' (resident, Warrington)

> 'People have lived here forever – some here are great grandparents, with families grown up.' (resident, Liverpool)

> 'My grandfather, my father's father, came from Middlesbrough to work here. There's quite a few people with a long history, a long connection to the place. [There are] people whose parents are still here. Their children are grown up and married and they live here to be near their parents. It's quite a community in that respect.' (resident, Derbyshire)

A neighbourhood that contains several generations of families is counter to wider trends for people to live further away from their families – 44% of adults have no relatives they feel close to living nearby (Coulthard et al, 2002). At the extreme end, these trends were discussed by one group of Chinese women in Leeds. They described cultural shifts in the Chinese community away from traditional ideas about filial duty and children's responsibility for parents. There was a "cultural conflict" because the "expectations of the second generation" were not the same as those of their parents. The parents "expect to be looked after" and only spoke Chinese, while the children only spoke very limited Chinese. Some families had their parents living in the house but the children ignored their parents "They are forced to move if their children are not happy living in the same house" (community worker, Leeds).

Neighbourhoods with extended family networks

In the study neighbourhoods, there were still strong extended family networks, with sons and daughters of tenants moving into their own homes nearby. Nationally, people without educational qualifications, or in manual work, were also still more likely to have close relatives living nearby, and saw relatives more regularly than people in non-manual work or with higher education qualifications. For example, in the 1997/98 Survey of English Housing 57% of respondents had relatives living in the local area, and 65% in the same survey said they had relatives in the area with whom it was important to stay living close (Bridge, 2002). Three years on, in the 2000/01 General Household Survey, 69% of people without educational qualifications had close relatives living nearby, compared to 41% of people with qualifications above 'A' level. One in five (19%) of people in the manual socio-economic group saw relatives daily, compared to one in ten (11%) of those in the non-manual group (Coulthard et al, 2002). This shows that the Gatsby groups were typical of many other working-class neighbourhoods at the time in their levels of local family ties.

> '[There are] lots of extended families, they don't move away.' (resident, Bristol)

> 'Families live round here and their kids still live here.' (community worker, Kent)

> 'There was lots [of houses] bought years ago, when the kids had grown up. A lot of people don't want to come to this estate. It's still like a community. So people stay to see their grandkids. Most people still have got relatives on here.' (resident, Warrington)

> 'Some families have three generations on the estate.' (resident, Liverpool)

A play scheme worker working in the same estate in Liverpool also described the same situation: "I am now rearing the children of the kids I reared".

Supportive communities

The family networks and stable core populations in the neighbourhoods contributed to a feeling of a close-knitted and supportive community. People described a positive place where neighbours looked out for each other and respected each other (15 comments, ranked 2nd; see Table 3.3). In this the residents in the study had a similar take on neighbourhood relationships to 65% of respondents in the 1998 British Household Panel Survey who agreed with the statement 'The friendships and associations I have with other people in my neighbourhood mean a lot to me', with only 14% disagreeing (Bridge, 2002). The British Crime Survey shows that, since 1992, more of the population overall have thought that people in their neighbourhood 'go their own way' rather than 'help each other out'. However, the percentage of people who saw their neighbourhood as one where people help each other out rose from just under 30% in 1996, to 36% in 2000. The interviewees shared the views of the 43% of people in the Home Office's Citizenship Survey in 2001 who answered 'Yes, definitely' to the question 'Would you say that this is a place where neighbours look out for each other?', although it is worth noting that a further 41% answered 'Yes, to some extent' to the same question (Attwood et al, 2003).

The longer someone has lived in a place the more likely they are to see it as somewhere people look out for each other (Attwood et al, 2003). Given some of the resident volunteers interviewed had moved onto the estate when the places were built, their views could have been explained by that fact. However, perhaps counter-intuitively, people in better-off places were more likely to see their places as supportive neighbourhoods than those in the most deprived areas. In the Home Office's Citizenship Survey 2001 50% in the least deprived areas saw their neighbourhoods as places where people looked out for each other, compared with 32% in the most deprived (Attwood et al, 2003). This means the supportive relationships described here are more unusual than might be initially thought of in less well-off areas:

> '[Three local dads in the family support group] all drink in the same pub at the bottom end. It's a small town, you always bump into someone. It's only small, people know each other. [The area is] very communal, community spirited, with everyone playing together.' (member of a parent support group, Cheshire)

One play worker lived in a private estate where "you don't know your neighbours". In contrast to this estate, "I've never come across an estate like this" where people were friendly and knew each other. "This is a brilliant estate, everyone is willing to help one another" (play worker, Liverpool).

> '[There is a] good community spirit, people rally round.' (community worker, Kent)

> 'If something bad happens people are responsive, there is a supportive atmosphere.' (headteacher, Keighley)

> 'There is community spirit. People who live here won't go out of the area. Everyone sticks together.' (priest/teacher at local school, Liverpool)

These social networks were close, neighbourly relationships between people who lived in the same place. This is not to say that people on the estates did not also have contacts and friends outside the estates where they lived. Whether people came by social networks through work, home or leisure, it is acknowledged that having social supports and interaction is a key element of social inclusion (Burchardt et al, 2002; Coulthard et al, 2002).

Transient populations undermining areas

The interviewees felt that the presence of long-standing residents and extended family networks contributed to the stability of the neighbourhood. Alongside a stable core population, many of the neighbourhoods also experienced high turnover of sections of the population, for example newer residents and single people. The groups felt that the transient nature of parts of the estates contributed to a lack of stability and commitment to the area shown by residents. High turnover in other types of areas, for example in an area of young single professional renters, might reflect upward mobility and was not a serious threat to the neighbourhood. But people moving in and out of these areas reflected instability and undesirability.

This perception based on experience is backed up by research evidence (Power and Tunstall, 1995; Burrows, 1997; Young and Lemos, 1997; Coulthard et al, 2002). Residential stability and a high density of families with children as described result in strong local friendship ties (Sampson, 1988):

> 'An area of neglect in itself attracts problems. I'm talking about fly tipping. There is a general feeling of nobody cares, and that it's always been like that and it always will be. Also, there is rapid turnover. The builders leave rubble in people's gardens. Whoever moves in has to deal with it. We're careful not to blame the local community.' (director of a voluntary organisation, Birmingham)

> '[Private tenants] get evicted from one bloke, or move when they can't pay the bills, then move to a house round the corner.' (resident, Wakefield)

According to residents from Wakefield, many properties were boarded up and the abandoned houses had collections of dumped rubbish and furniture in the backyards. The homes that were occupied were run down and not cared for. Residents in Rhyl said that people built up big bills with catalogue firms like Empire Stores and then moved to avoid repayments:

> 'It's like a gypsy encampment, people move flats, they don't rest where the caravan stops! They try and better themselves. You regularly see people with prams going down the street with TV sets and wardrobes in them.' (resident, Rhyl)

Closed communities

Stable, long-standing populations contributed to area viability according to the groups. However, the positive aspects of close-knitted and tightly bonded communities were in contrast to some of the negative consequences of closeness. References to the problems with 'closed' communities ranked second in comments about negative aspects of communities in the interviews (14 out of 48 comments; see Table 3.4). The downsides of community ties have been explored elsewhere in the literature (see, for example, Portes and Landolt, 1996; Aldridge et al, 2002) and the interviewees were extremely conscious of the issues. This suggests that their advocacy of 'community' was not wholly based on a simplified and idealised notion of the purely positive aspects of communities. The negative aspects of closed communities raised by the groups were:

- wariness of 'outsiders', and isolation of incomers
- problems within the community were hidden or covered up
- feelings of lack of privacy
- negative social behaviours or anti-social cultures were protected and encouraged
- restricted aspirations and insularity
- divisions between and within sections of the population.

Unwelcoming of 'outsiders'

One aspect of this was that the established community was wary of, or hostile to, outsiders, or 'incomers'. 'Outsiders' felt isolated. According to a parent support group in Cheshire, the majority of the group were "born and bred" and "old [X place] people". But one person said "I still feel like a newcomer, an outsider and I've been here for 12 years". Other examples included:

> 'I was here a whole year before someone spoke to me.' (resident, Bristol)

Community workers in Preston described how the Asian community worked on strong family and extended family links. One of the group's users was a single mother. She said that she had no family links: "I haven't got a mother-in-law". She therefore felt isolated within the Asian community.

Some groups pointed out that closeness could lead to problems within a community being hidden. There were also hidden mental illness and health problems: "The community is quite closed, so problems are covered up" (headteacher, Keighley).

Strong ties in a neighbourhood could also generate a feeling of lack of privacy:

'Everyone know everyone else and they know your business before you do! It's that type of place. It's what you might call old fashioned. The fact that it's such a closed community can have drawbacks. You know, if they saw so-and-so coming in and they knew it was the day the debt counsellor was here they'd think I wonder what she's got to go there for.' (resident, Derbyshire)

Reinforcing an anti-social culture

Interviewees detailed the protection that close-knit networks of family and friends gave to people engaged in negative social behaviours, or how these bonds reinforced an anti-social culture:

'One lad, we had to ban him from the youth club. He went home and told his mam he'd been barred. He came back with a baseball bat. It was his mam what told him to do it.' (resident, Stockton)

And in a separate interview with a community worker in the same neighbourhood:

'Crime is practically non-existent, but there's very high fear of crime. There's four or five families. It's the same as you generally have anywhere.... We did have a youth club. It was volunteer led, but [it closed] when the parents sent their children down with baseball bats.' (community worker, Stockton)

Restricting aspirations

Solidarity can also mean insularity. Groups referred to the way that this insularity restricted the visions of the people who lived there, or reinforced a culture of low aspirations:

'[On an outing, the children] didn't know how to enjoy themselves. The adults are just the same. You look at the parents – they're kids themselves. They haven't finished their growing up before getting pregnant at 16. They just want someone to love, it's something that they *can* do. It's another world, and that's [this estate]! It's a bit insular. Some people have never been over the Humber. They wouldn't leave the estate to go to Beverley [20 minutes' drive away]. They might have been to Benidorm but ...' (community worker, Hull)

Causing divisions

The flipside of closeness is greater potential for division, both between sections of the population and within them. Outside of London, social housing is predominately made up of a white British-born population. There is an acknowledged problem for social landlords of trying to recruit minority ethnic tenants into social rented housing. For example, in cities such as Birmingham and Bradford Asian families suffer from overcrowding when living in private accommodation, while there are many empty council houses (Radcliffe et al, 2001). Ongoing racial tensions, as demonstrated by disturbances in Lancashire and West Yorkshire in 2001, have further strengthened the need for integration. The traditional local authority residents' associations in the study reflected the predominately white composition of those neighbourhoods, although, in the white areas, groups still faced issues connected to 'race', such as local Asian shopkeepers selling alcohol to underage children.

There were nine examples given of racial divisions in the neighbourhoods. These varied from relatively neutral comments about the separateness of different ethnic groups to more serious comments about racial harassment:

> '[The Sikh temple] don't like to become too involved in things.' (resident, Walsall)

One member of a group originally from Jamaica also described incidents in the housing office where older Jamaican residents were ignored and treated badly in contrast to white residents.

In another example from Keighley:

> '[The Asian community] don't mix. They never invite us [to their events], not that I'd go mind. They've got their own culture. It's the village culture transferred over here.' (resident, Keighley)

The groups picked up on differences between the levels of perceived integration of the Asian community versus the West Indian community:

> 'The Asians are playing catch up. They speak a different language, you can't go round their houses, you can't go out with their girls. We're fourth generation [African Caribbean immigrants], and we're saying what is going on? They [Asians] think that black and white are against them, but they keep themselves to themselves.' (resident, Bedford)

One West Indian group in Lancashire described long-running tensions between the Asians and West Indians over additional resources for facilities through regeneration programmes.

Racial divisions

In some places, there had been more polarising and divisive racial dynamics, leading to 'white flight' or harassment of minority families. One area in West Yorkshire had 5% white families, which had been the case for the past 15 years. The population shift started gradually, once "it got to the 50/50 point then the white population went down quickly. This used to be an all white school. People voted with their feet" (headteacher, West Yorkshire). But there were small signs that white families were coming back. One white family chose this particular school because they "know it's a good deal, because of all the extra input. The teaching here needs to be good, especially if there are ESOL (English as a Second Language) needs" (community worker, West Yorkshire). Lots of white families, however, have "fallen off the end" and gone to social housing estates.

One family on a social housing estate in Hertfordshire was being harassed, for example people setting the pram shed and dustbins near their house on fire. The community worker only found out after this had been going on for six years. She found out socially when a local firefighter mentioned it to her. The family had tried to get help via the housing department, but had been told that it "was just a neighbour dispute". The families' problems "weren't taken seriously" (community worker, Hertfordshire), and only the eldest daughter spoke good enough English so she was having to try and do all the negotiation, at 15 years old.

There were also worries about the divisive potential consequences of provision for refugees:

> 'They [the local authority] have kept four flats for asylum seekers. They're furnished, with carpets and everything. They're reserved for five years. No one has taken them up. They may be void for five years if people don't. It looks bad. They're going to stand empty and not be available to people who've lived in the borough all their lives. But I'm not saying that these people shouldn't get a roof over their heads.' (resident, Walsall)

Pride in racial integration and tolerance

None of the groups defended segregated communities. The residents felt lack of integration between ethnic groups was negative. This view was put forward by minority groups, as well as white groups. For example in Leeds community workers explained that the level of integration of second-generation Chinese depended on how good an education they got. If they did not succeed academically, then they ended up working in Chinese restaurants and takeaways. There was also an expectation from their families that they would help with and continue the businesses. They worked long anti-social hours so also had problems integrating, although some were doing well financially through work or businesses:

'People point to the large cars, but it's quality of life.... Before 1997, thousands of Chinese came from Hong Kong [to the UK] with Portuguese passports and not very good English. They have found it difficult to integrate into British society too, because of cultural difficulties.' (community worker, Leeds)

Where groups felt they had achieved a degree of integration, they were proud of their tolerant communities:

'It's a multi-cultural place Bedford. There are two Asian chaps – they're as English as me. It's because of the overspill from London. Some areas are mostly African, and [a neighbouring area] is mainly Asian. There are Italians near us – they like the 1930s houses. It's a mix of everybody. There's a few of us who bring colour onto the estate, like [another group member] and myself.' (resident, Bedford)

Both of the white residents had partners from a minority ethnic background, and Bedford generally had "lots of mixed race children and mixed marriages".

'There are a few black people on the estate. On our committee there's [three people from a minority ethnic background]. A representative from the [council] came to ask if there were any black people because: We want to give them extra information. [One black group member] thought, Are you suggesting we are stupid or something that we need extra tuition?. She was furious, most upset. That's the council. That's how they see it, but that's not how the community see it.' (resident, Walsall)

Before this, the same black group member was asked by a council worker "why didn't she just work with black kids" in her youth work.

Summary

Communities are about both the people who live within particular geographical locations and about the services, facilities and physical environments that people experience within a neighbourhood. The study neighbourhoods were typical of deprived neighbourhoods in the range of problems that they faced. The residents interviewed gave priority to public service delivery issues, which was in line with public service users' preferences nationally. Residents wanted, and sometimes got, regular, attentive, polite management and upkeep of social rented areas. The priorities of the resident representatives in the study matched the priorities of social housing tenants more generally. Successive governments have struggled with the massive change agenda for public services, which is still ongoing.

The residents were frustrated by day-to-day problems of a lack of hands-on management and maintenance of their homes and of public spaces, including: inadequate and inefficient repairs service; poor tenancy enforcement and ineffective action against anti-social behaviour; poor customer care; poor management of public and communal space or facilities; inappropriate allocations; and poor quality housing refurbishment. In addition, things such as insensitive or discourteous service providers further compounded the residents' feelings of lack of status and power to command a response. It was basic tasks, and the attitude with which they were performed, that rankled most with the residents. The residents' dissatisfaction with public services was representative of a significant minority of unhappy customers across social housing nationally.

There are naturally bound to be many differences and shades of opinion within any large group of people – there were upwards of 50,000 households in the 56 neighbourhoods, and 20 communities of interest. Even within the community groups themselves, the volunteers had many different viewpoints. But there was a consensus within the groups on the key issues, and national opinion surveys show a consensus in national opinion on key indicators, such as confidence in public bodies. We found that the interviewees' comments chimed with national figures that show worryingly low levels of public confidence in the way that public bodies managed things. Ironically, the area where the opinions of the residents in the study differed from the majority was in their recognition of the positive achievements of service providers and public bodies.

The residents in the study had privileged access to information from service providers. They were aware of and praised emerging service improvements led by social landlords and others. Although public services have improved, public perceptions of change have not followed suit, and rising expectations mean that achieving high satisfaction levels is more difficult. The residents' praise for service improvements was in contrast to normal 'consumer' perspectives on service change that do not follow actual changes closely, or lag behind.

In their awareness of improvements and praise for reforms of service delivery, the interviewees were unusual, compared with a majority of residents nationally. This indicates that more needs to be done by service providers to communicate with a wider body of service users.

There was praise for recognition by service providers of area and service problems, and strategic planning for the future; practical change and good existing practice in day-to-day management; and increased transparency, accountability and involvement. Moves towards neighbourhood wardens and neighbourhood management – getting things done, sorting out day-to-day delivery, consulting and engaging with users and working to improve services in line with users' priorities – were therefore in line with these residents' priorities.

Moves towards better accountability of service providers to users were welcomed by the groups, and are thoroughly in accordance with people's views nationally. The issues raised by community volunteers, and their 'bottom-up' thinking on suggestions for improvements, resonated with 'top-down' thinking by landlords and policy makers on ways to improve service delivery and customer care, and to tackle anti-social behaviour. Their views reinforce the necessity for the positive moves towards reinventing social housing that are currently taking place. The direction of change that residents pushed for was in tune and coincided with the emerging messages about public service delivery from people in the professions and from government.

The comments overall suggest that government policy on public service reform and on neighbourhood renewal is going in the right direction as far as residents were concerned, although neighbourhood renewal still faces serious challenges to improving neighbourhoods to an adequate standard.

Residents felt passionate about the need for strong communities. Strong and stable communities were partly based on length of residence and the presence of extended family networks. This was typical of low-income families nationally, despite trends for people to live further away from their families. In contrast to trends towards increasing societal fragmentation the neighbourhoods stubbornly remained tight-knit closely bonded communities, as did other low-income neighbourhoods in the UK. The neighbourhoods represented what to many is a dead or dying 'golden age' of British working-class community openness. However, far from being a form of nostalgia for lost patterns of relations, residents described an ongoing reality for those neighbourhoods, and many other neighbourhoods like them.

Residents in the study placed a high value on 'community spirit'. Contrary to many debates about community as an outmoded idea, this actually reflected a wider longing for cooperation and shared understanding within local areas in the UK and across income brackets. People's sense of belonging to a neighbourhood across the country was high, they saw their neighbourhoods as places where people looked out for each other most or some of the time and they valued their place-based friendships. The evidence on the value people place on 'community' is compelling.

However, the residents held ambivalent feelings about how these close-knit and supportive networks could sometimes be isolating for outsiders, claustrophobic, protecting anti-social cultures or hiding problems. They could be insular and restrict aspirations, and be potentially divisive. The groups' advocacy of 'community' was not wholly based on a simplified notion of the purely positive aspects of communities, and they were able to articulate many arguments reflected in the academic literature about the downsides of community ties and place-based social networks. There were tensions within communities, for example racial divisions, which were counter to the residents' desire for more integration. Where groups felt they had achieved a degree of integration, however, they were proud of their tolerant communities.

One community tension that residents dwelt on was the negative consequences of inappropriate allocations of vulnerable families who disrupted neighbourhood life, and how concentrations of vulnerable people exacerbated neighbourhood stresses. People that disrupted or damaged community relations were an immediate problem facing residents in the neighbourhoods. In social housing this problem was particularly acute because of the bureaucratic 'needs-based' system of allocations. These problems were part of the wider residualisation of the social housing sector particularly since the 1980s when public housing became the 'tenure of last resort'.

Residents' anger at people disrupting the neighbourhood was not about wariness of newcomers or people who were different in some way. Some of the vulnerable families at issue had actually been on the estate for some time. It was not simply about labelling some people in a negative way. The groups made it clear that it was the lifestyle clashes, and additional stresses that vulnerable or anti-social tenants placed on their neighbourhoods that were at the root of their anger, rather than the fact of newness or difference. They backed moves in government policy towards a more proactive, interventionist position emphasising the duties of tenants to behave reasonably. The interviewees were supportive of new approaches to the allocation and letting of social housing, in line with new experiments by social landlords in allowing choice, while maintaining fairness.

Concern for the community in all its forms was a key motivator for people to get actively involved in volunteering and community self-help; we move on to look at this in the following chapter.

FOUR

Community action: so what?

'… what they've come in [to the advice centre] for is a cheap cup of tea and what they can scrounge. We want to give advice and support, and have more say in local government and to empower residents to change their own circumstances. The hard part is to help people to change their own lives.' (resident, Rhyl)

The community groups in the study were engaged in a huge range of small-scale activities, which included running community centres, organising parents and tots clubs, doing litter picks, organising barbecues, meeting with landlords and other public services and running youth clubs. While laudable enough as activities in themselves, it may be difficult at first sight to understand their role in tackling serious neighbourhood problems. Other writers have posed the same question in trying to explore the value of community activity (Hastings et al, 1996; Chanan et al, 1999; Ferguson and Dickens, 1999). And possibly even more puzzling is why a project such as the Gatsby Project would invest over £1 million in these activities as part of an attempt to tackle serious and deep-seated social exclusion problems. We refer to this as the 'fishing trips' problem (Richardson and Mumford, 2002) – one of the first projects in the study was a couple of fathers taking a group of 10 children sea fishing in Colwyn Bay. The response from some policy makers and many academics working in the field of social exclusion was 'so what?'. At first glance sea fishing seems a wholly inadequate response to serious deprivation. As a tool to rejuvenate deeply disadvantaged neighbourhoods, it can be difficult to match up the rhetoric of community self-help with the reality. This chapter considers how we reconcile the claims made for the importance of community activity with the modest undertakings of groups of perhaps four or five committed individuals.

As described in Chapter Three, the estates and neighbourhoods the groups work in faced several problems. They were physically and socially disorganised, and they were neglected or treated badly by the services that managed them and by some of the people who lived in them. We have used these underlying area problems as a basis on which to categorise and understand the underlying significance of the groups' work. In response to failures in the delivery of public services, and the mismanagement of neighbourhoods, the residents have tried to improve the delivery of public services, and upgrade the physical environment of where they live. They have tried to get people to take better care of their neighbourhoods, each other, and occasionally themselves, by doing things designed to increase levels of citizenship and social inclusion. They also attempted to tackle social disorganisation by bringing people together, and increasing opportunities for the creation of social networks and therefore social capital. In doing this, the groups sometimes created spin-off projects, and provided a beacon role for others doing similar work in similarly isolated circumstances.

We have chosen to use over 450 concrete examples of successful work by the groups to try and answer the 'so what?' question. These examples show how the groups help neighbourhoods and people in them in very direct, practical ways – some minute, some on a more significant scale. However, 450 examples do not conclusively prove the case that community activity is of value and benefit. Before looking at the examples of the groups' work, therefore, evidence on the benefits of community engagement is reviewed. There is then a detailed look at what the groups do under five headings:

- improving public service delivery
- increasing levels of citizenship and social inclusion
- increasing opportunities for the creation and strengthening of social networks
- improving the physical environment
- creating spin-offs and providing a beacon role for other projects.

The benefits of community activity

Credible evidence

Policy to increase community engagement generally is based on many different sorts of benefits it is said to produce. The argued benefits of community engagement in policy form a long list, including: improving neighbourhoods, public services and local government; rejuvenating democracy including voter turnout; helping people feel less powerless and more valued; more resident satisfaction with the places where they live, and with decisions made that affect their lives; health and education improvements and reductions in crime; strengthened community cohesion and social inclusion; and value for money in public spending (Home Office, 2005a; ODPM and Home Office, 2005). Government documents make reference to research and 'evidence-based policy' making and policy delivery are very much in vogue (Cabinet Office, 1999), but many key policy documents contain only very cursory evidence or simply assert the value of involvement. Some policy summaries of the evidence have ended up making the arguments sound somewhat facile:

> As Robert Putnam argues ... communities that are inter-connected are healthier communities. If we play football together, run parent–teacher associations together, sing in choirs or learn to paint together, we are less likely to want to cause harm to each other. Such inter-connected

communities have lower crime, better education results, better care of the vulnerable. (Blair, 2002, pp 12-13)

And in the academic community, where the evidence for government policy came from, things are not quite so clear-cut.

The first of the five categories of the groups' work is about their involvement with mainstream services, particularly housing. Much of the evidence about the benefits of 'community engagement' is actually just about people's engagement with mainstream services rather than the sort of work that comes under the other four categories (Burton et al, 2004). These are about the groups' community self-help work, things the groups do by themselves not directly related to mainstream service providers. Much of the evidence about community self-help has been from the 'social capital' field, where the waters of evidence are muddied by arguments over one particular thesis by Robert Putnam (Putnam, 2000).

The consensus in the academic field is that, on the one hand, the jury is still out on the impacts of community engagement because the evidence is not robust enough. One summary states:

> A review published by the Home Office's Civil Renewal Unit in 2004 suggested that ... there is little systematic and comparative evidence on the impact of community engagement, or on what works and what does not work in terms of effective and cost-effective community engagement (Burton et al, 2004; Rogers and Robinson, 2004; Wilson, 2005). A more recent review of the costs and benefits of public participation concluded that 'there is a severe lack of data on the actual costs and benefits of public participation' (Wilson, 2005). (White et al, 2006, p 65)

The author of that report has concluded elsewhere that, without evidence, continued political commitment to community engagement is vulnerable, but that providing this evidence presents considerable methodological challenges.

Many academic commentators note that there is more advocacy, enthusiasm and evidence of perceptions of benefits or processes that might lead to benefits than strong evidence (Tunstall, 2000; Cole and Reeve, 2001). Stronger evidence would be based on research that was quantitative, large scale, with use of controls or comparators or attempts to take counterfactuals and context into account. However, even in the US where there are larger-scale studies of community development projects, and greater willingness and funding for more 'credible' methods such as randomised experiments, it is acknowledged that there are 'severe limitations in practice' in using these methods (Rossi, 1999). There is little information on the financial, non-financial or opportunity costs (what the time or money could have been used for instead) needed to make a full evaluation of effects. The limitations of the available literature mean that it is hard to accurately assess things such as:

- what level and form of user participation might lead to the claimed effects
- through what processes these effects could be produced
- under what circumstances they might be repeated
- whether there are any other effects.

The measurement of the impact and effectiveness of tenant participation in housing management has been said to be very complex (Cole et al, 1999). It is hard to find 'a series of precise indicators' to measure tenant involvement and its impacts (ODPM, 2000).

Positive research findings

On the other hand, even where researchers were concerned about the lack of reliable evidence, they ended up concluding either:

- that the costs of community involvement were modest and generally outweighed by the benefits to services or neighbourhoods, especially in specific services (Cole and Reeve, 2001; ODPM, 2005a)
- that involvement had other benefits, for example for empowering the people involved (Goodlad et al, 2005)
- that despite the limitations of the available evidence there was a large body of evidence pointing in a similar direction (Burton et al, 2004)
- that engagement has the potential to provide benefits (Rogers and Robinson, 2004)
- or at the very least that hypotheses about the value of involvement are worthwhile being tested further (Burton et al, 2004).

For example, in one of the literature reviews mentioned above the researchers say: '[several factors] have got in the way of more rigorous empirical research design [on impacts of community engagement]....That said, the sheer volume of usually qualitative case study research, and its broad agreement on what constitutes good practice in this field, provides an impressively large body of overlapping and similar advice on aspects such as appropriate processes and techniques of involvement' (Burton et al, 2004, p 48). Another review of the research (Cole and Reeve, 2001), despite criticisms of the evidence, argued in favour of user involvement based on the available evidence. Notwithstanding the many health warnings about the evidence, there is much material on the benefits of community involvement and community activity.

Official bodies that are responsible for ensuring that public money is spent economically, efficiently and effectively have made the case for community engagement as good business sense. The former head of the Audit Commission argued for tenant involvement in large-scale capital spending programmes in housing to maximise satisfaction with capital projects, and therefore value for money that he says is 'clearly demonstrated for the schemes in this research' (Foster,

2000, p 5). The National Audit Office has argued for participation in regeneration to make the benefits sustainable (NAO, 2004).

Tenant involvement in housing

There is considerable qualitative and anecdotal evidence showing that staff and tenants believe that participation has direct and positive effects on social housing services (Bines et al, 1993; Power and Tunstall, 1995, Cairncross et al, 1997; Audit Commission and The Housing Corporation, 2004). This includes things such as: reducing the number of empty properties; reducing repair times and costs; better re-let times for vacant homes; more appropriate allocations of homes, and customer-friendly lettings; decreasing anti-social behaviour; improving estate cleaning; and better design of homes/refurbishment.

Increased tenant participation has been shown to increase resident satisfaction with their homes, estate and the management service (OPM, 1999). Increased contact and improved relationships with service users may improve staff information or morale, and may make some aspects of management easier over time making the job more fulfilling (Watson, 1994; Power and Tunstall, 1995; Cairncross et al, 1997). And 'some initiatives can have lasting impacts of the attitudes and behaviour of local government officials' (Stewart and Taylor, 1995, p 58).

Evaluation of tenant participation compacts after the first year showed significant benefits in terms of positive cultural change in organisations, changes to the way housing organisations did business planning and engaged with users (Albourne Associates, 2001). Other research shows tenant participation can help overcome paternalist service provision (Reid and Hickman, 2002).

If community groups are the answer, then what was the question?

Community groups' activity at the scale discussed in this chapter is not by itself going to turn round an area. Part of the problem is that claims for the impact of community action are often overblown. We have argued previously the obvious but important point that 'small community groups cannot, by themselves, combat the effects of exclusionary forces like poverty, polarization and depopulation. A fishing trip is just a fishing trip' (Richardson and Mumford, 2002, p 225).

Paul Henderson has argued: 'Equally important is the need to avoid presenting community development as a panacea. The commitment to be found among those people involved in community development, as well as its idealistic, principled language, make it vulnerable to this tendency' (2005, p 55). The experiences of community development approaches to urban revitalisation in North America has led one prominent writer to argue that 'effective policies for increasing the capacity of communities to supply social capital' (Sampson, 1999, p 270) would learn from the following lesson about structural aspects of the neighbourhood: 'policy [to develop social capital] must seek to join the forces of informal social control, local institutions, and extralocal (public) control while at the same time ameliorating the constraints imposed by economic inequality, racial segregation, concentrated poverty, and residential instability' (Sampson, 1999, p 270).

It is hard to show what impacts individual small projects have, but the idea is that on a grand scale the cumulative impact of all the small projects added together creates positive outcomes for society and the people in it. These arguments about the role of 'social capital' associated with Robert Putnam (Putnam, 2000) have excited much interest, but also polarised the debate into Putnam supporters and detractors. As a result, attention has perhaps been drawn away from some of the positive things about what the groups do. The groups' work is made to bear the weight of proving the case for social capital when it may well stand up by itself. For example, it could be argued that telling mothers new to an area where local schools are, persuading young men to go to college or organising a fun evening with singing and food are all good things to do regardless of whether they help reduce national crime rates, or make the nation healthier or more economically productive.

Understanding the Gatsby groups' work

The groups inevitably described the successes of their work more than anything else – we collected 476 examples of successful work by groups and 16 examples of unsuccessful work. We now look in detail at what the groups did, summarised in Table 4.1.

Table 4.1: The groups' work against social exclusion

Work against social exclusion	No. of successful examples	No. of unsuccessful examples
Public services	128	8
Citizenship	115	0
Social capital	98	3
Built environment	75	0
Beacon role	60	5
Total	**476**	**16**

Improving public service delivery

Resident representatives in predominantly social housing neighbourhoods are very aware of their dependence on social landlords in order to effect neighbourhood change. The social housing neighbourhoods in the study were very clearly 'publicly managed' areas, many at that time with near monopoly public landlords. These were places where somebody was supposed to be in charge, of the housing at the very least (Power, 1997). Moreover, where social landlords owned large amounts of stock in a neighbourhood they had an obvious stake in making it viable (Power and Richardson, 1996). Local authorities had general overall responsibilities for aspects of mostly privately owned areas, but the higher profile and greater visibility of social landlords meant that the landlord body had a clearer responsibility in predominantly publicly owned areas, not just for each individual unit, but also across the whole neighbourhood. In addition, as a result of their additional problems and stresses, these low-income neighbourhoods had a high degree of contact with other public service providers such as the police, social services, welfare benefit services and regeneration agencies. In fact, three quarters of the neighbourhoods where the groups worked were the subject of special regeneration initiatives.

The Gatsby Project supported groups that were bringing about improvements in public services that were relevant to residents. Out of the five categories of direct work by the groups shown in Table 4.1, improving public services was mentioned most often. This work took different forms, as shown by Table 4.2.

Table 4.2: The groups' work to improve public service delivery

Action taken	No. of examples	Rank
Housing and neighbourhood management	36	1
Visible improvements	34	2
Signposting to services	19	3
Accountability and customer care	17	4
Replaced services	12	5
Services more tailored	10	6
No results yet	8	7
Total	**136**	

Lobbying for better housing and neighbourhood management

The residents interviewed gave priority to public service delivery issues, which, as shown in Chapter Three, was in line with public service users' preferences nationally. Successive governments have also struggled with this massive change agenda, which is still ongoing (DETR, 1998; ODPM and Home Office, 2005). We also saw that public services improved, although public perceptions of change have not followed suit, and rising expectations mean that achieving high satisfaction levels is more difficult. The public service reform agenda has not just emphasised public perceptions; there has been a significant emphasis on public engagement in all of its forms in making services better for users (Home Office, 2005a; ODPM, 2005a; ODPM and Home Office, 2005). There is still serious debate over the value of user involvement in service improvement, for example much of the mainstream performance management literature has lacked a strong emphasis on user involvement (HM Treasury et al, 2001; Audit Commission and IDeA, 2005; Richardson, 2005a).

The following examples show through detailed practical cases how the groups worked with services to make changes for the better. The direction of change that residents pushed for was in tune and coincided with the emerging messages about public service delivery from people in the professions. For example, residents argued that a different treatment of empty homes, putting up net curtains instead of security grilles, would not draw unwanted attention to those properties. This was a new idea and a subject of debate in the profession at the time (Pawson et al, 1997). Indeed, some residents felt that they had been ahead of the times, and were only glad that public and other agencies had caught up with their thinking.

Resident activists seemed to have fewer qualms than professionals about arguing in favour of controversial measures such as vetting social housing tenants or being tough on anti-social behaviour, working from the first principle of what was best for the neighbourhood as a whole. In some cases residents argued for a 'tough to be kind' approach, for example residents in one group persuaded the local authority to reduce the amount of time before they took action on arrears, so that people did not get into serious debt before anything happened.

The messages on improving service delivery from the groups were:

• common sense principles of flexible and people-friendly delivery, as also outlined in the Priority Estate Project model of localised, responsive and flexible hands-on housing management with frontline decision making (Power, 1987);

Institutions sometimes made decisions that created brutal or inhuman outcomes. Residents promoted common sense principles of people-friendly services.

- taking more care with small maintenance and cleaning jobs, in line with the improved efficiency required by BestValue in housing (the duty of continuous improvement for local authorities as set by the 1999 Local Government Act);
- multi-agency work against anti-social behaviour, considered to be good practice in the literature and recommended by the National Audit Office (NAO, 2001; Scott et al, 2001);
- making services more sensitive, and achieving good quality customer care, as stipulated by The Housing Corporation (The Housing Corporation, 2003).

Common sense principles: lobbying to improve the management of homes and of the neighbourhood ranked top in the groups' successes in improving the efficiency of service delivery (36 examples). They illustrate the potential for community consultation to stimulate and direct service and area change, and the examples were often of basic and common sense principles of flexible and people-friendly delivery. Successes for one residents' association in County Durham included a change to the policy on void units. Previously houses would have been boarded up, but it was felt that this "looks shabby" and would attract damage. Residents suggested they put nets up instead, and install burglar alarms. This happened and was successful – there was much less vandalism and glass breakage. Residents also persuaded the council to change allocation policies on family housing as demand dropped. The local authority reduced the age of eligibility for family houses from 30 to 25 years old. The director of housing said: "Through working with residents they pointed out the issue and helped back up officers who thought it was daft that at 26 you couldn't allocate".

One group in west London had some success in improving their estate, for example environmental improvements where parking was restricted. Previously there had been a problem with people illegally dumping cars. Residents persuaded the council to put up security cameras and security locks/entrance systems to the communal entrances so all had locked doors. One major thing was to get the council landlord to name the blocks on the estate, because previously they had just been lettered A, B, C, so the residents all used to joke about it being Prisoner Cell Block H.

Many of Hull's terraced houses have back alleys known as the '10 foots', and people put their bins out in these 10 foots. "These huge lorries trundled up but the 10 foots were cracking up" under the weight, said one resident. "So, the council decided in its wisdom it couldn't collect from the back, people would have to put their bins to the front." This was not a good solution because people would have to take the big bins through their houses:

> 'There was public pressures, and it got changed – the council uses smaller lorries, and are making good some of the 10 foots. Around 400-500 people turned up to meetings – people felt strongly.' (council officer, Hull)

Taking more care with small maintenance and cleaning jobs: some problems were that the landlord or local authority and its staff were not taking enough care in the tasks they should already have been performing, such as in the case of poor street cleaning. The residents in the study were unusual, however, as they referred to policy tools designed to improve local government, such as Best Value. This was at a point when nine out of ten people had not heard of the concept of Best Value in relation to local government (Grant et al, 2002).

Pressure from residents on existing responsibilities not being carried out resulted in staff paying renewed effort and attention, sometimes alongside more effective ways to do jobs, such as motorised street sweepers. A residents' group in Stockport started with a list of 19 basic maintenance jobs that it wanted the landlord to complete. The list included installing and mending street lighting, closing off dangerous alleyways and mending broken steps. "Once they got to know us and they knew we were serious, they changed overnight – they couldn't do enough to help us" (resident, Stockport).

In another example from Walsall:

> 'There is a problem with drainage on the estate. The DSO [Direct Service Organisation, the local authority in-house maintenance team] came. They turned up in a van, looked at the puddle and the drain and then drove off. I rang [the housing manager] and he said that he'd had the bill through already! That's not getting Best Value. We promote Best Value and if we question it then [harrumph harrumph].' (resident, Walsall)

Multi-agency work against anti-social behaviour: one major responsibility the tenants fought to get landlords and other agencies to take on board was enforcement of sanctions against anti-social tenants (tenancy enforcement). There were some examples of multi-agency work to do this. In Nottinghamshire, for example, there was now multi-agency work in the area, and every couple of months, 12 agencies including the Neighbourhood Watch group, the local authority housing department and the police "chuck names into the hat and share information. It's a question of letting the left hand know what the right is doing" (resident). This had had positive outcomes. For example, in one cul-de-sac, the Neighbourhood Watch group had been videoing vehicles coming in and out they thought were related to people dealing or buying drugs. The group gave these videotapes to the police, and the police were going to use them as evidence for a warrant on the perpetrators before the housing department evicted them for rent arrears. The suspect drug dealers had rent arrears of £400:

> 'We work together, for example, we issue a warrant the day before, and seize their money so they have no means to pay the arrears, so it helps with the eviction, but it means that the police get the money because of the Drug Trafficking Act and the housing department loses

out [on the bad debt]. In one case we seized £1,200 and £10,000 worth of gear.' (police officer, Nottinghamshire)

Making services more sensitive: it is a relatively major action to change the policy of how social resources such as subsidised housing are allocated to people in need, or to change the way that drug enforcement is done, as in some of the examples above. But not all the groups' successes were of this magnitude. Other examples were of seemingly minor changes that made the way that services operated more sensitive to the needs of its customers:

'There are a lot of mixed feeling on the estate about the redevelopment, especially people who have been on the estate for a long time. They hate the thought of having to move into temporary and then move again. So we suggested that there's help for the pensioners moving.' (resident, Liverpool)

This included the groups' work to improve standards of customer care in public service organisations. In the interviews 17 examples of where groups had achieved this were gathered, as shown in Table 4.2. The perceived negative or indifferent attitude of service providers and their staff towards their customers exacerbated the residents' feelings of anger and frustration at what they were getting. The residents' groups felt that their contact with providers had in some cases caused an improvement in the way people were dealt with as clients, as well as in the accountability of the services more generally.

Lobbying for capital investment to make visible improvements

The examples given above are all of ongoing day-to-day housing and neighbourhood management, but some of the neighbourhoods were in such a poor state of physical disrepair that residents also lobbied for more thoroughgoing improvements. We collected 34 examples (shown in Table 4.2) where the groups had played a pivotal role in persuading the landlord or local authority to make capital investments in the neighbourhood for its longer-term future. 'Housing investment alone is unlikely to "turn around" estate decline and bring long-term changes', but capital investment has been shown to benefit neighbourhoods if it is done using resident involvement, and if it is integrated into wider strategies tackling physical, management and social issues (Cole and Reeve, 2001, p 5).

On one of the estates in Wrexham, the three-storey houses had some structural problems: "To us it looked like their backs were broken" – they were sagging badly. So "we pestered and pestered" (resident). They were built on a concrete plinth and:

'... the surveyor said that birds had been pecking away at the concrete, then he said it was thermal nuclear movement, then he said we wouldn't understand the survey because it was too technical. It turned out that he hadn't done one! He'd only done a soil sample, not a structural survey as such.'

The surveyor also told them that:

'… in fact, the buildings can't move because of their metal structure, and the gap between the buildings is a three foot cavity, but [a local councillor's] mum proved you can put a knitting needle into next door's house. You've heard nothing like the rubbish they were giving us. It ended up it wasn't cost-effective to repair them, they knocked them down. We had them by the short and curlies, we were asking too many questions and put too much pressure on. That's the start of a different understanding.'

"Where people were scare mongering" about the houses being unsafe, "we supported the council" (resident). This was in 1989/90, and the houses were not knocked down until 1995:

'It took ages, they tried to fob us off. The actual survey took two years. If they'd have spoken to [an elderly resident] who lived here he'd have told them there was 80 foot mine shafts under the houses [which was what was causing the subsidence].' (resident, Wrexham)

Guiding the direction of large-scale change: as well as pushing for major physical improvements, resident involvement also helped to guide the direction of these large-scale physical changes, for example where there was large-scale redevelopment of social housing and landlords consulted extensively with residents about the major decisions being taken about people's homes. The following examples illustrate the importance of resident involvement in pushing for resident priorities, giving people information about major changes to their homes and allowing them a say in this.

On a Liverpool estate the block of flats we met in was not considered by the landlord to be among those in the worst condition. The landlord's policy was worse first, so no work had yet been done on these blocks. There was an option appraisal and some tenant consultation but "some of the [community development staff team] are unhappy about the way it was done by development" (community worker). The staff responsible for physical redevelopment did individual visits, a questionnaire and a public meeting with tenants, but "only one option was presented". "They said they were going to refurbish it all, but they've actually demolished most. We'll be lucky to get anything in 2004 when we're due. If tenants want refurbishment they'll have to fight for it" (resident, Liverpool).

Minor capital improvements: there were some examples of successful lobbying for smaller value capital spending, such as replacement windows and roofs, environmental improvements and traffic calming. A residents' association in Manchester was set up to improve the sheltered housing scheme. The association got a chairlift on the stairs, fenced round the outside of the grass, and installed walk-in showers, handrails in the corridors and heating in the lounge. "We've fought hard for things. We got told we couldn't have the fencing so we went to the *Evening News* about it"; "Even [a senior officer at the housing association] said we wouldn't get the chairlift – he was amazed when we got it" (residents, Manchester).

> 'The committee started it, then it needs someone to make it happen like the broken flags, the handrails for the disabled, the coal bunkers taken away, all sorts of bits and pieces like putting in plants with big thorns to stop people cutting across, getting salt bins installed.' (resident, Keighley)

All these improvements were done after lobbying by the group.

Liaison, advice and brokering with services

Even where there were capital improvements, the process of doing extensive work on people's homes was sometimes fraught, and the groups found themselves playing a smoothing function while work to homes was going on. For example, on an estate in Derbyshire the residents' group started in 1993 because of problems during refurbishment work on the houses: "They came and ripped down the houses around our eyes". The residents were not moved out while the work was happening: "there were so many complaints from residents", as well as the contractors, that a group started to liaise between residents and contractors, "a place to vent your spleen" (residents).

The residents' groups played a liaison, brokering and advocacy role between residents and public services more generally. A common example was the work of the tenants' and residents' associations to chase complaints about outstanding repairs with the landlord on behalf of residents. As one group explained, the landlord preferred to deal with batches of complaints with the residents' association acting as an intermediary instead of getting a series of individual complaints. In Keighley, one housing officer saw the tenants' association as "the link between the collection of tenants and the housing office. Their role is letting us know what is going on."

Several of the groups brokered between people needing housing and the social landlord. This is a more hands-on aspect of the groups' work lobbying to improve service efficiency on the allocation and letting of housing:

'There were three bungalows void. [The housing manager] said they're going to go hard-to-let, I've got no tenants. [The chair of the group] said you can't do that, they're gorgeous. So, I got onto one lady who I knew because her mum needed a place. If [the housing manager] was doing his job properly, he should know his tenants. He doesn't door knock. They're all occupied now – we found tenants.' (resident, Walsall)

In another example, County Durham Council were going to sell off six empty houses. Residents heard about this and did not want to lose the social rented units. They said they knew of people who wanted to live on the estate and referred new applicants to the housing department. The director of housing confirmed the residents' role in changing the Empty Property Strategy:

'The community said we know people who want to live in them, so we changed to three for sale and three for rent.'

The groups dealt with a range of issues and service providers. While the examples above are about housing, other groups played a similar advocacy role in relation to other services such as healthcare:

'We've also campaigned against doctors who visit people in their own homes to do medical assessments. For example, one who visited someone in a bungalow said that they could climb stairs! We keep an eye on malpractice. They can visit any time of the day or night. It's not appropriate to what people do everyday.' (volunteer, Cheshire)

Some doctors got claimants to "sign a blank form", which was particularly bad for "elderly people, they think that doctors are God, so they can pull fast ones. They lose benefit and it can't be challenged [easily]" (disability advice worker, Cheshire).

We collected 19 examples of this liaison role through which residents had directly changed or improved public services. In total, we collected 80 examples of the broader brokering work of groups to link up residents and existing services, shown in Table 4.3.

Advice and 'signposting': many groups gave ad hoc advice or ran drop-in advice sessions (26 examples). They described their role as one of 'signposting' people to the right forms of help and helping people negotiate complex, often bewildering, bureaucracies of public services, especially of local government. Indeed, there is now a website called DirectGov (www.direct.gov.uk) designed for use by individuals looking for local and national government and public services that brings together information in a single place because of the complexity of provision. It illustrates recognition of the need for 'signposting'.

Table 4.3: The groups' liaison and brokering role

Action taken	No. of examples	Rank
Advice and signposting	26	1
Advocacy and representation	21	2
Base for outreach services	17	3
Publicise existing services	10	4
Referrals to services	6	5
Total	**80**	

Seventeen examples provided a base for outreach services where agencies could provide locally based provision. On an estate in Rhyl, one of the groups' volunteers lived in a bedsit locally:

'We're helping him get onto college courses, he's had alcohol problems, but he's got himself straight now. We found him a nice landlady and got him out of a bad landlord. He needed basic help really – the bus fare to get to college. He's now finding a job – he applied for one recently. We provide support and encouragement for him. People think there's a magic wand. We've got to help people understand the bureaucracy you've got to go through.' (resident, Rhyl)

A centre in Wolverhampton was also a help point for residents. While we were doing the interview, a couple of residents dropped in to get a copy of their Family Allowance book to get free school meals: "People always come in for help"; "Anything people ask, we always try and help, like helping older women read letters, CVs" (residents).

Advocacy and representation: twenty-one actions were to negotiate directly with specific services on behalf of residents. Examples of this were where residents helped people to deal with family or school problems. On an estate in north London parents developed a relationship with the youth club: "they have come to rely and trust us". One boy was being bullied at school, and the young person felt that his teacher was actually helping lead the bullying – the teacher called him things like a dull boy and his classmates picked up on it. The youth club advised the parent to talk to the teacher first, then try and reinforce the child's confidence: Yes, you can do it. The teacher apologised and it got sorted out.

Social services in North Yorkshire use a group to help them intervene with families in their care. For example, relations between one mother and the social worker had broken down. Social services asked the group, who had good relations with the mother, to persuade her to let them into her home and explain that if she did not, her children may be taken into care. The group persuaded her for her own good to let them into her home.

Publicise existing services: groups also helped to publicise existing services. A Hertfordshire group put elderly Caribbean residents in touch with dominoes clubs. A Bedford group produced a 'Welcome Pack' for new residents containing details of schools, shops, clubs and other facilities, as did a West Midlands group:

> '[We did the Welcome Pack] so when people come to the area they know where the schools are, and there's a little article by a mum saying what they're like. When I came here I got a list of the schools but I had to trudge round and find out myself what they were like and go on gut feeling.' (resident, Walsall)

In Walsall and in Liverpool, groups were access points for families to affordable warmth schemes. There was a national scheme to install central heating and energy efficiency measures in people's houses for free. One group was helping promote this through the office:

> 'One family had two young babies, their house was freezing and damp. I gave them the forms, passed them on. When I first heard there was free central heating, I thought "as if"!' (resident, Liverpool)

In this case (the scheme is now called 'Warm Front') the body administering the scheme welcomed the role of local groups in helping to publicise the service as one way among others to reach the 20% 'hard-to-reach' (Beck et al, 2005).

Increasing levels of citizenship and social inclusion

There were 115 examples of work by the groups to increase levels of citizenship, shown in Table 4.4.

The social inclusion and citizenship agenda has become prominent in recent years, crystallised in the 'Respect' agenda and government *Respect action plan* (Home Office, 2006). Work to increase citizenship has focused on young people, for example through the citizenship curriculum in schools. A group was identified of around 10% of 16- to 18-year-olds,[1] termed 'Generation Zero', who were out of touch with any mainstream institution, that is, school, college or work (SEU, 1999). One teacher working with excluded pupils on an alternative-to-school programme described how the young people had "fallen off a cliff face":

> 'I don't know why they're not in school, they seem reasonable enough kids, I don't know what happened for them to be excluded.'

The effect was that "some of the kids are very angry, very angry". All had either learning difficulties, behavioural difficulties or both. The majority had problems outside of school, for example home problems or were involved with the police. Some had been or were currently in care.

Table 4.4: The groups' work to increase levels of citizenship and social inclusion

Action taken	No. of examples	Rank
Leisure activities for young people	21	1
Anti-social behaviour	14	2
Educational work with young people	13	3
Decision making by young people	12	=4
Job training/incomes	12	=4
Educational work with adults	12	=4
Team building with young people	8	=7
Vulnerable residents and families	8	=7
Outreach to 'tough' young people	9	9
Emotional support for young people	6	10
Total	**115**	

> 'The kids get involved with gangs and maybe end up taking a knife to school because someone's threatened them and then they get in trouble. It's when they get kicked out of school and have nothing to do all day that they'll start taking a few drugs then, but it doesn't usually start with the drugs.' (teacher, Central London)

Even where the situation for young people is not so bleak, youth issues are a major priority for the groups, and poor neighbourhoods more widely. For example in 2000/01, 45% of householders wanted to see opportunities and facilities for children and young people improved in their area (ODPM, 2002b).

The citizenship policy agenda also includes responsible behaviour by adults. There have been government-funded experiments to try and increase citizenship by adults (Mayo and Rooke, 2006). Citizenship means a range of different things, including being an active citizen like the active residents in the study, but also people taking on moral and social responsibility as individuals. We look here at citizenship in the sense of people being more responsible for themselves. First we consider attempts to bring young people back into the fold and to help them behave in a more responsible way, and then at the dilemmas the groups faced when trying to change adults' behaviour.

Preventative work with young people

The groups expressed their feelings of responsibility and obligation as:

'You always look after the old and the young, because the young are with us forever, and the old aren't with us for long.' (resident, Wrexham)

They emphasised the need for preventative early work with young people. In North London one group's leader had a background in engineering; he joked that this helped his work with young people. If you can fix things then you can "fix human things! Human beings have dents like cars". The group worked with up to 25-year-olds but felt they needed to look at younger ones because:

'It's like [African style] smoked fish. Before they're smoked, they bend. Then you smoke the fish, and it becomes rigid and cracks.' (resident, North London)

In another example from Walsall:

'We can catch them at this age before they start [getting into trouble], they are at the sort of age where you can still imagine them in their pyjamas and their mums tucking them into bed!' (youth worker, Walsall)

Youth work

Half of all the examples of work to increase levels of citizenship and social inclusion were related to young people – leisure activities, educational work, team building, outreach to hard-to-reach young people and emotional and personal support:

'… hear them, they talk in the [resident-run] coffee bar. They, used to shout up the road to me, You big fat XXX. Now it's: Hello.'

There were problems on one Warrington estate with children lighting "fires on the back fields and in bins. This estate was the highest" for fire incidents:

'They [fire service] wanted to set up a group of kids, so me and [another volunteer] did it. I just asked them, would you be interested in meeting with the fire brigade and telling them what you want changed on the estate. The first thing we did was give them cameras. That's how it all started. They loved it.'

The children went round and took photographs of the estate and what was bad about it: "Then, we asked, Are you interested in doing the batteries? We did three visits to the fire station first of all." The young people learnt about fire safety. They then did a scheme where they went round houses on the estate to sell people smoke alarms and batteries:

'It was funny. People were shocked. It was the same kids that had been harassing them, now turning up on the door to help with batteries. They took nine off this estate for fire cadets. They love their uniforms. They're so proud of them. See, this field used to have a lot of fires but you can see the grass is growing back now. People can see we work with the bad kids and want to do more. It has got quieter on the estate. There are less fires. The kids work better together.' (resident, Warrington)

Assertiveness and education:

'What we've done must be working because the young people are accessing training. We're bringing them closer to Yale! This is a closeted estate, they think that's all there is.' (resident, Wrexham)

'We do poetry construction, words and their contexts, verbs, adjectives and metaphors, and confidence when performing. We give people techniques. When they're more confident they look at education in a different way – more motivated. You'll find schools where there is a lot of [racial] segregation, so we put everyone together so they feel a new relationship and break down stereotypes and barriers.' (resident, Manchester)

Opportunities and facilities for children are a priority for poor neighbourhoods generally. One of the key motivators for the groups' own work was their concern to help children and young people.

Giving children a chance:

> 'The children come here to release energy. We don't know what happens in homes, so we give them a chance to run around and play. We like to encourage social learning – like teaching each other to play. Some of the children on the estate have hard lives, they need a place to feel safe, escape, and get away from aggro at home.' (play worker, West London)

> 'Kids aren't born evil – you got to give them a chance.' (resident, North Yorkshire)

One group had been working closely with one teenager who was having family problems, also providing informal foster care at times: "She's learning to respect herself and not sleep with any lad who asks". She was now living in the local YMCA and doing job training in NVQ Business Administration.

Trying to change adults' behaviour

As well as work to increase levels of citizenship and social inclusion with young people, the groups also worked with adults and their families – half the examples were of work with adults. However, in contrast to the face-to-face work the groups did with young people, most of the work trying to change adults' behaviour was from a distance, for example by setting standards or trying to behave in an exemplary way. Far fewer groups attempted to alter the way that adults lived their lives on a direct face-to-face basis. This is partly because they felt that trying to tell adults how to behave was a more delicate task than guiding and directing young people. Getting people to change their behaviour to be better citizens, or more responsible for the environment, or to look after their own health more was a complicated and difficult task that government, academics and others have also wrestled with (Peters and van Nispen, 1998; Ekins, 2003; Bastow et al, 2007).

Aside from educational work with adults, for example through adult education classes in IT, the majority of these efforts were around trying to reduce anti-social behaviour. Mostly this work was in conjunction with landlords to tackle the problem using enforcement of tenancy conditions. While it may seem contradictory to some to say that residents advocating eviction was helping social inclusion, the residents' support for punitive action against anti-social behaviour was a way of re-establishing standards of behaviour. Their landlords supported them, for example:

> 'If people are causing problems, if they are made to feel excluded it will push them out. [Resident engagement is about] sustaining the area, if we can keep the hub of the community, if we can keep quality

[people], people who want to be here, then we can attract people to live on the estate.' (director of housing, County Durham)

Promoting better ways to behave

A few groups had bravely attempted to promote different models of behaviour directly. Residents in Hull, for example, bought a mop and bucket. This was because the cleaners only did the communal landings, not in front of the flats. People had to sweep and mop their own areas, but some residents were not: "We bought it because the young people were using it as an excuse for not mopping. They said they'd only pinch it but they didn't!" (resident, Hull).

According to the director of a voluntary organisation in Exeter:

'Everyone told us that the need was for parenting and youth work. We went in with an open sheet and an open mind. We had no preconceived ideas. Parenting wasn't even in our heads.'

The voluntary organisation then ran a series of parenting courses. "For £5,000 we've reached 50 families, that's £100 a family, £20 per family per session." The written feedback from parents was all very positive. It showed that people valued the courses and it helped them in their lives as parents. People enjoyed meeting other parents, sharing problems, finding out they were not alone and finding coping tools. For example, one comment from a parent was "it made me realise how important being a parent is, and it has helped with discipline".

Shifting patterns of behaviour

A few groups explicitly debated the tensions they faced on shifting patterns of behaviour. Groups helped to prop people up and deal with immediate crises, but they sometimes found it frustrating not to be able to help people make longer-term changes in the way they lived that might prevent problems from happening. Despite this frustration, groups were very wary of doing work to change adults' behaviour. This was because it would shift them into a more ambiguous position in relation to their neighbours, from representation and advocacy to what might be seen as moralising. On these grounds, some groups had rejected this option. Some did want to try and change adults' behaviour, but had not had much success. Based on their drop-in advice work on an estate in Rhyl, some groups felt that it could be difficult to support vulnerable people in need. They gave the example of one person who had come in with stolen televisions to sell, and "the following day the same person came in: Can I go to Vincent de Paul's [local Catholic charity] for a television? We have to sort out those in need, sort the wheat from the chaff" (resident). One person came in one day and they helped them get some furniture from Vincent de Paul, and:

'… the next day they were shoplifting out of Dr Barnardo's. We don't discriminate but if they've not followed up the advice, if they come back two days later when their money's ran out there's not more we can do, but we do try and help.' (resident, Rhyl)

Healthy eating was a good example of this debate at the time, although it has become more popular and mainstream since these debates first started. The following examples illustrate the groups' understanding of the challenge as outlined by one government think piece: '[public policy to change behaviours] is not just about the government and its agencies learning a few extra techniques to "make people eat their greens". Rather it is about helping individuals – and communities – to help themselves' (Halpern et al, 2004).

A group in Stockport had mixed feelings about promoting their community allotment as a health project. They called the vegetables they produced 'chemical free' and 'home-grown' rather than 'organic'. They also saw how difficult it was to change lifestyles overnight. For example the health promotion worker had been trying to promote walking and healthy eating, but lost support from some residents because he took the bacon butties off the menu in the community cafe: "Healthy eating's okay, but people must have a choice" (resident, Stockport).

In Leyland, one group thought that their food cooperative went wrong because "we were not only trying to change shopping habits, but people's eating habits as well" (resident), and this was too much all at once. "People's priorities are all wrong", for example they wanted their shopping there and then, even if it was more expensive. People do not plan ahead enough to make the system work.

And in Preston:

'I always thought that we needed a food co-op on the estate because of the poverty, people need to eat healthily. There's a lot of things that take parents' minds off their children – if you don't encourage them it's just a bag of chips, a bag of chips…. People have good intentions, but you've still got to remind them.' (resident, Preston)

Winning trust first

For others, they planned to resolve their dilemmas about giving unasked-for advice by first winning residents' trust – giving people things that they wanted and reacting to people's expressed needs. The groups hoped that this would develop a relationship with other residents where they could start trying to guide people more proactively.

In County Durham, the approach the group took was to tackle "functional problems", first, the "small everyday things" that most people found a nuisance such as drugs on the street, lack of facilities and physical improvements to the housing. They hoped that would build up trust gradually. They wanted to go from sorting out people's immediate problems to "trying to improve the way people live" (residents, County Durham).

In Rhyl, the group helped to temporarily solve people's most pressing immediate problems, which is why people came in. It wanted to do more, like "sitting people down and saying, Why don't you go on a college course?", but found that people in crisis could not respond to this well. The chair said the big vision for the group was "for helping people of this area through advice on their everyday needs and going ahead.... The hard part is to help people to change their own lives" (resident, Rhyl).

Increasing opportunities for the creation and strengthening of social networks

As discussed in Chapter Three, the groups felt passionately about their communities, and a big driver for many of the groups was their commitment to creating and maintaining a sense of community, both people and place.

For one group in Rhyl, it had no venue and felt it could only restore community spirit if it had a focus and base, and the survey of the views of residents on the estate backed this up. People wanted a place to have a youth meeting-place, things for older people, for example bingo, and a general meeting-place to stop people from being isolated and to help them get to know each other.

The biggest drive behind the existence of a minority ethnic umbrella group in Hertfordshire was always the establishment of the community centre:

> 'The driver to work together is to get a base where we can work together. We want to give an identity to multi-cultural communities. At the moment, if you're not part of a church, and you don't drink, then there's nowhere to meet. We want somewhere positive where people feel good about going to, not a hut on the hill.' (community worker, Hertfordshire)

As with the groups' attempts to increase citizenship, their work to increase social networks was also something that government, academics and others internationally wanted to achieve (Grootaert, 1998; Aldridge et al, 2002; Policy Research Initiative, 2005). The groups may share the goal of wanting to increase forms of social capital with such institutions as the World Bank, but they are, of course, in a different position to be able to achieve this. National and local governments struggle with the limits of the tools available to them (6, 2004). It is hard to imagine how the council could 'force' people to be friends, for example, although some innovative local authorities have put thought into this issue (Khan and Muir, 2006). In contrast, the groups' positions in their localities mean that they were able to directly influence the development of friendships between their neighbours in very practical, and often fun, ways.

We now look at the groups' work to build the community in terms of relationships between people. In total there were 103 examples of attempts to bring people in the neighbourhood together, both successful and less so, shown in Table 4.5.

Table 4.5: The groups' work to increase opportunities for the creation of social capital

Action taken	No. of examples	Rank
Regular events	35	1
One-off leisure activities	23	2
Good neighbours	14	3
Help for pensioners	12	4
Meeting spaces	8	5
Family contact	6	6
Tried and failed/difficult	5	7
Total	**103**	

Successful attempts to develop social networks

There were 98 examples of sucessful work by groups that created or increased opportunities for the development and strengthening of relationships between residents, shown in Tables 4.1 and 4.5. These opportunities took different forms, for example regular (35 examples) or one-off leisure activities (23 examples) like Tai Chi, line dancing, cross stitch clubs, social evenings with music and food, trips out, holidays, summer fêtes and Christmas parties, bingo, coffee mornings, cycle trips and lunch clubs:

> '[On trips out we take] a bus full. We throw it open to other groups and they do the same for us. It's families and old folks, everybody. People in here take their grandbairns. We never have seats left. This year we're starting BBQs – because we've just got funding for them.' (resident, Hull)

> 'We were really taking off. We did these nights out – this place was bouncing! We charged this time. The first time ... we got 40 people – it was a success. We decided to do it again but charge £1.50. Ninety per cent of the same people came back. Now we do it once a month.' (resident, Wrexham)

Most of the people who attended the social events in Wrexham were from the village and the estate, not the sheltered complex where the group was based. They ran a lunch club every week, which was on during our visit, and it was packed out with around 40 people eating and chatting, and a buzzing atmosphere with lots of mingling between customers, saying hello and passing the time of day.

Outcomes of more social contact

Groups described how they had encouraged people to build relationships through the activities, and what outcomes the contact had resulted in:

'We got £500 and took them to [a pub restaurant], we got a bus, you can have a three course meal, a bit of bingo and some dancing. Half way through on the way there, I got everyone to swap seats, so by the time we got there everyone had started to talk to each other. That started the community spirit.' (resident, Keighley)

The lunch club in Leeds for Chinese women is:

'... a venue to meet, to discuss problems between themselves, and they can approach the workers. Also the majority don't have anywhere to go apart from the Casino, not necessarily to gamble but because it's warm, you can drink tea, you save electricity! Quite a lot are either not diagnosed [as depressed] or are depressed and given tablets but they don't know what they [the tablets] are. They are depressed but they don't know what depression is.' (community worker, Leeds)

According to one community worker, most of the people eating there were older Chinese women who spoke only a little English. The women said they liked coming because of "the very good chef, the warm atmosphere", "make happy", "talking", "tasty fantastic food", "mingle with other elderly" and "have nice chat" (lunch club members).

Some of the groups are explicitly self-help/mutual aid clubs, where members provide each other with support:

'We meet once a month, and we talk on the 'phone a lot. Like I'll ring [X] to see how he's doing, or if I'm having a bad week I know I've got someone I can call on.'

'It's a shoulder. I don't like burdening someone but you can offload.'

'[It's] fun and sanity! It helps my sanity. And friends I didn't have before, I didn't know anybody.'

'It's helped me as much as I've helped other people. I go mad if I don't talk to anyone else – it's social contact.' (members of a parent support group, Cheshire)

'People's expectations are just of what it is, a place to talk. There is no obligation, it's a drop in.'

'The group are a listening post [where] people are sharing experiences.' (members of a mental health support group, Cheshire)

Others provided ad hoc 'good neighbour' support and help for older people (26 examples in total; see Table 4.5), such as fetching prescriptions and shopping for elderly residents. Much of this ad hoc work was related to older residents.

Communal spaces create social relationships

We included groups' development of general gathering spaces such as community gardens and cafes in this category (8 examples, ranked 5th; see Table 4.5). The creation of a public communal space could lead, but not necessarily, to social relationships being formed or strengthened (Amin, 2002). However, the groups' detailed comments suggested that, in practice, this had been the case. At a community cafe, "the single mothers from the nursery have started meeting together on Tuesdays and Wednesdays here" (cafe worker, Liverpool).

According to a headteacher and community workers talking about a school entrance in Keighley, the group put in landscaping, shrubs and plants, a water feature and three benches. They tried to incorporate the school pupils' ideas. The mostly Asian mothers used the area to congregate and chat when picking up and dropping off their children, and now they had extra benches it was well used.

Failed attempts to develop social networks

Five groups faced serious difficulties in bringing people together. For example, the residents' association in Sunderland "tried socialising and all that ... but people aren't interested". Residents used the group to resolve specific problems:

'... they grab us in the street if there is something they've already seen council about and it hasn't been sorted. That's all they're interested in, we've tried bingo, pie suppers, car boot sales but they just don't want to know.' (resident, Sunderland)

Improving the physical environment

We have described the run-down physical appearance of some of the estates. A neglected built environment is a public signal of an area's low status, for example

The groups improved public spaces, for example by demarcating green spaces as places people could use

derelict buildings and boarded-up homes are visible indicators of area decline and unpopularity. Equally, good quality green and public spaces contribute to the popularity and viability of a neighbourhood (CABESpace, 2005). Surveys show a high level of public concern with the built environment (MORI, 2002), and policy has coalesced around the 'liveability' or 'cleaner, safer, greener' agenda (ODPM, 2002c).

Community involvement in improving the built environment has been shown to deliver benefits that outweigh the costs, and has been integrated fully as part of policy on liveability (ODPM, 2000c; Williams and Green, 2001; McInroy and MacDonald, 2005).

We collected 75 examples of work by the groups to improve their built environment, shown in Table 4.6.

Table 4.6: The groups' work to improve the physical environment

Action taken	No. of examples	Rank
Green space/external communal space improved	35	1
Derelict building or site improved	23	2
Play facilities created or improved	9	3
Better internal space or private green spaces	8	4
Total	**75**	

Public and green spaces

We collected 35 examples (ranked 1st) of where groups had rescued or improved public spaces. Sometimes this was through simple actions, such as a litter pick, or demarcating green spaces as places people could use.

A tenants' association in Hull put up a couple of bird boxes at the front of the high-rise blocks: "It's surprising how many take an interest and give £1 for bird seed". They are looked after by two brothers: "they compete to outdo each other!". The group persuaded the caretaker to do a flowerbed: "[The caretaker] took out the shrubs and gradually filled it up. Tenants buy flowers, some buy them in memory of someone". People used to litter the grounds but the group have tried to stop this: "People don't mind doing naughty things but if other people know about it they don't like it. So we put a poster up – 'used condoms and underpants garden'!" (resident, Hull).

A project in Wakefield was to secure, clear and landscape a piece of waste ground behind the houses that had previously been used to dump rubbish. A private landowner owned it, and was persuaded by the group to lease it to them. They organised tidy-up weekends and consulted young people on designs for the landscaping. Bollards were installed to prevent people driving onto the land and dumping washing machines and mattresses. From the before-and-after photographs, the land already looks much better.

Every year a group in Kent organises a beach clean. One of the members lives in one of the large Edwardian houses facing the sea and organises a barbecue after the beach clean for all the helpers. According to one resident, they are due to have the clean-up soon – they walked down to the beach and it was covered in litter such as crisp packets and old paint cans.

In Liverpool, residents and a housing officer said: "We sponsor a community skip programme". They bought a skip for £300 and put it on the estate every week to a fortnight. The local authority took it away for free:

> 'It's been very successful. Only one has gone back empty. It's surprising how quickly it gets filled. It's been a good result on the estate. It's stopped lots of fly tipping. We change roads regularly. It's got our logo on, sometimes it goes elsewhere, so people ring up from other areas wanting one!' (residents, Liverpool)

Derelict garages on an estate in Stockport were given to the tenants' association by the council. The group bought new padlocks and some paint; for a total of £50 they refurbished 14 garages. They replaced doors and rebuilt the brick walls themselves: "we went round the houses for bricks. We've improvised" (resident, Stockport). They then let them back out on a first-come-first served-basis – the new tenants do not pay rent, but they have to maintain them themselves.

Eight examples (ranked 4th) were of work to improve private green spaces or internal communal spaces, for example through tool banks, where residents could hire garden tools at subsidised rates.

Rescuing buildings

The groups, desperate for premises, managed to use empty shop units or empty houses, themselves often a consequence of the lack of demand for these neighbourhoods and the withdrawal of services from the areas. There were 23 examples (ranked 2nd) of groups bringing derelict sites or empty/disused buildings back into use.

In early 1997 on an estate in Derbyshire there was a group of young people congregating at the parade of shops on the estate. They focused on the shop owned by an Asian family, but other shops also had smashed windows and graffiti. There was a crisis point and at public meetings 200 people turned up. Some of the traders wanted to ban the children. Instead, as a result of discussion, people ended up keen for something positive to be done about the youth problem. A project was started by a resident on the estate. It was based in a previously empty shop unit in the parade of shops where the trouble had taken place. There was a:

> '... group of kids who wanted somewhere to meet, and she saw this place was empty and she asked if they could have it for a youth club. The council said they could have it provided they had it as an advice and information centre. The kids did all the decorating. The young people made the curtains, covered the chairs. I don't think it'd have opened if it weren't for them.' (resident, Derbyshire)

Another example was of a high street cafe. The building was brought back into use from a derelict state, with capital works of around £50,000, not including help in kind, and the value of volunteer labour to do some of the work. The cafe/shop unit and office spaces above were then in a condition for use, with potential for a change of use: "We have rescued a building and brightened up the High Street" (resident, Lincolnshire).

Creating spin-offs and providing a beacon role for other projects

The Gatsby Project did not have the possibility for the replication of grant-funded projects as an explicit criteria for grant funding. However, it was very keen to encourage groups to develop spin-offs from their work – it hoped to see groups' work evolve and spread to a wider audience.

We collected 61 examples of where the groups' work had been exemplary in some way or had been a beacon for others doing similar work, of which five had been unsuccessful, shown in Table 4.7.

Table 4.7: The groups' beacon role

Action taken	No. of examples	Rank
Groups' work first in area	15	1
Set up spin-off groups	14	2
Individual members have recognition	10	3
Model for others	7	4
Recognised by wider body	6	5
Failed to create spin-offs	5	6
Others want to replicate	4	7
Total	**61**	

Groundbreaking and pilot projects

In four examples, the local authority was deliberately using work involving the groups as a pilot for possible replication on other troubled social housing areas. This is linked to the fact that these neighbourhoods were often the least desirable or most problematic to manage and to live in for those particular authorities. In 15 of the examples (ranked 1st), the work by the groups was the first if its kind in the borough. These were pilots by default, and formed the basis for replication even where this was not the original aim. Again, the activities were often linked to the negative status of the neighbourhoods, attracting additional attention from the landlord or local authority.

In local authorities in County Durham and in North Wales, groups were the first to win permission to convert an empty social unit into a community house. We know of other community groups in those boroughs that have now done the same. In Walsall and Keighley, the estates were the first to produce a local tenant participation compact as part of a new government policy to encourage tenant involvement, introduced by what was then the Department for Environment, Transport, and the Regions, in April 1999. Many local authorities were late in developing and producing their compacts:

> 'People are buying our compact off us, we were one of the only ones to finish on time.' (resident, Keighley)

Two of the other study estates were the first in their local authority to introduce an estate agreement that specified levels of service the landlord would provide, allowing tenant monitoring of service delivery. On a third estate problems letting homes had pushed the staff and tenants there into arguing for special dispensation from the housing committee to change allocations and lettings policies to 'vet' new tenants and reinforce rights and responsibilities.

Stimulating replication

In 11 examples of the groups' work (ranked 4th and 7th) there was a clear expectation by the local authority, or evidence from other estates in the area, that other community groups or estates wanted to replicate the activity.

A welfare rights manager and residents in Derbyshire described how their neighbourhood was "in the top half dozen for deprivation". The manager of the county welfare rights service said, "we have no resources for community-based work. We were aware that we weren't seeing as many people from [this area] as we should have been". The Gatsby grant was funding one session a week on the estate with a welfare rights adviser from the county's central service. The pilot was also sparking off other projects. The manager said that a nearby area was getting a local welfare rights service funded by the Single Regeneration Budget, partly because of the Gatsby-funded project's work on the estate. Another deprived neighbourhood was about to put in for one too, "if [this place] can have it, why can't we ... they've got it, we need it. It puts pressure on the council to do what they should be doing. It's only a small investment but it delivers results."

In another example, a director of a voluntary organisation in Exeter said:

> 'Several churches have set up their own groups [parenting classes]. People ask us how we did it. I said, Well, you've got the congregation, and the building, go ahead! We showed them our leaflets and how we did it, and the materials – we told them they can use these overheads. But they do their own thing – we give mutual support.'

Recognition of members

The quality of the groups' work was partly a result of the quality of their individual members. Ten groups had members who were also personally exemplary as community leaders, as evidenced by recognition from local external bodies under 'Community Hero' award schemes, or people's elected roles as heads of borough-wide and regional organisations. For example, one of the groups' members won a citizenship award organised by the borough council called 'Pride in [X Town]'.

Some of these groups had also been recognised by national bodies such as the Chartered Institute of Housing, the Department of the Environment (as was) and the National Association of Neighbourhood Watch Schemes.

Difficulties in cultivating spin-off organisations

Some of the groups created new independent organisations as a spin-off from their main group. This put the groups into the role of community development workers, and was not always easy. Five groups had tried and failed to develop spin-off groups. This was because the spin-off groups faced similar barriers to organisational development that the main groups trying to help them might also face. For example:

'It's a major problem with local people that getting them to accept that it's public money and they have to account for it. They'd say, Are you calling me a thief? – No, but I need the receipts because I need to put them through the books. [They] had never been involved in a formal organisation.' (resident, Rhyl)

People's experience was of things like running the darts team "and keeping the subs in a sock in the bottom drawer, they thought you could run in that way" (resident, Rhyl).

In another example, the group in the study was helping a group of men set up a fishing club. The group persevered but had reached a temporary impasse when interviewed:

'A group of men five years ago wanted to take [ownership of the fishing pond] over. They were loud. I asked one of them what his name was and he said Nutter – you know the sort of thing I mean! They weren't good at discussion, but they were good at demanding. So, it fizzled out. Now, there's a new guy interested. We're meeting with them to try and help them do their constitution and rules, and we're desperately trying to do equal opportunities. They don't see the point and they're a bit prejudiced. They want to show the little kids how to fish, but they've drawn a blank on the paperwork side. I can't take it any further with the council until they do it.' (resident, Walsall)

Groups created spin-off organisations

There were 14 examples (ranked 2nd) of the groups successfully creating new independent organisations, such as girls' clubs, slim and trim clubs, football teams and women's environmental groups. One group explained this 'incubator' role using an analogy:

'The Community Business Partnership is like a mother hen – it rears its little chicks and they set off on their own.' (community worker, Dudley)

A girls' club in Leyland was something that one group helped get started, but it was now run independently by the daughters of one of the group members. The original group donated £50 to help the club set up. It was for 7- to 11-year-olds, and they did art and craft, for example salt dough. They were also doing a show with music and drama. The adult helper said: "they decide, I haven't got a say! But I oversee if there are problems". They had their own membership cards that the girls made themselves, and paid 30p a week to cover the cost of materials. The aim was that the original group would be the umbrella for the girls' club, as well as the other projects such as a magazine and a garden project and that the projects would all flourish individually: "We're going to be big one day!" (resident, Leyland).

A slim and trim club in Liverpool started when:

> '… someone came in and said they'd lost weight, But have you seen the price of those slimming clubs, can you do it instead? So, we put it in the newsletter for people to turn up. We helped the first time with how to organise, we made up little cards to put weights on, but they do it themselves, because we can't do it.' (resident)

The philosophy of the club was for people to do things for themselves so the core group was not left organising all the activities. They helped get people going.

Summary

The argued benefits of community engagement in policy are many, but credible evidence is less easy to find. In the academic field many feel that the jury is still out on the impacts of community engagement, and there are considerable methodological challenges in getting more credible evidence. However, there are positive research findings, even from the sceptics. Research has shown that the actual or potential costs of community involvement were modest and generally outweighed by the actual or potential benefits. There is a large body of evidence pointing in a similar direction, and ideas about the value of involvement are worth being tested further.

We used over 450 concrete examples of successful work by the groups to help answer the 'so what?' question. These examples show how the groups helped neighbourhoods and people in them in direct, practical ways – some minute, some on a more significant scale.

The community organisations were engaged in running a variety of small-scale activities. Examples of these activities included running community centres, organising parents and tots clubs, doing litter picks, organising barbecues, meeting with landlords and other public service providers, giving advice about welfare services and signposting people to services, creating allotments and community gardens, running parenting classes, organising line dancing sessions and taking young people on fishing trips.

However, community groups' activity at a very small scale is not by itself going to turn round an area, and claims for the impact of community action are often overblown. Small community groups cannot, by themselves, combat the effects of exclusionary forces such as poverty, polarisation and depopulation. In fact their work may initially seem relatively insignificant in the face of deep-seated neighbourhood problems. We call this the 'fishing trips' problem. As a tool to rejuvenate deeply disadvantaged neighbourhoods, it can be difficult to match up the rhetoric of community self-help with the reality.

We try to understand the value of this small-scale work in tackling aspects of social exclusion by exploring how it contributed to addressing the immediate problems of social and physical disorganisation, neighbourhood decline and neglect. These underlying area problems provide a basis on which to categorise and assess the underlying significance of the groups' work. We show that in its own way a fishing trip is a valuable contribution to community building. A big driver for many of the groups was their commitment to creating a sense of community, both people and place.

In response to failures in the delivery of public services, and the mismanagement of neighbourhoods, the residents tried to improve the delivery of public services, upgrade the physical environment and tackle visible signs of the undesirability of neighbourhoods. They tried to cope with neighbourhood neglect and disorganisation by getting people to take better care of their neighbourhoods, each other and occasionally themselves. They tried to do this by doing projects designed to increase levels of citizenship and social inclusion. They also attempted to tackle social disorganisation by bringing people together, and increasing opportunities for the creation of social networks. They developed opportunities for the creation and maintenance of social capital. In doing their work, the groups sometimes created spin-off projects, providing a beacon role for others doing similar work in similarly isolated circumstances. They were models for replication.

The messages on improving service delivery based on the groups' achievements were all based on common sense principles of flexible and people-friendly delivery; taking more care with small maintenance and cleaning jobs; multi-agency work against anti-social behaviour; making services more sensitive, and achieving good quality customer care; investing in neighbourhoods; resident involvement in large-scale change; having a liaison, brokering and advocacy role between residents and public services; and offering signposting help through bewildering bureaucracies.

Some residents felt that they had been ahead of the times, and took heart that public and other agencies had caught up with their thinking, as they saw it. Resident activists seemed to have fewer qualms than professionals about initiating a discussion of controversial measures such as vetting social housing tenants or being tough on anti-social behaviour, working from the first principle of what was best for the neighbourhood as a whole.

In their citizenship and social inclusion work, the groups emphasised the need for preventative early work with young people. Creating and enhancing opportunities and facilities for children and young people was a major priority for the groups, and poor neighbourhoods more widely. However, trying to tell adults how to behave was seen as a more delicate task than guiding and directing young people. Getting people to change their behaviour to be better citizens, or more responsible for the environment, or to look after their own health more was a complicated and difficult task that government, academics and others have also wrestled with.

Much of the groups' work was reactive and responsive to other residents' expressed needs and immediate crises. But they sometimes found it frustrating not to be able to help people make longer-term changes to prevent problems from happening. Despite their impatience, groups were very wary of doing work to alter adults' behaviour and to increase levels of civic responsibility, for example persuading people to eat more healthy food. This put the groups that attempted such work into a more ambiguous relationship to other residents, from representation and advocacy to what might be seen as moralising. The groups were reluctant to openly moralise, while some still wanted to promote positive models of behaviour, and to generate a sense of civic responsibility, especially in neighbourhoods where it was difficult to get people to take individual and collective responsibility. They aimed to resolve their dilemmas by winning residents' trust first and building relationships before trying to guide people more proactively.

There were many examples of successful attempts to develop social networks. As with groups' attempts to increase citizenship, the groups' work to increase social networks is also something that government, academics and others internationally have wanted to achieve. National and local governments struggle with the limits of the tools available to them. The groups' positions in their localities mean that they were able to directly influence the development of friendships in their neighbourhoods.

Surveys show a high level of public concern with the built environment, sometimes called 'liveability' or the 'cleaner, safer, greener' agenda. The groups were contributing to the creation of good quality public and green spaces, which in turn contributed to the popularity and viability of a neighbourhood.

The groups' work had been a beacon for others doing similar work in isolated circumstances. In a few cases, the local authority was deliberately using work involving the groups as a pilot for possible replication in other troubled social housing areas. The groups had created spin-off community organisations.

Together the examples of the groups' work demonstrate how residents' concern for community, good quality neighbourhoods, environments and neighbourhood services was put into practice, and how the complementary community self-help role was worked out.

Note

[1] Officially termed 'NEET' (not in education, employment or training). The proportion of people classed as NEET nationally had remained at around 10% for over a decade. As of November 2004, the work of the Connexions service had reduced this figure to 7.7%, exceeding the government's target of 8.1% (Connexions, June 2005, http://www.connexions.gov.uk/partnerships/).

FIVE

The value of volunteering

One person argued that "It's a bugger if ordinary people have to do it for themselves".Another resident replied "but we *want* to do something for ourselves". (residents, Stockport)

Area problems may be distressing to those who live there, but they do not automatically trigger people to try and solve problems for themselves.There are many efforts being made by government, local authorities, voluntary organisations and others to increase levels of community involvement and volunteering, and the profile of volunteering and community participation has been raised within government over several restructures of government departments in order to push the citizenship agenda with more vigour. There is a cross-departmental government action plan called *Together we can* promoting local people working with government to solve problems that covers 12 different government departments (Home Office, 2005a). Other political parties are also promoting the role of the community and voluntary sector to tackle social problems (SJPG, 2006).

In terms of active engagement, the focus of the New Labour administration has been on increasing the amount and range of people who participate in their communities in different ways, particularly from groups that are currently least engaged.The official measured target between 2005-08 is 'to increase voluntary and community engagement, especially amongst those at risk of social exclusion' (Home Office Public Service Agreement No 6, 2004), which includes the proportion of those at risk of social exclusion who regularly volunteer, formally or informally, and the capacity of the voluntary and community sector to deliver public services, although the whole *Together we can* agenda is much broader than this.

In addition, moves to reform public services, revitalise local democracy and build a new concord between central and local government have focused on the need for active citizens.Termed 'new localism', the idea is of a 'double devolution', 'not just to the Town Hall but beyond, to neighbourhoods and individual citizens' (Miliband, 2005). One definition is:

> ... a strategy aimed at devolving power and resources away from central control and towards frontline managers, local democratic structures and local consumers and communities, within an agreed framework of national minimum standards and policy priorities. (Stoker, 2005, p 2)

New localism holds out many possibilities for community engagement, including: citizen control over decision making at the neighbourhood level, made tangible through devolved local budgets for environmental improvements and neighbourhood 'contracts' specifying minimum standards of service provision; community ownership of assets; and service delivery opportunities through commissioning for community and the voluntary sector (ODPM and Home Office, 2005). All of these possibilities require volunteers to be part of new governance and delivery arrangements.

Policy to increase community engagement is based on many different sorts of benefits it is said to produce. We have already looked at concrete examples of positive outcomes created by the groups, and reviewed the available research evidence on the benefits of engagement in Chapter Four. The central argument is that citizens and government should work in partnership, sharing responsibility for tackling problems and making an active contribution to improve the quality of life, particularly in low-income neighbourhoods.

There is an opposing side to the debate (Imrie and Raco, 2003), including from those in support of participation in principle, based on a long tradition of critical self-reflection within the community development profession (Cooke and Kothari, 2001). Some argue that it seems unfair that those who have the least resources should have to give their time and energy for no financial return, just in order to create the sorts of liveable places that better-off households enjoy. We consider whether people who receive poor service delivery are forced into doing things themselves because of the ineffectiveness of other organisations – a sizeable minority of volunteers (four out of ten) when asked felt that if the government fulfilled all its responsibilities there would be no need for volunteers (Davis Smith, 1998).

The chapter considers a range of questions, such as: is community participation just a way of distracting people from bigger structural and power inequalities without improving the position of poorer people (Kearns, 2003)? Are people being hoodwinked, manipulated or undergoing 'subjection' (Henkel and Stirrat, 2001) by agencies to justify their own actions or poor performance (Brett, 2003)? Will they genuinely be able to influence things (Cochrane, 2003)? Should we be encouraging people to put in voluntary effort to their communities? What makes people give their time when others do not?

Here we look at what the community volunteers' own views were about volunteering, about what motivates residents to be community volunteers and what the costs and benefits are to community volunteers. We discuss what people told us about their attitudes to:

- why they felt residents should do what they could to help
- what function consulting and involving residents played
- what motivated and sustained community volunteers, and
- what personal costs and benefits they experienced from volunteering.

Residents helping themselves

We saw in Chapter Three that residents felt ambivalent about the nature of their communities. They described negative aspects such as lack of privacy and divisions. Yet, overall they were passionate about the importance of strong and stable communities. Much of the groups' work was aimed at creating forms of social bonding, for example people put a great emphasis on the need for community facilities where social activities involving residents meeting together could take place. We also saw in Chapter Three that the residents were frustrated where mainstream service provision was not up to scratch, and were concerned about the disadvantage they experienced in their neighbourhoods.

But a belief in the importance of community, or frustration over failures of service delivery, does not appear to explain how people make the leap to deciding to act on those beliefs, since many people do nothing about their beliefs or frustrations. We did not directly ask about groups' attitudes to the principle of community self-help in the abstract. To gain an understanding of people's impetus to act, and their attitudes to the principle of self-help, we asked groups about the history of their organisations and how they began. We got people to narrate the chronology of their work and to give examples of the roles they had played. Through the discussions of the history and work of the groups in practice, some clear messages emerged about the general principles on which the residents based their work. In total, there were 139 comments on this topic (Table 5.1).

Taking views at face value?

What is missing from Table 5.1 are comments about how people might be going into volunteering because they were being manipulated or misled as to the real underlying problems. We chose to take at face value people's own explanations of why they volunteered. As we saw in Chapter Three, many of the residents were well aware of wider structural issues affecting their neighbourhoods, such as economic change leading to unemployment, or the way that local governments' record of poor administration had impacted on the places where they lived. They had chosen to deal with the immediate ways that those things impacted on their lives, rather than (or perhaps as well as) take political action to change the bigger system. There are many routes to tackling the causes and effects of disadvantage, and these residents had chosen the options they had chosen, possibly alongside other options they were engaged in that we did not discuss.

Of course, if people are being manipulated in a very sophisticated way then they may not be aware of the con. But as we saw from what residents said in Chapters Three and Four, they expressed their irritation when they felt agencies were not taking them seriously. In this chapter residents demonstrate their advanced ability to differentiate between situations where they had chosen to take on responsibilities because they saw it as preferable, and circumstances where they felt they were taking up slack from poorly performing agencies. They distinguished between

Table 5.1: Attitudes to the principle of community self-help

Attitude	No. of comments	Rank
Residents provide unique advantages	30	1
Complementary role of self-help	22	2
Action due to service failure	18	3
Positive role of mutual aid	15	4
Increases civic responsibility	13	5
Residents want to contribute	12	6
Need for community activity	10	7
Need for community development support	7	8
Creates sense of ownership	5	9
Self-help failed/inappropriate	4	10
Thorn in side of service provider	3	11
Total	**139**	

successful involvement where agencies responded, and unsuccessful involvement where agencies did not respond in the expected way. Far from feeling they had been put in an unfair position, however, residents argued for the advantages of local control, and wanted more of it.

In the Gatsby Project generally, through training courses, we had many conversations with thousands of residents to challenge their existing views, and to offer facts and new information. The 'dialogues' (Freire, 1972) we had were seen by the participants as empowering and confidence boosting, as can be seen by the feedback on the project in Chapter Eight. During the courses some big issues were covered, such as what the reasons were for high crime rates in particular areas, why some estates had a poor reputation, what role social enterprise could play in poor communities, what caused racial and ethnic tensions, and what environmental problems were being faced and why. We discussed what sorts of solutions worked best, for example challenging people who wanted CCTV (closed circuit television) with evidence that an extra security guard would cost the same, was just as effective, and also gave a local person employment. However, we did not attempt to persuade people that they should be engaged in a fundamentally different sort of activity to the one that they had chosen. We did not try to politicise residents out of a 'false consciousness' by taking them through a process of 'conscientization' (Freire, 1972) leading to radical political action to overturn the status quo.

'Bob' and his onions

In the history of the tenants' and residents' movements in the 20th century, resident action arose largely out of anger, in response to landlords letting residents down, or worse (Grayson, 1996). This is the classic model of community action, protest-based and driven by neglect by authorities. Some single-issue groups wind down once the problem they were set up to challenge is resolved. Many of the Gatsby groups did spring out of a strong feeling that something must be done to deal with intolerable conditions, and some were continuing to offer services because of their negative experiences of other organisations, which we describe in this chapter. However, as we will see in Chapter Six, the groups in the study liked to think of new things to do once they had completed a project. The list of things the groups wanted to improve was long so they did not run out of problems to tackle, but, also, they moved from sorting out the most urgent matters to having the luxury to do things to enhance their neighbourhoods. A medical analogy would be that the groups moved from treating a serious illness to wanting to get fitter and healthier.

One example was a communal allotment group from Stockport we saw using an entrepreneurial approach in their communal allotment. The group did not start, however, by growing onions and lettuce. We saw the group in Chapter Four lobbying for better housing management before they started digging and growing. The chair, who we have called 'Bob', presented to the council a list of 19 urgent outstanding maintenance jobs that had to be fixed. It was only after the group had got the repairs done that they could look ahead to making the estate a greener place.

The story of 'Bob' and his onions is one that is reinforced by the other groups. Overall, the message from the groups was that people were as prepared, or more prepared, to act if people felt agencies were pulling their weight. They preferred to be volunteering in a situation where they did not feel forced into it, and where they did not feel other people were letting them down. Our other research has also shown that a positive perception of the effort authorities are making is a key factor in people deciding to do something themselves to help the neighbourhood – the more effort authorities made the more people were willing to help (Richardson, 2006; Bastow et al, 2007). It has also been shown that local government modernisation has had positive effects on participation levels by people in deprived areas. For example, modernised local authorities have higher user involvement levels than unmodernised and less responsive authorities with similar levels of deprivation (Barnes et al, 2003a).

Everybody doing their bit

As may be expected, the unique advantages of resident action ranked 1st in comments about why people helped themselves, shown in Table 5.1. Residents also recognised that their work had to be part of wider work by others to regenerate their neighbourhoods (22 comments). They welcomed their complementary role in relation to work by statutory agencies. The message was clearly not one of 'go it alone' – the groups did not think that their action in isolation could solve problems. Residents supported policy and good practice thinking about shared responsibility between citizens and agencies for tackling neighbourhood problems on the grounds that problems affected them and agencies, and that all parties contributed to problems:

> 'That's the point of this. We can do a bit but we can't solve the problem.'
> (resident, Bedford)

Nearly all of the groups were involved in regeneration partnerships with other agencies, such as the police, local authorities, landlords, social services, drugs organisations and colleges – each playing the part they could. Residents saw their work in the wider context of regeneration work performed by a range of organisations.

Residents and a council officer in Walsall told us about how the local authority was using area committees as an experiment with delegated budgets across services, with consultation on how they were used. The council officer said that this group "fits in well with our work". The local authority saw the group's work, such as the allotment project, as "part of the wider regeneration of the area to make it more environmental and greener". The residents described the multi-agency working as "we all get interlocked to know what we need to know".

Another Walsall-based group tried to include all the interest groups in the area as well as the residents, including the schools: "We asked them to get involved because of the times when the young people are hanging round when they are meant to be at school." They also drew in leisure services and the police, "and the one shop! So far he's not been very supportive. He charged us to put a poster up. I don't know how [we can get him to] see it [the need for links]. He has problems with the kids, shoplifting and setting bins on fire" (resident, Walsall).

Several groups had been involved in clarifying the division of responsibility between themselves and statutory agencies, such as for dealing with anti-social behaviour:

> 'There are still people on this estate who have their own laws. "Normal" people are supposed to tone it down, but that's not what happens. Instead, one person causes hell for the others. People have got to understand that your home starts when you walk in the gate not your front door. This is my home, I've got nowhere else to go. I have a life here, and want to build something, so I got involved. I represent people who pay the rent and want to live here. I heard on You and Yours [Radio 4] that Glasgow City Council are giving training for anti-social families, being proactive instead of just moving them from one estate to another. We need to address behaviour. They're our neighbours, but they are their [the council's] tenants.' (resident, West London)

Indeed, the groups' lobbying work with landlords to improve service delivery is itself an indication of their acknowledgment of the different responsibilities of residents and service providers.

What can volunteers do, and what they cannot

In the Gatsby Project training courses, the messages about what role residents could reasonably play in relation to others' work were key. One aim of the training was to help residents distinguish between 'things we can do on our own', or 'with a little help', and actions 'we cannot do, but we can tell other agencies what needs to be done' (Gibson, 1996). Other organisations in the field emphasise a similar approach to community attempts to tackle problems such as high crime and anti-social behaviour. For example, residents can be effective within their 'circle of control' and their 'circle of influence'. They need to identify which actions they could implement directly, which they could work in partnership with the police and other agencies to implement, and which actions fall outside both their circles of control and influence and need action at a national or global level (Silverlock, 2000).

Professionals versus volunteers?

For some specialist work the lines of responsibility between professionals and lay people were difficult to agree. For example, the first training course in the Gatsby Project's programme on tackling substance misuse was not effective in helping residents take action because the trainers told residents that helping drug users was a job for specialists. The residents came away more 'aware' of the different drug types, their effects and sources of professional help, but they also came away feeling impotent.

This message was echoed in the groups' local experience, for example for one support group for families of drug users:

> 'They [professionals] hate us. We get shouted down in meetings, like you can't do parenting classes, you're only volunteers.' (member of a family support group, Cheshire)

Education is another field where there are fierce debates about the potential roles for lay people, such as arguments over the use of classroom assistants in primary schools, or the ongoing debate over volunteers in the Further Education sector.

Several of the volunteers at a Saturday club in North London were actually teachers in their 'day job'. However, the Saturday club did not have any status with mainstream education providers, or any real links with the schools. For example, they had to track the young people's progress through parental feedback rather than academic results: "That's a difficult area, we're not the school, we are only complementary for three hours a week" (resident, North London).

A group in Hastings ran an after-school club. One of the members was a special needs helper in a school so she had some experience. But the group felt strongly that the helpers did not need to be teachers: "that's where people see it wrong, we're not supposed to teach them, if they need to know how to spell a word, you help them look in the dictionary" (resident, Hastings).

This partly reflects reluctance on the part of professionals to let go and allow residents to play a role. Professional protectiveness over their domains is a long-acknowledged issue (Weber, 1978; Parkin, 1979), and where 'an elite corps of experts' has emerged to protect privileged scientific or technical information then one consequence is 'less participatory citizens' (Schneider and Ingram, 1997).

However, in most cases, the opposite problems existed. The interviewees were trying to get agencies to take on what the groups felt were the other organisations' responsibilities.

In North Wales a clean-up day for litter and dumped rubbish was organised for October 1998. They had skips donated from the local community agency, the community association, countryside services and an agency doing the refurbishment scheme in the area. The probation service offered 20 boys who "muscled in and did the heavy work". But the county council, which was responsible for rubbish collection and street cleaning, only gave them 50 black bin bags with the less than encouraging message to:

'... take any we didn't use back! We ended up buying extra ourselves. Isn't it barmy? The people, the department responsible, are bad contacts. The people in charge of refuse gave us 50 black bin bags, and countryside services who have nothing to gain from this chipped in with a Land Rover.' (resident, North Wales)

In addition, many groups wanted or had professional staff to help with their own work (7 comments, ranked 8th). The groups were open to outside expertise to help with things such as project management and development, administration of large community facilities, or intensive and structured work with troubled young people. They recognised their own limits and the value of professional input.

In Stoke a group had experienced youth workers doing detached youth work with the older youths outside: "The volunteers feel more secure. [The professional youth worker] calms the situation down. Two months previously there was lots of trouble outside" with children with baseball bats. "The workers are better at spotting things, like when they're on drugs and drink, whereas I'm oblivious" (resident, Stoke).

And in Liverpool:

'[X] is the manager of the community building. She reports to someone in town. She was seconded to us from community development. We decided that we couldn't manage as a community a centre like this. So we left it in the hands of the council, and we'd rent rooms. We hoped that [X] would get the job, because she's been through from the beginning. We'd be lost without her.' (resident, Liverpool)

It was in this context of all stakeholders in a neighbourhood playing a role that the groups promoted the value of their input. Several groups (12 comments, ranked 6th) definitely said they were happy to 'do their bit'. They saw their work as more positively motivated:

> 'My little son was a right tearaway. It's done him the world of good. I enjoy it, putting something back in, so I carried on doing it.' (member of a parent support group, Cheshire)

There were 15 examples (ranked 4th) of the benefits of the groups as informal mutual aid, or just being 'good neighbours', which they saw as an appropriate role for them to play:

> '[X] is a member of the committee for the estate, and also chairs his own residents' group for his block of flats. People in the group for his block are much more active socially than the committee. The group just for the block of flats have a coffee shop, do fish and chips together, and help the frailer residents out with shopping. [X] helps over-50s by things like taking an older lady to the shops, and collecting prescriptions.' (resident, Walsall)

Sometimes residents are better

In relation to the provision of services that are more normally delivered by public services, we now look at how residents saw their own work in contrast to that of other agencies. The point the groups made most often was that, under certain circumstances, residents were the most appropriate group to offer support or services because of their unique position, for example: unpaid, same status as people being helped, live in neighbourhood and insider's perspective (30 examples, ranked 1st). Nationally in 1997 the views of other volunteers were similar, with seven out of ten respondents in a national survey of volunteering feeling that volunteers offered something that the state could not provide (Davis Smith, 1998).

The groups commented that their volunteer status, and the fact they were permanently resident in the neighbourhoods, meant they could offer a greater level of continuity and commitment to service users:

> '[We got] everyone together – youth service, drug and alcohol. [We spent] 18 months trying to get a constituted body together. [Then] the well-intentioned professionals had their budgets cut so they just stopped coming.' (resident, Wrexham)

A housing officer in Keighley said the tenants' association's "role is letting us know what is going on. Because I'm largely working in the day I'm not aware of things". He heard that the police had a similar problem.

> '[Being a volunteer] is a 24-hour job. Paid workers leave at the end of the day.' (resident, County Durham)

In Derbyshire, the Citizens' Advice Bureau (CAB) did a surgery at the community centre next door. The group had a relationship with CAB, but their work was different because CAB "don't know people and they're only here two hours a week, they go off at the end of the day" (resident).

Groups felt that they had more space to be flexible in what they did, unlike some more bureaucratic provider organisations. The groups presented examples of their sensitivity to users' needs as a result of shared experience and the equal positions of those helping and those being helped.

In Nottinghamshire the dedicated beat officers responsible for each police area were a recognised point of contact for each of the Neighbourhood Watch areas. All the beat officers would contact Neighbourhood Watch coordinators once every three months and feed back to the sergeant: "Neighbourhood Watch is a sea change in terms of the involvement of local people. Neighbourhood Watch is more approachable and user friendly because it's local, small and condensed" (police officer, Nottinghamshire).

> 'Because we're so small and can change direction easily, we've found the relationship with the council quite hard – not individuals, but bureaucratic structures. It is frustrating, disappointing and downright annoying. We've had to be innovative and flexible – and they aren't.' (development manager of a voluntary organisation, West Midlands)

> 'I've been bought flowers [from users of support line]. I haven't known any services that get that! They say thank you for being here. Thank God there's someone who understands. Statutory organisations are clinical and formal.' (member of a family support group, Cheshire)

In Devon there is a project that advises people about unwanted pregnancies. The project is run by a "group of ladies, all volunteers". The women are "midwives and teachers. One has been helped herself through an abortion and she wanted to help others" (director of a voluntary organisation). They also help people who are coping with the effects of previous terminations.

The value of having an understanding of clients' needs based on personal experience was also applicable to paid staff:

> 'The assistant housing manager is an ex-heroin addict and was in prison. He met some Christians, and now he's working with young

people. It's been a transformation of the young people – from self-harm to mended lives. He's someone to rely on.' (director of a voluntary organisation, Devon)

The organisation felt that this staff member provided a possible model for the young people they work with.

Against dependency

Public service providers have already been responsive to new cultures of organisational change and improvement, as we were starting to see in Chapter Three. Public sector organisations are becoming more efficient. Many local authorities and other organisations have taken this to heart, with continuous improvement, voluntary benchmarking clubs, restructuring of corporate services to create performance management teams and so on. It is easy to see why this would translate into a need to educate and actively engage users in delivery – a more responsive service needs more responsive (and responding) clients. Central government and regulators have focused on changing provider organisations. Providers, in turn, have focused on changing users. There is some agreement that greater service efficiency without reduced dependency and demands will not fully tackle needs in deprived areas. In research done on neighbourhood governance, a neighbourhood manager in a deprived area of Bradford gave the example of whether the agency should put in extra litter bins and increase the frequency of rubbish collection, or if they should instead concentrate on getting people to stop dropping litter or dumping rubbish in the first place, or indeed do both:

'The more local people get involved in thinking about the neighbourhood the more likely we are to get improvements. [We need to] counter a dependency culture – how can we make a difference and own things for ourselves? It's not *us* delivering for *them*, it's them starting to take part. We need to stop residents seeing us as the answer to everything. It's not the council or us that drops litter. The problem we are trying to tackle and turn round in neighbourhood management is the expectation that more things will be done *for* people without them having to change too.' (cited in White et al, 2006, p 217)

Debates about the 'dependency' of people on services or the state can often sound like agencies trying to offload responsibility in a one-way deal with residents, who then end up getting less. However, the boundaries of this debate are being redrawn, with recognition that some residents, like those in the study, agree with people doing more for themselves as an empowering approach.

The groups are, by definition, committed to the principle of people helping themselves. This meant that they felt their activity was, in some cases, fundamentally more empowering than work by charities or the welfare state, where residents were seen as the beneficiaries of help:

'[The community centre] was built by [a local charity 'Challenge']. We thought it was a community centre but it's more adult education. It's a charity thing more than a community centre. [A local brewery] used to finance it. It's not a bloody community centre because the kids aren't allowed in there.' (resident, Warrington)

'[The X Project] is church types. They expect gratitude for doing "charity" work and all that – it puts local people off.' (community worker, Manchester)

They made the point that getting 'outsiders' in to give help could exacerbate their dependency where those organisations were not already involved in providing long-term services to the neighbourhood, or did not have a long-term stake in neighbourhoods. They felt there was a danger that outsiders of this kind would take benefit from the neighbourhood, then withdraw:

'Our achievement has been to take control, very largely, of the socio-economic programme in the regeneration of the estate so that it is led by residents and is genuinely community based. There was an assumption by the partnership [of social landlords] that they could carve up the money between themselves! [Another of the social landlords have] got their own community unit. They sent so-called experts in. The idea was that they would dispose of all the regeneration money. They lied on their outcomes. And that was our regeneration money. In the end, [we fought for] the partnership to establish that all providers had to apply to the socio-economic sub-group, so there's no advantage to people just because they're in the partnership. It took a year to sort that. We are now a provider, because we fought for credibility.' (resident, South London)

In Lincolnshire externally funded regeneration projects were being delivered by "big players" such as the health authority, and the Further Education colleges, "outsiders from Lincoln" (resident). This "exacerbates" the problems because "people come in from outside" (resident).

In Lancashire, a community worker was currently working part time with a group of Asian women. She planned to apply for another job in community work soon as the money was running out. Another worker linked to the Asian women's group commented that the group "gets used by people who go up the ladder" then realising that the community worker was also there added quickly "I don't mean you, [X]".

In West Yorkshire the Single Regeneration Budget Partnership "did everything through external agencies for the first three years. Then the environmental group struck out by itself" (community worker). The environment group started off as a sub-working group then decided they wanted to be independent so they bid to be a deliverer of parts of the programme: "we went from involvement to delivery" (resident). The external agencies were charging high professional fees: "What we're getting as results proves it. We knew things would happen. Other projects haven't worked", like the toy library that did not take off, and other projects run by "outside agencies" (resident).

Resident action builds civic responsibility

The interviewees saw the advantage of community self-help as creating more civic responsibility and a sense of ownership in the community (13 comments, ranked 5th; see Table 5.1). We saw in Chapter Four how the groups were actively trying to persuade people into responsible behaviour and to increase citizenship through their work, based on the negative consequences for areas discussed in Chapter Three. They argued that people helping themselves generated increased levels of civic responsibility and community engagement created feelings of 'ownership'. These are perhaps overly familiar phrases about the benefits of community activity that are now routinely found in government documents and are parroted by many. Because of this, the arguments may have lost their impact, but it is a strong advantage to be able to generate a sense of ownership in neighbourhoods where it

Community volunteers wanted to help themselves, and felt empowered by working collectively

is extremely difficult to get people to take individual and collective responsibility, and where cynicism about change is high.

In Birmingham residents argued that a history of state provision of services had created a lack of ownership:

> 'There was no real tradition on the estate of self-help. Birmingham was very protective and did everything in-house. The nanny state idea is rife in Birmingham, people are reluctant to let go of the reins. People have grown up with healthcare and everything provided.' (resident, Birmingham)

While in Liverpool the residents' group described how people's attempts to care for their neighbourhood were undermined by the withdrawal of services:

> 'The council stopped giving people bins, so people bought their own bags. [But] the council just left them, people had 10 bags in the garden. It is killing people's spirits. There's a malaise about. People couldn't care less, they are accepting all things, there's no respect. It's not the hearts of the gentle people, it's the others. There's less respect, we need a change in attitudes.' (resident, Liverpool)

In Derbyshire and London the groups said that civic engagement was reduced when residents did not feel listened to by those in charge of making decisions:

> 'Whether they'll bother to vote [on whether to transfer housing stock to a new landlord] is another matter because they feel that it doesn't count, because they think the council will do what they like anyway.' (resident, Derbyshire)

> 'We learnt by coming back with recommendations [for changes to local authority services] that whatever we decided could be overruled for no reason.' (resident, South London)

Some pointed to a general lack of desire by people to help themselves:

> 'For the category of 16-25 they've got the support and facilities here but it's sad because one day they'll wake up and it will be too late. They're wasting themselves. An average of 6 in a 100 want to try it. The other 100 throw it back in your face. You try a few times but if they let you down a few times then why waste time when you could be helping someone else? If they don't help themselves ...' (youth worker, South London)

There were some positive examples:

> 'A man on [X] Road saw a bloke with a TV, so he rang the police and because he knew where the other man lived they went round and the TV was there. Because he lived local you know if someone's not supposed to be there. It creates community spirit. If a car pulls up – you go and ask what they want. We could impose a subscription [for joining the Neighbourhood Watch scheme] but we don't want to. We don't want to charge people for being a good citizen.' (resident, Nottinghamshire)

Sometimes residents feel forced to help themselves

It could be argued that the residents' case for their superior position says as much about their negative experiences of other organisations as it does about whether they were actually better qualified to offer help, for example other providers' lack of long-term commitment to an area, or paid staff's insensitivity to residents' needs. There is national support for the idea that a small group of 12 to 15 'ordinary local people chosen at random' (Chivite-Matthews and Teal, 2001) would make better decisions about the neighbourhood than local government. In a well-respected annual survey of the public (the British Social Attitudes Survey) in 1998 only a third of respondents felt that they would trust councillors 'just about always'/'most of the time' compared to two thirds who said they would trust a citizens' jury (Chivite-Matthews and Teal, 2001). This is a relatively strong response, that the respondents in that survey would rather trust people chosen at random than their elected members to 'come to the best view' about something like 'a proposal for a major new building development in your neighbourhood'. The residents in the study were interested in influencing both big and little decisions about the neighbourhood. They were also deciding to take on doing some things themselves.

This feeling that residents were better placed to help people in their neighbourhoods under certain circumstances was often in contrast to the poor service they felt that statutory services provided, particularly in relation to youth work. A resident in North Yorkshire said: "We don't agree with [the local authority youth worker's] approach". The council-employed youth workers allowed drinking on youth club premises, and swearing and smoking. On a trip to Blackpool that a group member also went on, the council worker went drinking with the young people. The group has discussion sessions about these issues with the young people when they talk seriously.

In another example from Walsall:

> 'At the time I was totally fed up. There was a hut on the land that was used as a youth club. It was badly managed. They were selling

E[cstasy] tablets at £1 a time. The youth workers let it happen.' (resident, Walsall)

And in Cheshire:

'[The high school] had a youth worker. She was a waste of time because the kids don't relate to her. She used to run the youth centre. The way she spoke to the kids – effing and blinding. That's not acceptable. She said, You will fucking do this. She speaks to them like they are little children, but I speak to them like mini-adults. They're our future tenants, and to the council – they are future voters!' (resident, Cheshire)

In Wrexham, the youth service "seem to think that youth work equals the youth club" (resident), which they already provided so they would not give them anyone to help do outreach work. The youth club was 15 minutes' walk away and was "awful. It looks like a prison." The club was underutilised, partly because "it is stuck in a time warp, they have a set way of doing it" (resident).

Comments about poor service delivery prompted groups to take action more generally. In the West Midlands the group took over management of the estate, and were heavily involved in the economic and physical development for the area, such as the new leisure centre. The impetus for this came from the general decline of the local economy, and the group's and residents' perception of the failure of the local authority to manage the estate well. There was an estate redesign where the local authority replaced streets with shops, so the local shops disappeared. The residents argued that low demand for the estate was exacerbated by the council's allocations and lettings system that was all done centrally: "[A central office] allocated 140,000 properties, so you can imagine the nightmare" (resident). There was very little accountability, and potential for "bribes and backhanders". "At one time we never had a waiting list, just an escape list"; "There's only one way to go when you're at the bottom" (residents). The group ran its own waiting list for housing on the estate alongside the local authority list.

Another driver for a group starting was that "originally" the organisation responsible for spending Single Regeneration Budget funding employed a publicity officer who was an "old officer from [the local authority]" who was "useless" (resident). The local authority had "no policy of compulsory retirement" (community worker), and they thought that the council had given this person the job "in lieu of redundancy" to keep them occupied. He was an ex-professional journalist. They were so "annoyed" at his work that they started their own community publicity group.

Comments on how community self-help activity had been triggered because of the failures of other organisations to deliver good quality services (18 comments) ranked 3rd (see Table 5.1) and were a running theme through the narrative of groups' histories:

'[In this neighbourhood] like a lot of [the] inner city [in this city], waste and rubbish are big issues. The Consortium … gives priority to inner-city communities, because that's where issues of waste and rubbish are strongly felt, and also where there's little recycling infrastructure. Most recycling facilities are in supermarket car parks. That's fine if you've got a car, go to that particular shop, and have the motivation to do that. But here there is very low car ownership, it's an Asian area and people shop locally because of their culture. Our conclusion is what [the city] needs is kerbside recycling. The Audit Commission summed it up that the council's recycling service is "an umbrella service run on a shoestring". [We] have proposed to do a kerbside scheme [in the city]. We've already done it on a small scale here. We collected 1,200 bags of waste over the season. We've also encouraged household composting by providing discount compost bins. We did community compost sites so we can give people soil conditioner back for their gardens.' (director of a voluntary organisation, West Midlands)

Not letting failing services off the hook

Despite the advantages of self-help the residents identified, the interviewees were still in the position of having to take action themselves because of others' failures to properly manage and deliver services to neighbourhoods. In these circumstances, self-help could be seen as 'letting services of the hook'. However, this was not always the case for the groups in the study. There were three examples of how the groups' aim was conversely to pressurise services into doing more rather than less. They intended their actions not as a replacement but as a 'thorn in the side' (ranked 11th).

Residents in Rhyl said that the group bought a trailer for £25 for dumping rubbish at the tip and it was well used. Other voluntary groups also used it, as well as estate residents. The local authority used to have skips on the estate, but removed them when there was a fire, even though a fire brigade report proved it was caused by accidental dumping of ashes from a coal fire, not started deliberately. They got their own trailer to "show them [the council] up really more than anything" (resident).

Some of the interviewees felt that their hand had been forced by a lack of a viable alternative (18 comments, ranked 3rd). The implication was that they may have chosen to put their time and energy elsewhere if others took over the role effectively:

'We want funding to better people round here, not be giving them money, but a better life, all the money in the world wouldn't help some, we give in kind not in cash. If you had a £1 going spare, get some sugar and milk on a cold morning. People say, Somebody ought to do something about this, but "somebody" has never turned up yet, do you know them? Who is going to do it?' (resident, Rhyl)

Limits and failures of self-help

Residents commented on the failures of other organisations. The groups also referred to their own failures and limits. There were four clear examples given by interviewees (ranked 10th) of where community self-help was inappropriate or had failed. Residents recognised the limits of the level of organisation and responsibility they could offer or that particular groups without experience had been able to deliver:

> '[The recycling project] employed two local people, bought vehicles, etcetera, etcetera. It was going nowhere. It was only very small scale – two mornings a week. [Then the] two paid people left, and all the volunteers. Because the housing renewal people wanted them to be [financially] accountable for X, Y, Z, and they couldn't. When I took over it was being run as a boys' club. They were coming in drinking tea. But, with a kerbside service you have to be there on the button, at the same time every week, or people don't bother any more. Previously people [the volunteers] did it to suit themselves. They all left … why? Because I expected them to go out if it was raining! And I gave them a timetable, and they didn't like it. Once I'd been here a few weeks, I stamped some rules down. I got a placement agreement with the voluntary sector. I organised six-month placements. Everyone who's stuck it out has got full NVQ Level 2…. All that have stuck it out with me have got jobs.' (manager of a voluntary organisation, West Midlands)

Even where the groups were more confident of their abilities, the message was that community organising was a difficult activity that required support, for example a significant minority of the grants given by the Gatsby Project were for paid administrative help for the groups. Some of the groups had reached a crossroads stage where their lack of experience or confidence coupled with rapid growth in size and level of responsibility meant they sought out external help:

> 'To be honest I don't know what we'd have done without [the paid staff] now. Before, you manage but we were walking round like zombies. We've got the building, it's huge, we felt so unsupported.' (resident, Wrexham)

Consulting and involving residents

The residents were unusual in that they were active in decision making with mainstream service providers. This was only one way that services could consult and engage with residents. Other forms of engagement, such as one-off open day consultation events, were more effective at getting views from a large number of people. However, mainstream providers liked to use existing informal groups such as tenants' and residents' associations for ongoing community involvement because it offered service providers the opportunity to develop ongoing two-way dialogue with the public in a stable context. This was a relatively simple way to generate meaningful discussion on complex issues. An ongoing relationship was a more supportive environment for developing mutual understanding of expectations and constraints, and then adapting to generate more realistic expectations. Established community organisations and active volunteers also offer possibilities for what has been termed co-production of services, that is, people taking on more responsibility for providing services to themselves, and thereby reducing both their dependency and the level of demand being made on services (Richardson, 2005b).

Here we look at the residents' views about community consultation and involvement, at why they were keen to be involved, what the plus sides of involvement were for residents and at how community involvement works. We collected a total of 145 comments about community involvement in the interviews (see Table 5.2), of which 132 in total were positive and 13 comments (ranked 5th) were negative. We asked people about specific examples of their work rather than questions about community involvement in the abstract. Through this, we categorised residents' views based on their actual practice.

Table 5.2: Attitudes to community involvement

Attitude	No. of comments	Rank
Community involvement is a positive thing	30	=1
It helps improve service delivery	30	=1
Linked to multi-agency working	22	3
Key to area change	19	4
Involvement has negative aspects	13	5
Conduit for information and accountability	12	6
Direct link means services more likely to respond	11	7
Residents act as intermediaries	8	8
Total	**145**	

Residents' desire to be involved

The set of comments that ranked joint first were general statements about the positive aspects of community involvement and how this helped improve service delivery. These positive comments were often in the form simply of a list of all the working groups, forums, committees and other consultative mechanisms the groups were involved in. The message from the lists was broadly that residents were pleased with the commitment and respect they earned from the consultation by service providers, including those that had previously ignored or patronised residents. Political engagement, by voting or campaigning or lobbying, is another element of being socially included (Burchardt et al, 2002).

The examples of successful work by the groups to improve service delivery in Chapter Four indicate that the residents did have some genuine influence with agencies, that is, they had the power to effect change.

How community involvement works

How does the community consultation actually work? The outcome of more information and involvement was to elicit feelings of satisfaction from residents. This was a consequence of the opportunity to make consensual decisions, the increased ownership of decisions by recipients, better decision making due to better information and prioritising and better delivery due to closer monitoring.

Involvement works as a mechanism for residents to effect change (11 comments, ranked 7th), and it gives residents direct contact with managers and staff. This face-to-face contact with the people delivering services to the neighbourhood was significant in helping residents implement change. The relationships that service providers and their staff built with residents may generate a sense of obligation that it would be more difficult to feel towards a nameless group of 'customers'. Community involvement gave opportunities for residents to access officers' time directly, and make personal relationships that eased negotiations between staff and residents. It gave residents a greater understanding of the constraints that services were under.

We also talked briefly, where possible, to service providers during our visits. Their views on the overall role of community involvement reinforced the arguments made by the residents' groups, and some of their comments have been included here.

In County Durham, the council's attitude to community involvement at the time of the visit was very supportive. This really started since the "Labour Government"; "It was a change from 'this is what you're going to get' to 'what do you want'" (director of housing). For example, consulting on demolition or refurbishment, "previously we would never have done that and asked. Some officers are still struggling with it" (director of housing, County Durham).

A housing officer from Walsall said:

'We have a very good relationship, a nice rapport, we don't fall out and they know they can come in and see me at any time. Tenants are our ear to the ground, we're not there on site. They've got a good idea of how the council works and ask for achievable things. People say to me, You go home every night, and they're right. We rely on tenants to come and tell us what the problems are. Tenants now have an idea of how the council works, so they can ask us for reasonable things and ask us in the right way. They're a well-experienced group. They have the knack of asking the right questions. You build up a nice relationship with people. It makes your day-to-day work a lot easier when you've got rapport with tenants. Hopefully they just come and explain what they want not shout.'

And the residents said: "We ask rather than demand, that's why we've done so well. We ask if it's feasible".

In another example from Stockport:

'It was all red tape with [the council at first. Now] we meet with the team leaders every month, religiously…. Once they got to know us and they knew we were serious, they changed overnight – they couldn't do enough to help us.' (resident, Stockport)

Involvement makes services more transparent and accountable

The other factor that helps us to understand what makes the groups feel so favourably towards involvement structures is that involvement was a key way of the groups getting information, and holding services accountable (12 comments, ranked 6th). Occasionally community accountability had been formalised through mechanisms such as an estate agreement, a document specifying what levels of service a landlord would provide to residents. For example, a landlord might promise to sweep the hallways once a week, answer the telephone within 30 seconds or re-let empty homes within three weeks. The landlord then provides management information about which targets they met against which residents could monitor their performance. The estate agreement also specifies what action would be taken in the case of inadequate performance. Estate agreements were early versions of what are now being proposed as 'neighbourhood contracts' (ODPM and Home Office, 2005; DCLG, 2006).

In Walsall, the local authority had a borough-wide 'compact' laying out an agreement between residents and the council about services and service monitoring: "It's got target dates, who is monitoring and accountable. We want and are seeing results" (resident).

A new housing liaison board in Birmingham was linked to the tenants' quality promise, "an appalling name" (resident), but good because it set out loose performance standards for local authority services. The board was the monitoring body not just for housing but for transport and leisure so, for example, it included street lighting. They could issue an improvement notice to the director of the department responsible. It was a pilot, "it's a brand new idea – dead new" (resident).

Other examples included:

'Previously we had sub-committees for the council. Two years ago the Local Government Act devolved to area committees, apart from the statutory social services committee. So, we have monthly meetings with the councillors for the area. It provides clarity of mechanisms of how the city is run. It makes democracy clear to everyone. They have opportunities to feed in. The area committees are meetings held in public, so people can see how we're performing on your behalf. This is a major breakthrough.' (council officer, Hull)

'The information from the likes of the community drugs team is an eight-week waiting list – so we need an overseer, because we've got parents coming to us saying it's longer. So we want parents to go to the community forum because that's community accountability. They continue with no opposition. Parents have no one to complain to.' (member of a family support group, Cheshire)

Residents pass on useful information

Information flows can be two-way. Residents' experiences of living in the neighbourhoods meant that they were able in some cases to provide ground-level intelligence to service providers:

'Any group banding together gives us that feedback. When [the resident representative] speaks I know that she is not just speaking for [herself].… She's the eyes and ears of that block. It is two-way feedback, she tells the residents what's going on.' (regeneration worker, Hull)

A housing officer in Keighley liked to liaise with the tenants: "Because I'm largely working in the day I'm not aware of things".

The police in Nottinghamshire "collate information on crimes coming in and see the hot spots and then allocate the van to night patrol" (police officer). They used to just go out around 6pm, but this was too untargeted so they gave active residents pagers to contact police with information:

'So someone rings in for example a youth nuisance, and we say, Okay, we'll monitor the situation, if it builds up it becomes a hot spot. Then we give a leaflet to that person, so if they ring we converge on that area from different angles. It comes back to giving out the pager number so we can target trouble instead of driving around aimlessly.' (police officer, Nottinghamshire)

People want to know about things that affect them

In Chapter Three we discussed residents' desire (nationally and in the groups) for better transparency, accountability and communication with service providers. Residents were understandably upset where they had been denied information about decisions on the places where they lived:

'Unfortunately, [the] housing committee has now made the decision not to re-let vacant properties. Well, it depends on whether you want to believe the papers, the actual report, housing committee, the staff or the rumours. The thing that got me was I saw [the neighbourhood manager] that day and he said [the] housing committee are meeting today but he didn't tell [us] what they were going to be discussing – I had to buy the paper to find out. After I'd seen the article I spoke to the senior officer and he said the "no letting" policy was just until they decide what to do.' (resident, Walsall)

And some residents started attending local resident group meetings simply to find out more information about decisions being taken that would affect them:

'I'm nosey, found out what was going on on the estate and wanted to find out more and then [X] roped me in.' (resident, Wrexham)

'I've always been interested in the block. I wanted to know what was happening. I went to a meeting to find out, and somebody said "I vote [you] for secretary!" And that was the start of it.' (resident, Hull)

Community involvement by facilitating the flow of information can make the job of services easier by building trust with clients and easing anxieties about watershed decisions. For some major decisions about the neighbourhood, such as the transfer of ownership of housing stock, residents' consent is obligatory:

'The offer document [for possible transfer of housing stock to a new landlord] goes out at the end of the month. The ballot should be May/June. It should have been the end of March but the government review of rents delayed everything – it was RPI plus half a per cent, then they decided on rent convergence so.... The government changes it mind. The tenants were told at that time it would be RPI plus half a per cent and improvements on top. Now they've been told it's RPI plus 3% and no extras for improvements. It'll probably be a yes [vote] because people round here want value for money – if they see by switching to a new company they can get double glazing and central heating. If they stay with the council it's the same rent and nothing done. They will say yes. The general feeling is that people would rather be with the council but if they weigh it up....' (resident, Derbyshire)

Problems with the involvement process

Residents may have liked the principle of being involved, but they did not always feel positive about the process, as has been the case elsewhere in the UK (Hastings et al, 1996; Burton, 2003; Policy Commission on Public Services, 2004). There were 13 examples (ranked 5th) given in Table 5.2 of where groups felt that they had not been respected by professionals, or where consultation had had a negative effect, or where people's views had been ignored. There was anger where consultation did not appear to lead to action, or where the speed of delivery was slow.

In Derbyshire a national environmental organisation are doing some work on the square. Unfortunately, the residents on the estate had been "consulted to death" (resident). There were lots of plans for the square, but nothing had happened yet:

> '[An environmental organisation] have been talking for a long time about a ball park. It was supposed to be done for the summer. They did a Planning for Real. Now people don't believe it's going to happen. They think that anyway about things.' (community worker, Kent)

The delay was because of an initial funding shortfall of £2,000 which the environmental organisation was then going to fundraise for. Because it was "dragged out", the shortfall increased to £5,000. Also "the time they're spending on it has to be paid for" (resident). The community worker said "I would have used the money to put a spade in to show people" that something was actually coming to fruition. "The kids were all excited but ..."; "We've not been told it's on hold, we've not heard anything" (residents, Kent).

In Lancashire some Single Regeneration Budget projects had not been successful: "The ones that have been contrary to what the community wanted in consultation" (community worker, Lancashire). One example was CCTV: "It lasted seven hours". They put it up without asking people, so "the young lads pulled it down" (resident, Lancashire). The youths also harassed the workmen paid to put the cameras up again. "A couple of firms pulled out" of the contract because of this. "There's stanchions there but no cameras."

Multi-agency working

Nevertheless, overall residents in the interviews were supportive of the principles of community involvement, often in the context of many different organisations working together via the groups and forums. Support for multi-agency working with residents involved as consultees ranked 3rd in the comments about community involvement in the interviews.

A community forum in Hull organised a Millennium Conference in October 2000 to develop a "way forward" for the estate. All the different services and organisations working on the estate were there alongside residents. They developed ideas about how to tackle education problems, for example bullying and children with special needs. The workshops were facilitated by a mix of residents and workers. Hull Participatory Appraisal network also helped to facilitate. There was a list of the solutions people came up with, for example youth radio, lunchtime clubs in schools and for housing, more park keepers and "being able to deal with issues at any housing office on the estate" (resident). "We're now in the process of doing policies on each of the subjects through the forum" (resident).

In another example from South London:

'Now there is joint training – members, officers and tenants. A change in the attitude to the job and a change in approach. The officers got a lot out of it. It started small – a few working groups. Now every estate is doing estate plans with an officer and a councillor on the working group. [This] neighbourhood did that.' (resident, South London)

Motivating and sustaining community volunteers

So far in this chapter we have concentrated on residents' views and beliefs about the principles of community self-help and community involvement as an explanation of why they became active in their communities. There are many background factors that make it statistically more or less likely that people will volunteer, such as income, ethnicity or age, which we look at later in Chapter Eight. The residents in the study did volunteer, despite this being statistically unlikely for people in deprived areas, as they wanted to see improvements in their neighbourhoods.

But there is another piece of the explanation about why people make the personal commitment to become active, and what sustained them in their voluntary efforts. There were personal benefits (and costs) from their work that sustained (or threatened) their continued involvement (Burton et al, 2004). Previous studies of why people volunteer have also found people were involved for a mix of motives – altruistic and self-interested, including the meeting of one's own needs and those of family and friends, responding to a need in the community and learning new skills (Davis Smith, 1998).

We asked interviewees about what made them personally get and stay involved. We focus here on what motivated them.

The groups found it a challenge to recruit and retain volunteers. Even larger organisations with paid staff wrestled with the problems of maintaining motivation. Nearly all of the groups struggled to recruit volunteers against what they saw as a climate of 'apathy'. Only a minority got actively involved or made a big volunteering commitment. All this makes it important to have a greater understanding of the circumstances under which volunteers become and remain involved.

We gathered a total of 185 comments, shown in Table 5.3.

Table 5.3: Motivating and sustaining volunteers

Comment	No. of comments	Rank
Personal development/employment/training	34	1
Like to feel useful and achieve	33	2
Join friends and make friends	27	3
Care about neighbourhood	19	4
Personally affected/ex-client	17	5
Difficult background/empowering	15	6
That 'type' of person	14	7
Care about young people	13	8
'Dragged'/persuaded	10	9
Ego/status	3	10
Total	**185**	

'The importance of the ask'

Some of the respondents phrased their comments about how they got involved in a negative, but light-hearted way. They joked that they had been pushed into volunteering against their own better judgement, and were reluctant volunteers. These comments ranked 9th out of those about motivation – nationally in 1997 47% of volunteers said the reason for them being a volunteer was that 'someone asked me' (Davis Smith, 1998).

One member of a Nottinghamshire group got involved when he was "dragged" to a meeting to set up a tenants' association in his area: "I was totally disinterested, and I walked out as secretary!". Another member ended up as chair because he was "lumbered with it, because there's no one else!".

> 'I attended a meeting and they were looking for volunteers, so with a bit of arm-twisting! ...' (resident, Wrexham)

The reluctant construction was indicative of volunteers' modesty, or at least their concern not to appear self-aggrandising in public. The comments also indicate what has been called 'the importance of the ask' – that is, being asked to participate is a key factor in mobilisation (Independent Sector, 1999; Birchall and Simmons, 2002):

In 1998 [in the US], more people (49% versus 43%) had been asked to volunteer than in 1995. Approximately an equal number of respondents were asked or not asked to volunteer. The number of respondents who volunteered after being asked was astonishing. Ninety per cent ... of those asked actually did volunteer in 1998, but only 22% of respondents did so when not asked. Comparable results were found in previous surveys. The volunteer rate among respondents who were asked to volunteer was nearly four times greater than among those who were not asked. (Independent Sector, 1999)

Getting volunteers involved at the beginning sometimes takes a proactive approach to encourage people who may not feel confident about what they have to offer, or feel nervous about taking on what is a big responsibility. For example, volunteers talked about how the process of being active in the community had boosted their self-confidence that was low at the beginning of their volunteering.

One volunteer said she really did not like talking in a big group. She was very embarrassed by it and this was the same when she went to college: "It's okay if it's just about yourself because you know it, but anything else ... ooohh [shivers]" (resident, Sunderland). She used to be secretary of the group: "it was daunting at first, the first time I took minutes my hand shook". And another resident from Rhyl said: "Last year I became chair. At the time I wasn't confident. I wouldn't say boo to a goose. Now, it's a different story".

On the other hand, volunteers have to have a degree of self-confidence to put themselves forward, particularly where the result of volunteering is that they are criticised for being self-selecting and unrepresentative. Comments about being almost forced into their roles are also related to the more general issue of 'apathy', which we discuss in Chapter Eight. Some felt 'lumbered' with the role because:

'No one else could be bothered.' (resident, Derbyshire)

Concern for young people and the neighbourhood

Comments about people getting involved because of their personal concern about their neighbourhood or the young people in it ranked 4th and 8th respectively. In the 1997 National Survey of Volunteering, around a quarter (26%) volunteered because of a 'need in the community' (Davis Smith, 1998):

'I wanted to do something for the children that included literature and reading because I realised that lots of them were behind for their age in grammar. [I have] always been a poet. I want to pass it down to the kids. I want to include kids in the ghetto as we say. If you can get them interested in art and literature.... It is very hard to get inner-city kids interested in the arts – I want to transform all that.' (resident, Manchester)

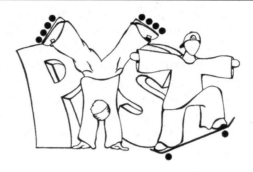

Parents Youth Support Team Ltd

PYST

Working with Young people In Northwich

Groups used creativity in their work with young people, for example this group uses humour in its name, and helped young people to organise their own skateboarding events and live music gigs.

This resident wanted to help the pupils and children find "their own way of expressing themselves and do what they think is creative".

A resident from Wrexham explained their rationale for working with children:

> '[The young people have] always followed us around. Children are our future tenants, and our future problem [unless we act]. From the tenants' point of view it's always been a focus, we've always thought that — if we want sociable tenants we have to teach the kids to be sociable, and if we want people to be employable.'

Concern for children and young people more generally was one of the key motivators for the groups to set themselves up in the first place. One resident talked about an incident in Lincolnshire four years prior to the interview in 1996, when there was a lot of concern in their town about a drugs problem. This culminated in an incident where some young boys were killed in a car accident coming back from a nightclub. The nightclub was "notorious" for drugs and the driver was under the influence of drugs at the time. One of the boys who was killed was the brother of a local councillor, who was a councillor at only 22. She was one of the people who started the youth project. The first request from young people was somewhere to play pool, and generally somewhere to go and some activities/things to do. She gathered up a group of people and set up a youth action group "to deal with the 'problem', I say 'problem' in inverted commas" (resident).

Rootless young people

'[The project] is for rootless and purposeless young people. We meet the kids where they are, like in the hostel. We say, Your life is upside down at the moment, so you need a foundation for it.' (director of a voluntary organisation, Exeter)

This voluntary organisation in Exeter offered accommodation to young people:

'At the beginning we'd get the youngsters jobs, but they all lost them. Because, you can't tell your boss to eff off, you have to get up on time. We needed to change the attitude of the young people. So it was difficult to get funding because it's the hardest to measure a change in attitude, but the government's now realising this.' (director of a voluntary organisation, Exeter)

Something to do

'The main aim then was to get a community centre. For a long time the thinking was that we want something for the kids. The kids were growing up, and it wasn't like it was when I was a kid. We went fishing in the brook.' (resident, Bedford)

'The neighbours wanted [a middle-class family living on the estate] out so they could knock through, so they got the kids to do it for them. The kids used to knock on the door, throw things at the windows, I know because when I moved in they did it to me! I thought bollocks to this. My kids were at the high school at the time. So I used my kids to get to them. I went out the front of the house and said, What can I get for you? They wanted discos, football and trips.' (resident, Warrington)

Altruism?

In addition, another 14 people (ranked 7th; Table 5.3) said that they were involved because they had 'always been the volunteering type'. People's genuine feelings of social obligation were motivating factors; 35% nationally said they volunteered because they 'want to improve things and help people' (Davis Smith, 1998), and internationally it was people's desire to help others (Independent Sector, 1999). But this (rather altruistic) portrayal still does not fully explain why those individuals at that point in their lives were community volunteers.

To add to a more complete picture of why people become and stay involved, we need to also look at the fun, friendship and personal development that volunteering represented to the interviewees. It has been argued that a 'major factor' in volunteering is the 'pleasure and enjoyment' people gain from voluntary activity (Roberts and Devine, 2004). These authors also argue that there has not been sufficient focus on the pleasure and happiness of being involved in the community, but that it is hard for volunteers to translate their own personal pleasure to convince others to get involved. In the interviews, residents communicated a great sense of excitement and pleasure in their 'jobs'.

Fun and friendship

Residents pointed to the desire to be useful in society as motivators, which implies that volunteering is partly a consequence of not having alternatives like paid work to fulfil this function, or of having more spare time. Nationally 21% of volunteers said they were involved because they had 'time to spare', although this was a reason more often given by older volunteers than younger volunteers, who were more likely to volunteer to add to their CVs by learning new skills (Davis Smith, 1998).

Although half of the groups were predominantly made up of people not in paid work, it is not necessarily the case that people in full-time paid work do not volunteer. For example, in 1996/97, 57% of householders in full-time work were involved in voluntary work, compared to only 4% of unemployed householders (Howarth et al, 1998).

What stood out from the comments people made about why they liked being a volunteer is how much they related to aspects of social exclusion. Overall, people were pleased and proud to be performing a socially useful activity, and derived a sense of self-worth from being useful in some way in wider society. Social inclusion is based on participation in socially valued activities, such as having social networks and social interaction, and participation in productive activity of some kind. These are benefits of volunteering quoted by residents. In these ways, volunteering seems to contribute to reducing people's social exclusion, for those who do choose to participate in it.

Personal circumstances

We felt privileged that people sometimes felt trusting enough to open up about difficult personal circumstances that led to them becoming involved, and how volunteering had helped people to overcome some of these issues. There were 15 examples (ranked 6th) given in interviews of this. There were another 17 examples (ranked 5th) of how volunteers had been personally affected by the issue the group was working on. Nationally in 1997 (Davis Smith, 1998) 42% said they volunteered because of 'their own needs or interests'.

In many cases people had moved from being a user of a service provided by the group to being a helper or organiser.

One volunteer was a founding member of the group that helped the families of people involved in drug misuse:

> 'Since I've got involved here I've done courses through the voluntary sector and community work via voluntary action. I've done psychology, sociology, criminology, any 'ology! I've got a "degree" in being a parent of a drug user. We've all got "degrees" in life.' (member of a family support group, Cheshire)

A group of mothers in Bristol "decided to set up a mother and toddler group straightaway in the community centre. Our [own] kids were that age"(resident, Bristol). They got a small one-off grant to start of £320 that they used to buy equipment. Three of the mothers organised the mother and toddler group, which ran one morning a week and had 20 parents plus their children. "Then our children got too old." At the same time as the mother and toddler group they organised a play scheme for the following summer. "That year everything burst into life" (resident).

Status, pride and power

Finally, we look at the issues of status and ego. Volunteering is often a thankless task. One of the accusations levelled at volunteers is that they are primarily motivated by the superior position it gives them. It is a criticism that community consultation and involvement increases satisfaction with services more because of a greater feeling of importance on the part of those involved than actual change. There were only three examples given in the interviews.

A local resident gave his perspective as an outsider to the group:

> 'When I first heard about it I thought, oh yeah, because the people involved in it were in it for themselves but [the chair is not]....There's a lot more going on now. The people in it before, well, how do I put it, were in it for their own benefit. [The chair] weeded them out because that's the way [she] is.' (resident, Walsall)

In a different group in Walsall the picture was not so good:

> 'This tenants' association is a talking shop, they only like to have meetings with officials but that's not the point. The committee is not here for individuals, they are here for their own glory. We are [supposed to be] here representing the residents not ourselves.' (resident, Walsall)

A couple of groups specifically denied that they were involved for purely egotistical reasons, without being prompted by the interviewer. For example:

> 'I'd rather be in the background. I don't like to stand out. I don't do it for the credit, I do it to get things done, I don't care who gets the credit.' (resident, Keighley)

Several groups did recount with pride stories of their personal connections, developed through their community work, to people in positions of power or influence, such as the leader of the council. We have already outlined the positive effects on self-esteem volunteers felt had emerged from their work, which is important given the feelings of residents of low-income neighbourhoods not being respected, disempowered or looked down on. There is obviously a fine line between this and volunteers becoming overly self-important about their position as an authority speaking on behalf of a neighbourhood. Many volunteers come from a relatively low power base, and as a result some of the groups were aware of the need to guard against overconfidence (or arrogance) developing in its place. One group learnt to be more self-aware through good community development support:

> 'When I first took over as chair, I said to [the community worker], get me an assertiveness course or something.' (resident, Rhyl)

But although the course helped the volunteer personally, it took a while for her to pass on this new knowledge to others: "I was selfish"; "I didn't like letting go [of control]!", "When it came time to pass on my skills, it was difficult, I knew I had to, and people were telling me but…".

Summary

Area problems do not automatically trigger self-help. It is relatively difficult to generate involvement. The government and other political parties urge the need to increase volunteering and citizen responsibility, especially among those at risk of social exclusion. Moves to reform public services, revitalise local democracy and build a new concord between central and local government need active citizens.

The community volunteers chose to get involved partly because of their belief in caring and strong communities and in a decent quality of neighbourhood life.

On a personal level, they were motivated and sustained by feelings of social responsibility, alongside the personal benefits of fun and friendship, personal development and feeling socially useful and therefore socially included. There has arguably not been sufficient focus on the pleasure and enjoyment that people get from being involved in the community. Many were persuaded by a friend to get involved – nationally 47% of volunteers said they volunteered because 'someone asked me'. This indicates what has been called 'the importance of the ask'.

The residents saw their work as a complementary part of wider work by other agencies to regenerate neighbourhoods, and recognised the limits of self-help. Nearly all the groups were involved in regeneration partnerships with other agencies. They sometimes did extraordinary things themselves, but the message was not to 'go it alone'. The groups did not think that their action in isolation could solve problems. Residents argued for shared responsibility between citizens and agencies for tackling neighbourhood problems. The community organisers pointed to some unique benefits that, under certain circumstances, resident volunteers could provide for neighbourhood residents, such as high levels of commitment, flexibility and an insider's understanding. Nationally seven out of ten volunteers felt that they could offer something that the state could not provide.

More importantly, the principle of communities helping themselves was seen as fundamentally more empowering than residents being the passive recipients of help from others. One potential advantage of community organising was to increase feelings of civic responsibility in a neighbourhood context where lack of confidence about the chances of change was high. Their promotion of the positive benefits of volunteering and the desirability of civic action in practice as well as principle were contrary to some arguments against community volunteering. These arguments included the suggestion that participation was unfair on low-income people pushed on to poor neighbourhoods without people being aware of the 'over-demands' being made on them. Residents expressed their irritation when they felt agencies were not taking them seriously. They differentiated where they had chosen to take on responsibilities and circumstances where they had taken up slack from poorly performing agencies. Far from feeling they had been put in an unfair position, residents argued for the advantages of local control, and wanted more of it.

As well as doing things for themselves, the residents were keen to be consulted about the work that others were doing. The residents we talked to were unusual in that they were active in decision making with mainstream service providers, who liked to use existing informal groups for ongoing community involvement because it offered ongoing two-way dialogue and was a relatively simple way to generate meaningful discussion on complex issues.

Dialogues with community volunteers on bigger issues, such as the structural causes of area decline, could be empowering. There are many routes to tackling the causes and effects of disadvantage, and the residents had chosen to deal with the immediate impacts of those things on their lives. We respected residents' choices of action, rather than argue for people to be politicised.

Residents overall were pleased with the commitment and respect they earned from service providers during consultations, including those that had previously ignored or seemed patronising to residents. Their experiences stand out against many concerns and examples of residents being unable to exert influence. While generally residents wanted to do their bit, there were cases of them feeling pushed into taking action because of the poor quality of services they had received. Some of their work set out not to replace services but to be a 'thorn in the side' of failing agencies.

One lesson, illustrated by the story of 'Bob' and his onions, was that people were as prepared, or more prepared, to act if they felt agencies were pulling their weight. They preferred to be volunteering in a situation where they did not feel forced into it, and where they did not feel other people were letting them down. In some cases, particularly services such as children's education or specialist healthcare, there was reluctance on the part of professionals to let go and to allow residents to play a role, as national debates over potential roles for lay people also show. Residents wanted to help but could end up feeling impotent.

Community consultation and involvement gave channels for two-way communication and information flows between residents and services. It was a way that residents could hold services accountable. Face-to-face contact with the people delivering services to the neighbourhood was significant in helping residents implement change, and also gave residents a greater understanding of the constraints that services were under.

Community accountability in some cases had been formalised through agreements specifying levels of service provided to a neighbourhood. Residents in the study and elsewhere liked these 'estate agreements' and found them effective. The agreements were early versions of what are now being proposed as 'neighbourhood contracts'.

In the next chapter we look at how the groups organised themselves internally to achieve their goals.

SIX

How the groups organise themselves

'There are two salesmen sent to [a far off place] to sell shoes. So they go off, and the first salesman rings back the office and says, It's no use, no good, they don't wear shoes, I can't sell any shoes here. The second salesman rings up and says Send me more shoes, I'm going to make a packet – no one here's got any shoes. There's no ifs or buts, if we want to do something or make something happen – we will.' (resident, Wrexham)

The majority of community groups in the study were informal associations of people, which were small and often not legally incorporated. The people active in the groups were nearly all volunteers, and the groups were not within formal systems of accountability or regulation (other than basic local authority registration criteria for tenants' groups). So in order for the groups to operate effectively they had to organise themselves into a functioning team and create their own vision for their work, ethos and approach, organisational systems, structures and working practices. Any organisation, whatever its size, and regardless of sector, can be vulnerable to the common problems of poor communication and teamwork, high staff or volunteer turnover, bureaucracy, power struggles, differences over direction, financial management, funding crises and bad leadership. This chapter looks at how the community groups faced up to these issues.

Community groups are sometimes characterised as disorganised, ineffective, lacking transparency in decision making and insufficiently concerned with quality standards or equal opportunities. Under four topics based on the comments made in the interviews we look in this chapter at how the groups created their own forms of leadership, kept motivated, developed a vision, created structures, worked together and generated income:

• teamwork and leadership
• recruitment and turnover of volunteers
• the groups' ethos and approach
• organisational systems and standards.

We then look at our own work to define a 'good' community group. We based this on a combination of what we had learnt from the groups and a literature review. The working criteria for a 'good' community group we developed and tested were:

- the need for a shared vision
- positive internal dynamics in the group
- strong relations with their local community
- links to their external environment.

We found that, where successful, the groups had developed small self-managing teams, good teamwork, strong leadership and vision, flexible systems capable of growth, a risk-taking, entrepreneurial outlook, shared information and a customer focus. This is the exact blueprint for a 'high performance organisation' as outlined by many management 'gurus' (Peters, 1989; Katzenbach and Smith, 1993; Mohrman et al, 1995), although the groups were not familiar with this literature.

Tables 6.1 and 6.2 show the range of 236 positive and 107 negative comments on this topic – the highest number of stated opinions for any single topic. This reflects one focus of the interviews, which had the explicit aim of seeing how the groups operated. However, more often than not the trigger question for these conversations was a general one about who was in the group, or how the group started, rather than any direct questions about how the team got along, if all members were equally involved, or if they had experienced problems. These direct questions, when asked, generated somewhat stilted responses. A less direct approach did generate lots of discussion on the internal workings of the groups.

Teamwork and leadership

The groups interviewed were recipients of grant money from the Gatsby Project. To be awarded this money they had already had to demonstrate that they could work together well. One criteria for grant awards was the presence of a good team. For their effective operation the groups emphasised the importance of teamwork, inclusion of all members, good internal communication and a clear and equitable division of labour (63 comments, ranked 1st).

Table 6.1: How the groups operate – positive comments

Comment	No. of comments	Rank
Good teamwork	63	I
Good internal systems and development of volunteers	53	2
Entrepreneurial	34	3
High commitment of volunteers	24	6
Good leadership	20	7
Informal culture	I4	6
Other	(28)	n/a
Total	**236**	n/a

Table 6.2: How the groups operate – negative comments

Comment	No. of comments	Rank
Divisions in team	31	1
Problems with leadership	27	2
Need administrative help	18	3
High turnover of volunteers	17	4
Need for base	14	5
Total	**107**	

'Everyone does something, everyone contributes, for example, for the "do" over there [at the local social club], [one volunteer] ran the bingo, [another volunteer] ran the raffle, I did the door, someone else will sell tickets, and so on.' (resident, Keighley)

'We get on very well. It's very important. We always have a consensus ... we've never had to have a vote as such. The thing about this association, as opposed to the others – they're here just for the business. They don't have other agendas like the others do. We don't do disharmony.' (resident, Wrexham)

The groups resembled one management thinker's view of how a non-hierarchical organisation should operate, where 'the information system is the key to effective co-ordination ... but is particularly crucial in a high involvement system.... The information system must provide the capability for people to co-ordinate and manage themselves' (Lawler, 1986, p 198):

'A lot of what we do is visible. We are doing it, so we don't need long meetings because everyone knows what is happening because they can see it.' (resident, Warrington)

'[It's] unanimous decisions more or less. There's no "I'm the boss", there's no gaffers here. We're no better than [the volunteer] who comes in and cleans the toilet. I'm the chair in name only. It's not a position that's held in high esteem! [We are not] undisciplined. We may get more structured if we get more in. We treat each other as equals. Each one knows what they've got to do. [With new ideas] first we talk amongst ourselves, weigh up the pros and cons, then we cost it out, figure out where the money's coming from, then thrash out who and how many we're going to need.' (resident, Rhyl)

Shared values and friendship

Good team working was often based on friendship, or at least friendly relationships or shared values between group members. Many of the women in the groups had known each other through their children for many years before they formed an association. Other groups' members were drawn together by similar interests, for example a 'sound system' in Oldham made up of a loose collection of friends and acquaintances who were musicians. The group started as a sound system in the late 1970s, and most of the musicians were now in their thirties. They did music for the events as a reggae sound system, then out of that they started playing in a live band. They carried on from then doing parties and community gigs, before starting to do more community work and work with young people.

One example where shared values were articulated was of a YMCA where the members shared a common faith:

> 'The people running the YMCA are Christians, but the work we do is much more outward-looking than that. We don't force things down people's throats, we wouldn't have so many [clients] if we did that. There is shared love in the team – like it says in the Bible, "love thy neighbour"! We put that into practice everyday. We value each person for their own worth. The board are very nice to the staff. It's a privilege to work here with my wife. It's the only YMCA in the country where all the staff and volunteers have shared faith. I hope it doesn't put you off but there you are!' (director of a voluntary organisation, Devon)

Only four of the 90 projects had religious affiliations, so it was more unusual for shared values to be focused around faith, although obviously some groups' members had their own faith. But the core principle of shared values between members was shared in a secular way by other groups.

In Liverpool, a community cafe had had a change of staff in the two part-time posts since they started "because one woman fell out with us after the three-month trial. She had the wrong personality for a cafe like this. She used to work in a restaurant so she was making comments" about customers negatively. She saw the staff and customers as different, and was nasty about people who used the cafe, whereas the group, as community volunteers, felt closer to the customers who were their neighbours.

A place for all-comers

Equally important was the ability of groups to absorb difficult people and accommodate the idiosyncrasies of volunteers. A chair said of one member of a family support group in Cheshire:

'… he adds humour to a serious issue. He's our resident cynic, he keeps us off-track. He is involved because he has lots of spare time. He doesn't deal directly with the families. He takes messages, he's very helpful. We love him to bits really.'

The groups needed to accommodate a wide range of volunteers with different abilities and interests, and absorb people's idiosyncrasies.

As volunteer organisations with self-selecting members, the groups had to find a place for all-comers, regardless of abilities or interests. Some residents in Derbyshire talked about having 12 or 13 new names for potential volunteers since Christmas and that four of them were promising:

> 'Some are lonely, but it doesn't matter how bad they are, they can still make a brew, but it doesn't mean you can open longer hours because it's not suitable to leave new volunteers by themselves.'

The groups' comments show them working through how to manage the contradictions between including all, and allocating tasks according to skill, for example where jobs were taken by people who did not have appropriate skills:

> 'The secretary and treasurer have just resigned. They're the second ones since May. [The secretary and treasurer were a husband and wife team.] 'They agreed to do it but I don't think they really wanted to, but they couldn't say no. [The community workers] knew them and said, You can do it but…. They said yes but they didn't do anything

much. [The husband who became treasurer] did say he wasn't much good and he'd failed his exams. To be honest, he was abysmal. He couldn't cope with anything more than two columns. They resigned.' (resident, Derbyshire)

And in south London:

'[The treasurer] is a nice bloke. He's not any use as a treasurer but he likes the title so we leave it. We thought he'd be good as treasurer because he worked in a bank! But he's a loyal emissary and he's very sensible. If he thinks we're doing too much or going off the rails he stops things. He's got his feet on the ground.' (resident, south London)

Internal struggles

The groups suffered from internal rows, poor internal communication and conflicts over power within the group. In some cases, responsibility for tasks was divided unequally between members. There were no set mechanisms for 'making' people complete tasks or take on responsibility such as in an organisation with paid staff. Sometimes the task allocation and reporting back mechanisms fell down:

'[Other members of the group include X.] She's good, she helps out ... [Y] helps with the car boots ... [Z] doesn't do anything apart from talk. She's a talker. She says she is [doing things] but she never does.' (resident, Hull)

During the visit we then met 'Z' while we were walking round the block, but she didn't say anything.

'[There are about 10 people on the committee.] Two ladies do the bingo, they've done that since the word go, but only a handful do anything.... There's too many chiefs and not enough Indians.' (residents, Liverpool)

'[The community worker] always said to me when you open a place like this [community cafe] only the committed members are going to stay, and the weak ones are weeded out. That's what happened here.' (resident, Bedfordshire)

The chair of one organisation in Cheshire told us:

'Sometimes there's decisions taken behind closed doors. It can be a problem in a small organisation.... [For example] the bid to the health trust. Certain people were not involved because we got the application two days before the deadline.' (resident, family support group, Cheshire)

She explained that the tight timescale meant that in this case they did not check with one of the members but this was necessary to get the application done: "But it does cause problems in the group. I understand that people feel excluded but …".

Leadership and responsibility

Much of the tension within the groups was over the allocation of responsibility, in particular over leadership roles. There were contradictions between having equality between members while having a central coordinating member.

Good team working focused on the ability of members to persuade the others:

'I've told [the rest of the group] straight, to pull their finger out. But, there's never any animosity, and we're constructive if someone has a problem, we sort it, except neighbour disputes. That's like interfering in someone's marriage, you end up the wrong 'un, you end the bad guy. Communication is the answer to it all.' (resident, Keighley)

'The volunteers sit round, they don't know what to do, we have to tell them, but we don't want to be too bossy so we ask nicely!' (resident, Derbyshire)

> *Not The Way We Run Our Committee!*
>
> <u>*Whose Job*</u>
>
> *This is a story about four people Everybody, Somebody, Anybody and Nobody.*
>
> *There was an important job to be done and everybody was sure somebody would do it. Anybody could have done it but nobody did.*
>
> *Somebody got angry about that because it was Everybody's job. Everybody thought Anybody could do it but Nobody realized that Everybody wouldn't do it.*
>
> *It ended up that Everybody blamed Somebody when Nobody did what Anybody could have done.*

Allocating tasks between volunteers could be fraught

This was a consequence of the nature of the relationship between group members where all are self-selected, all are there by their own choice rather than in paid roles of authority or obligation and the hierarchies may be unclear:

'We're all on the same level so we can't tell each other what to do. We just want someone who's in charge.' (resident, Derbyshire)

'I'm not strict with my committee. I'm chair, I facilitate. People use it as an authority role, then more fool you! Because you can't force them because they are volunteers. I like football, they like the coffee bar, then fine. That's why it works.' (resident, Warrington)

Most of the groups had some form of basic committee structure with positions of chair, secretary and treasurer. People usually had to be proposed to these roles, then elected at an annual general meeting by a minimum proportion of members. Even so, the role of chair did not automatically imply a right to dictate to other volunteers. Leadership roles were won, not given or appointed like a manager in a larger organisation would be. The leaders of the groups had to use good delegating skills to retain their team.

Leadership roles were generally extremely difficult positions. There were several examples given by the groups (20 comments, ranked 5th out of positive comments) of positive strong leadership models that also showed attempts to be inclusive and equitable:

'All the group works together. We're all local. The atmosphere is brilliant, even the youth workers. That's why we've achieved what we have. Sometimes I have to make an emergency decision and go out on a limb. I need the group behind me. I say to them, come in if you think I'm out of order, tell me. They could do what I do but they work. We all have a common interest in helping the estate.' (resident, Walsall)

'For each project you get a project leader and volunteers.' (development worker, parent support group, Cheshire)

The development worker for the parent support group helped the parents develop this structure, for example naming a project leader and dividing tasks and responsibilities:

'It's like an octopus, with lots of tentacles here and there! [The development worker] brings us together, does the paperwork like you're doing, plays on the computers. She's the body of the octopus.... We're all involved in the group. [X] drives the barge.... [Y] is the real expert!... [Z] does the panto and publicity ... the lads do the raffle tickets. Everyone's equal.'

Problems over leadership and openness

There were contrasting examples given of overly dictatorial or secretive leaders or competition over the role. Those leaders that became too egocentric found other residents dropped off the group. The groups were advocates for what is sometimes called in management books 'open book management' (Gilbert, 1978; Stack, 1992):

> 'The chair was a megamaniac [sic]. We got another one who was worse!' (resident, Hull)

There had been some controversy over some additional funding one group in Derbyshire had received that one member did not tell the rest of the group about: "[she] wants the credit, it's her baby so she doesn't tell us" (resident). The junior youth club was not running over the summer because of the problems they were experiencing within the group.

> 'I am still concerned that the credit union is in the hands of one person and that is [X]. If he disappeared tomorrow we would be in a mess. He's so total in what he's doing and he doesn't let others help. He's so insular he doesn't welcome aid.' (resident, North Wales)

Reluctant leaders

Leaders of the group often said that they felt they were forced into the role because of the unwillingness or inability of the other members to take on overall responsibility for coordinating the group (27 comments, ranked 2nd out of negative comments; see Table 6.2):

> 'Over the last seven years I've been chair, treasurer and secretary. [Other group members were not keen to take a leadership role.] They don't mind being on the committee but they don't want to do anything that requires brainpower.' (resident, Hull)

> 'There are people on the committee who are scared of authority. People who just go on the committee don't want a more active role. It's just me and [X]. [X] used to be in the army. That's why she has leadership qualities. She can talk for England!' (resident, Warrington)

> '[The rest of the group] blackmail you to carry on – they say we won't go on if he goes. Every committee has its driving force. When I was on a [break], no one else was willing or prepared to take over the responsibility. [X] tried but it was a disaster. I stood down one meeting, you know, to let someone else have a go. And all the others stood down.' (resident, Keighley)

His wife added:

'If he doesn't run it there wouldn't be a committee because they don't want the responsibility, they can't be bothered because they're so old. It's alright if there's someone saying how about you but not taking responsibility…. It needed someone to take the initiative.'

Recruitment and turnover of volunteers

The internal debates in the groups over strong but open leadership, the voluntary nature of the members' commitment and the need for inclusivity in the team were reflected in the groups' ability to recruit and retain volunteers. For example, an inspirational leader helped to persuade people to join a group. One member got involved because:

'I met [a well-respected local resident] one day, I'd known him a long time, and he said he was thinking of setting a tenants' association up, so I said, When you're ready give us a ring. I'd never volunteered before. I thought, gosh, yes, we need a tenants' group because something's got to be done.' (resident, Liverpool)

Another member was also inspired to join by the same resident: "he was 79 years old, he was inspirational".

But a secretive or domineering leader contributed to members leaving a group. In County Durham, the previous chair of a group used to be a sergeant major, and worked as UK health and safety manager for a large firm for 20 years so was used to paperwork and committees and so on: "He held on to information". He preferred to chair meetings very formally. When he left: "it was like lancing a boil. [He] frightened and intimidated people. When he was in charge he wouldn't let anyone else be involved, you thought, Let him get on with it". Volunteers left because of this. "There was seven people here last night, that would never have happened" when the previous chair was in charge.

Including volunteers

The degree of inclusivity of a group was directly related to its ability to get and hold on to volunteers, for example by making all members feel part of the organisation and that they had a valuable role to play:

'We got another gentleman and two ladies just by them coming into the community room. They come in for some reason and I always take the time to say, We'd love you to come and get involved. For example if you're good at cleaning I'd say Please come and help us, you'd be a gem. I'm not saying about washing up [that it's a lower-status job]. You just give people jobs that they feel happy with and valuable.' (resident, Walsall)

A group in Rhyl had attracted three new members who turned up at the house and said they were interested. When new volunteers turn up, they were given "any office procedure we think they can handle", from copying, making tea, sorting cupboards, computer work, using DIY skills, making telephone calls, "anything that needs doing" (resident).

Some groups maintained relationships with lapsed members in order to have a wider pool of supporters to draw on when they needed extra help. On an estate in Liverpool, they held social events, for example the past four years they had had a social for members – past and present – and 50 people attended. People who were not involved any more "still offer help if they're ever needed" (resident).

A couple who used to be involved with a group in Kent lived four doors down from the community house. They still "pop in" (community worker). One of the couple did youth and community work at college and he did his college placement in the community house, which helped both parties. The community worker was really pleased about their progress and pleased they had managed to get on, although that meant she had lost them as active volunteers.

Turnover and loss of members

Being able to draw on a wider pool of casual volunteers was important because of the fluctuating nature of the groups' memberships (17 comments, ranked 4th; see Table 6.2). The groups faced problems with a lack of continuity of members and high turnover of volunteers, despite their often sympathetic understanding of the reasons for this. One woman in Warrington was involved but was not any more "because she works now and has problems with her kid who's hyperactive, so she resigned. People's circumstances change all the time" (resident).

> 'People move in and out, because the trouble with the project is that it takes ages to get things organised. The rewards take a long time to arrive.' (resident, Lincolnshire)

> 'Then we have other volunteers who come and go. Some have gone to university, but that's why [the group] is here. People drift in and out because of personal circumstances.' (member of a family support group, Cheshire)

Motivation of volunteers

Where groups had good continuity of volunteers and high levels of motivation, interviewees felt this was partly a consequence of the high level of commitment of members (24 comments, ranked 4th; see Table 6.1). Their self-motivation was paramount, given the voluntary nature of the job and the desire for equitable relations in the group, whatever the individual reasons for this were. Nearly all of the people involved in the groups were volunteers, therefore to keep them involved they had to be motivated, the work had to be fun and worthwhile and they had to be able to use their skills. Residents' groups had to keep up 'staff morale' otherwise their volunteer workers would simply not turn up for 'work':

> 'Volunteers need confidence and dedication. Whatever time you're prepared to give as a volunteer, you should then double it, because you're conscience won't let you walk away from what you're doing.' (resident, Derbyshire)

One group with paid staff described the differences they had experienced in organisational culture between their group and the social landlord organisations where one staff member had worked previously. The group had only just filled the new administrative assistant post:

> 'She's finding it a terrible culture shock. She used to work for [a London local authority] and [a large housing association]. The main difference here is no one tells her what to do – you have to use your initiative.' (resident, London)

The new worker had "given up her pension" to take this job, which the chair said, made it more pressured on both sides.

The groups' ethos and approach

The existence of a set of highly self-motivated group members was also based on the groups' overall ethos and approaches. Vital factors for the groups' continued survival were their shared vision and joint goals. The groups needed clear goals about working in the community to exist, otherwise their members could have started asking 'why are we bothering?' and 'what are we doing here?'. Because of the size and nature of the organisations, they were not good at self-perpetuation. The community groups had to regularly question their role and function to find reasons to continue putting in voluntary effort. This partly explains why single-issue groups often fold after a while. Group members' individual motivations for being and staying involved needed to be channelled in the context of a common appreciation of why the group existed and what they were trying to achieve. The groups discussed how they revisited their vision and goals in order to keep going. They also used their bigger vision as a way of preventing themselves being overwhelmed by the day-to-day slog of running projects.

A minority ethnic umbrella group was set up in Hertfordshire in 1994 and officially constituted in 1997. It had 350 members in total. Previously it was a user group for social services, and for a few years it met once a month – people "had a moan and went away" (community worker). Then the forum got a new chair and she helped shift the forum to being more stand-alone. It registered as a charity, but also had to become more "self-defining" in the process.

The residents' association's mission statement in County Durham was about advice and information, regeneration, crime, recreation for youth, physical environment and partnership work. They felt that the "way forward is well defined", and they agreed that they were in a lucky position as a group to have the house project to focus on: "Any residents' group needs an objective" (resident). A group nearby had folded after having success in getting estate redevelopment, because they had not generated any new goals.

> 'The bigger picture gets lost. The bigger picture for the centre gets lost, but then the picture for the area gets lost because of the [need for upkeep and management of the] centre. It's relatively easy to buy a big dog but to keep walking and feeding it takes energy.' (resident, Rhyl)

The material in this book takes the form of many different stories about why the groups were formed, what their goals are and how they operate. The groups we talked to told some enthralling stories. In this, they are close to what one theorist argues is *the* key to leadership, which is the effective communication of a story (Gardner, 1995).

The groups' mission

There were some internal debates in the groups over their purpose and approach. The ability to debate is important in helping groups come to shared understandings and assumptions about what they are doing (Garmston and Wellman, 1999), for example on the issue of targeting the most vulnerable or how much help to offer:

> 'There are middle-class kids [locally], but they still have development needs – careers, relationships, family and relationships to parents, emotional needs. The debate is do we positively discriminate for people in need, or provide a universal service?' (resident, Stoke)

Attracting the tougher children might mean that the project "didn't attract the majority of young people, and the volunteers feel uncomfortable. Why shouldn't nicer kids get the opportunity to use the facilities?" (resident). Whereas, another member was more concerned about those young people who: "are in trouble with the police, are drinking and smoking, not doing well at school, some are using cannabis". They agreed to keep discussing it: "We have different views, but we all agree we are here to meet the needs of young people".

Entrepreneurial outlook

The groups aspired to be proactive, entrepreneurial, outward- and forward-looking organisations that could learn and adapt. They felt these were organisational attributes that contributed to a successful group and also helped to increase the chances of success with their projects, thereby also helping to retain and recruit members.

The projects also had to conserve cash out of necessity. Nearly all of the groups had raised significant help in kind. Some generated income. They were inventive in the ways they equipped and resourced projects and had the incentive and flexibility to use second-hand equipment, to 'scrounge' and make do:

> 'People give [residents] ideas and the administrative background, but don't give people buttonholing skills, how to get and maintain attention, and how to persuade people of the benefits to them of giving you cash.' (resident, Wrexham)

> 'I got told there was cash here for set-up costs and wages.' (community worker, Manchester)

This turned out not to be true. The workers and volunteers spent the first month on the telephone "getting donations, help in kind, like from local companies, paint manufacturers ...". To move the Portakabins around the site they needed a crane. AMEC were using a crane in the area, so they went and persuaded AMEC to loan it to them. "Those heaters are donated, we did it like sales, I used to be in sales so no different. You just get out the Yellow Pages and go down the list" (community worker).

A group in Stockport decided to set up a communal allotment: "At that time we had money of our own, through the Lottery Bonus Ball" of between £25 and £40 a week. "We kept mithering [the health promotion worker] for money, so he gave us £750 for fencing, the potting shed and the greenhouse" (resident). Then they got £1,800 from the council for tools and materials. They had help from the Prince's Trust and probation service. They have used an old shower unit as a greenhouse and they adapted some old wheelie bins into wheelbarrows and water barrels: "We improvise". They used old tyres as planters for the potatoes. In May they raised £55 from a mix of membership fees for the year and a table-top sale of produce. They made a deal with the corner shop to take any surplus they could not sell. They want to grow bedding plants for sale: "they should go like hot cakes", which would give them a bit of surplus and allow them to "build funds up".

Organisational systems and standards

Aside from the groups' grand visions, day-to-day they had developed systems to help them implement their work. The projects illustrated the principle of 'best fit', that is, their organisational structures needed to fit with the type of work and the environment they were working in.

The groups' small size and voluntary nature also meant that they exhibited a high level of concern about financial probity and transparent accounting. None of the groups could afford to be victims of fraud in financial terms, and in terms of their local reputation and relationship with funders. They strove for high standards in terms of health and safety, or training of volunteers, and general regulation and legal matters partly in order to show that they were 'voluntary but not amateur' (Reason and Hayes, 2004).

Small groups with a strict division of labour were slowed down from achieving their goals. Some of the most active groups had a generic model of working that was more suited to the size of organisation and type of work. This ensured that if a job needed doing, someone did it.

Financial probity

There was a common concern expressed among the groups for financial probity and accountability, for example in jokes about the tight control of the treasurer over finances, or comments about the scrupulousness of the group:

> '[The treasurer is] mean, she's a dragon!' (resident, Bristol)

> '[The treasurer] doesn't like dealing with money! Anything over two figures. She doesn't like signing cheques. I showed her the Trafford Hall cheque she nearly passed out on me!' (resident, Walsall)

In Leyland, they were careful about getting receipts, although this was difficult at the car boot sale: "we said, Can I have a receipt! – we've been told to get one" (resident). The seller did not have a receipt book, so they managed to get them sign a scrap of paper, "anything!" (resident).

The use of group finances could cause tensions. One Manchester estate resident (who was also a signatory to the group's account) accused another member of using petty cash money to "get a taxi home for his girlfriend". The member in question heavily disputed this, and the debate degenerated into an argument about people gossiping "behind people's backs".

Fraud

Despite their concern for financial openness and control, the groups did occasionally fall victim to fraud or had misplaced their trust in members. In the North West in one group a previous chair and treasurer were a husband and wife team and were alleged to be "alcoholics, we had a terrible time. They took over, we weren't involved, no one was. The [landlord] had the auditors in. The books are straight now" (resident). Apparently the previous chair had been using the internet for downloading porn. Also £1,000 went missing. "Now [the previous chair is no longer in the group she] buys her [bingo] book with pennies". So their suspicion is that the old members were using the money for their personal spending.

> 'We were a very green group at the beginning. We had no experience. The treasurer eventually got threw out because he didn't pay the rent, so you can imagine. He was a young lad.' (resident, Hull)

And in another example from Bedfordshire:

> 'A lot of fundraising has not hit the bank. It put us back a lot. We think it was £4,000. The police are investigating it at the moment. We found out because of a problem with the shutters. [The previous chair] was holding things up so we wouldn't find out. He's a very plausible chap. That was the problem, he was a nice bloke. I got the bank statement. He was the chair and his wife was the treasurer. He told outright lies. We had an emergency meeting with the [community] workers. To this day he still won't admit he's done anything wrong. Everyone was quite shocked as well. He'd done silly things like gone to Bookers and bought 63 odd litres of orange squash, just for the youth club he said, and 21 kilos of sugar! The police took the books away. They realised that it had all been filled in on one day. At the moment he thinks he got away with it but he will get prosecuted and arrested.' (resident, Bedfordshire)

High standards

More generally, there was a clear desire by the groups to try and improve organisational standards such as health and safety, equal opportunities and discipline. One example was the groups' emphasis on training for volunteers (53 comments, ranked 2nd including probity issues; see Table 6.1).

> 'The more we go on, the more we find out we need to know about, it's not just homework.' (resident, Hastings)

The homework club were members of the association for youth clubs in the region: "The information you get from them back is really good", for example training you could go on, weekends away and training packs. They were booked to go on training soon on issues such as anorexia, child protection and steroids, and the youth service had also offered help.

Because they had so many volunteers in the advice centre and cafe in one group in Cheshire they offered training. They did an induction, health and safety training and:

'… a checklist of what their role is. We have a particular difficulty with people with learning disabilities in the cafe, with food hygiene. We use pictures and big models of bacteria in specialist training. We fund the advice staff to go through two lots of training. We have weekly team meetings and run catch-up training [on new legislation] in-house.' (disability advice worker, Cheshire)

In North London, some of the spending for one group was on training for volunteers at the homework club. One volunteer was doing a course in counselling through the local college every Tuesday that lasted a year and cost £100: "For example some of the children say I want to sit down with you and they tell you what they go through at home and school, so if you are not skilled you'll be surprised" (resident). The leader already had an NVQ Level 3 in Childcare/Youth Work.

Informal versus formal systems

Concern for probity and standards was common in the groups in the study. However, there were markedly varying approaches to internal systems and structures. One approach was to keep the working of the organisation on an informal basis with relatively few internal systems (14 comments, ranked 6th; see Table 6.1).

A group in Oldham was really a group of musicians. They were not a 'community group' in the traditional sense, but they needed a constitution to apply for grants. They adopted a constitution but in name only: "We don't bother [with all that] because we're musicians" (resident).

Other examples included:

'We're informal. If anyone came in they'd say this is a bloody shambles! But we know where we're up to! It's not like we got taught on committee skills training. We prefer to meet in people's houses – it's cosier, isn't it.' (resident, Warrington)

'We were given a booklet on how to chair a meeting on the way to a forum meeting half an hour before the meeting was due to start. You can't run meetings by this book … [in pompous accent] "I recognise the chair" … respect for each other is worth more than any rules.' (resident, Derbyshire)

They felt that plain language was best, but in meetings they put forward one of their members who could speak the same language as the professionals. And in another example from Bedford:

'If there is something to say we get quite a few [to meetings]. A lot of the time it's just [my neighbour and fellow group member] and me just sitting down and chatting, then we bring ideas to the meetings.' (resident, Bedford)

Whereas, other groups of a similar size and with equally close members had needed to develop more formal systems to help them maintain the teamwork and communication they valued:

'Every now and then we do a volunteers' meeting. We have a meeting once or twice a month, we discuss what's working, what isn't, what we'd like to do, and what plans we have. It keeps everything fresh.' (resident, Liverpool)

In Rhyl, some residents were running the office like a proper office, even though it was only staffed by volunteers. They had an office manager, job descriptions, a day book/diary, visitors book, a telephone call log and incoming/outgoing mail book. The community workers helped them to set up a volunteering policy for the office:

'... things like volunteers' chores, so they don't feel undervalued if they're asked to make a cup of tea, it's all volunteer management really. We do appreciate them, for example [X] cleaned the bathroom this morning.' (resident, Rhyl)

'We need a constitution, because it's a legal document that's our working basis. And if we row, we can use it to explain to people why we can't do something.' (resident, Walsall)

Organisational growth

Some of the larger organisations had developed more formal organisational structures and started to systematise procedures as a result of growth or taking on staff. In Cheshire, one group had such a big staff and volunteer pool it was difficult to get everyone together. They had team meetings for the advice team. They also had an "everybody meeting" where they had a meal or "strawberry tea"; "We have problems getting everybody together routinely" (volunteers and disability advice workers).

Managing staff in a south London group was also a learning experience: "I've just introduced time sheets for everyone. Because previously it was only casual" (resident), but because they expanded the numbers of staff, and people were all working different hours they needed to keep more of a track. "I want to introduce a weekly lunch on Fridays – like a team meeting. As chairperson I line manage [the paid coordinator of the community centre]. We're sending her on First Steps [a voluntary sector management skills course]" (resident).

Need for a base

Several interviewees pointed to the benefits of a base in relation particularly to the groups' ability to function as an organisation. A base provided both a physical place to organise from, and a focus for organisational coherence (14 comments, ranked 5th; see Table 6.2).

Previously, community activity on an estate in Kent was "like a load of bees but they had no hive to go to so they were just buzzing around. The hive is here now. A lot of the community were trying to do things before they started the house" (resident), for example play schemes, mother and toddler groups in people's houses and the community centre (now a pub). The idea was that "we wanted a hub for the wheel, we wanted a base. We wanted to be directed" (resident).

Definition of a 'good' community group

What makes a 'good' group as opposed to an ineffective or 'bad' group? As the study progressed, we decided to explore this question in a more systematic way. We used the material from the interviews, as explored above, together with literature from the community development field to develop a set of criteria for an effective and well-functioning community group. The work on defining a 'good' group brings together the issues already discussed in this chapter, and crystallises them into a working definition and set of practical tools for assessing groups' effectiveness. This work is described in more detail in Richardson and Sefton (2003) and in a report about the economic evaluation of social welfare projects by Sefton et al (2002).

To define what we mean by a 'good' group, we started by looking at what others in the community development field had to say. We used resource materials designed for community groups (for example those produced by the Community Development Foundation and by Community Matters), best practice guidance produced by government and academic texts. We used the information from the interviews to adapt some of the principles identified from other sources that were more relevant to larger community organisations (for example, Thake, 1995) or different types of community organisation (for example, Marriot, 1998). We used the interview material to check that as many as possible of the issues that the groups raised were covered.

Many of the same issues came up time and time again, although often with a slightly different emphasis. There was a large degree of consensus about what made a 'good' community group. We summarised the issues into four broad headings:

- the need for a shared vision
- positive internal dynamics in the group

- strong relations with the local community
- links to the external environment.

Having got the four broad dimensions of success, we broke each heading down into five criteria under each heading. We then used quotes from groups themselves (from the interviews) to illustrate a positive and negative version of each criteria. This allowed us to create a series of four quizzes, one for each heading (shared vision, teamwork and so on), where people could agree or disagree with statements that illustrated how far their group met each of the criteria. When the members of the group completed the quiz, it gave us a score for how far each person felt the group met the criteria. We then used the completed quizzes to assess the effectiveness of a group using a combined score based on each individual member's assessment and external assessments.

Table 6.3 shows the dimensions, criteria and quotes used on the quizzes.

Shared vision

A necessary, although not sufficient, condition for effective community group action is that they have a clear vision about what the group is for and how it is going to get there. The effectiveness of community groups is very dependent on using and developing the skills, knowledge and abilities of its individual members. To work effectively, a group needs to have a mix of people with different skills and abilities, including leaders, creative people, 'doers' and team players (Skinner, 1997).

Group work

In addition, individual group members need to be able to work effectively together as a team. We have already discussed the importance of strong, but open, leadership where decisions are not taken behind closed doors, and the ability to resolve tensions within the group so there is no bad atmosphere or simmering bitterness between particular individuals (for example, see Horton and Hughes, 2000). It is also important that group members are committed and motivated by what they do. Community groups rely on the voluntary effort.

The wider community

The litmus test of a group's effectiveness is whether it is having a noticeable impact on its local community. It is important that the group can point to ways in which they are interacting positively with their local community. The success of community self-help is dependent on the participation of the local community, through taking part in the activities organised by the group or helping to run those activities (for example, see Home Office, 1999). Like any business or institution, a community group is not sustainable if there is little or no demand for its services.

Table 6.3: Criteria and questionnaire for assessing small community groups

Assessment criteria	Questionnaire
SHARED VISION	
A Clear sense of what the group is for	+ "We know what our priorities are" – "We seem to have lost sight of where we're going"
B Strong belief that the group is needed and can make a difference	+ "We can make a real difference to this area" – "If the group wasn't here, I don't think we'd be missed"
C Everyone feels they have a say in the running of the group and is in the picture	+ "Everyone is allowed a say in the running of the group" – "Too many decisions are taken behind closed doors"
D Lots of ideas for new things to do; creative	+ "Once we've done one thing, we just move on to the next" – "We seem to be running out of ideas for new things to do"
E Group responds well to difficulties and is adaptable to changing circumstances	+ "When a problem comes up, we always seem to find a way around it" – "We're not very good at dealing with change"
THE GROUP	
F Strong leadership of the group	+ "We're lucky to have such strong leadership" – "Sometimes, it's hard to see who's in charge"
G Good balance of skills, knowledge and personalities within the group	+ "We complement one another as a group – it works" – "Some people are trying to play the same role – stepping on each other's feet"
H People enjoy working for the group (and this outweighs any negative aspects)	+ "It's really satisfying what we're doing as a group" – "Morale is quite low – people are fed up"
I Group members are committed – "won't be disillusioned at the first knock"	+ "People really put themselves out for the group" – "When the going gets tough, people don't want to know"
J Team works well together – no infighting/empire building	+ "Any disagreements tend to be over quite minor things" – "There's a lot of infighting – sometimes you could cut the atmosphere with a knife"

THE COMMUNITY

K The group has sought to involve different sections of the community
+ "We try to involve everyone in the local community"
– "People think we're just a clique"

L The group is seen to be representing their community
+ "I think we've won people's respect – they look out for us now"
– "People blame us when things go wrong around here"

M People are interested in and support what the group is trying to do
+ "Most people support what we're trying to do"
– "People aren't very interested in what we're doing"

N Events, activities and/or services organised by the group are popular
+ "The activities we organise are usually well-attended"
– "It's hard to get people along to events"

O People want to be actively involved in what the group is doing
+ "We can usually get volunteers when we need the help"
– "Apathy is a real problem – people don't want to get involved"

EXTERNAL ENVIRONMENT

P Has good relations with the local authority and is actively supported
+ "The authorities listen to us now. They know we're not wasting their time"
– "The council is always telling us there's nothing they can do"

Q Actively involved in local politics and plugged into the 'bigger picture'
+ "We're always being asked to sit on new committees"
– "We don't really know much about what's going on outside our local area"

R Good links with other community groups or local institutions
+ "We keep in touch with quite a few other groups like ourselves"
– "We don't get much support from outside – we just struggle on by ourselves"

S Able to obtain professional support from other agencies where required
+ "If we need advice or information, we generally know where to find it"
– "There are things we'd like to do, but we just don't have the expertise"

T Financial position of group is reasonably secure
+ "Getting money for projects has been easier than expected"
– "The obstacle all the time is funding – we're having to live hand to mouth"

This means that the groups had to have good intelligence gathering, and were forced to be close to the 'customer'. The projects that worked best took a proactive approach to reaching residents, and relied on face-to-face contact.

Nor is it sustainable in the longer term if people are not being drawn into more active participation in helping to run the group or some of its activities. It is also important how the group is perceived to be making a difference by other residents in the community. The community should be able to identify with the group; they should feel it is their group and be interested in and support what it is doing.

Links to the outside

Community groups are more likely to succeed if they are operating in a favourable external environment. This is partly dependent on their ability to win external backing and to persuade other agencies of their worth.

Do groups need to have all the attributes?

But what about the community group that is delivering substantial benefits to the local community, but is not necessarily functioning very well as a team? There are many examples of community groups, and indeed other organisations in the public and private sector, that have 'dictatorial' leaders, internal fragmentation and poor internal communication that still achieve results. By itself, this might suggest that team working is not important, provided there is strong leadership. However, an emphasis on delivery above all else can obscure the other costs that poor team working places on these groups, such as a high turnover of members, which adversely affects a group's ability to operate in the longer term. Over-reliance on one or two key people also makes the group more vulnerable, because it can place undue pressure on these particular individuals and yet make the group's survival very dependent on their continuing involvement. Thus, a strong team is likely to make a group more sustainable, even if it is not essential to achieve results in the shorter term. Figure 6.1 shows these different models of leadership in groups with different levels of openness and inclusivity.

Testing the criteria

We wanted to check whether the criteria made sense to the groups. We also wanted to see if we could use these quizzes to assess groups' strengths and weaknesses. We piloted the criteria with a small sample of four of the study groups. Each group member completed a quiz, then we used this to spark off a group discussion on the issues. The quizzes tested well against groups' own concerns and issues. The people we interviewed responded well to the exercises. The quizzes are a tool for helping groups assess their own effectiveness – they allow discussion to take place,

Figure 6.1: Leadership models

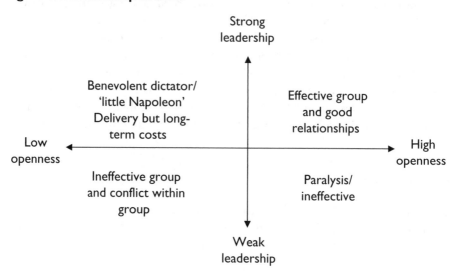

for example where different members of a group have given markedly different scores for aspects of how the group works.

The tool also allows for a more systematic evaluation of groups, for example comparisons of groups against each other, tracking change over time within groups, checks on internal differences of opinion within groups and internal consistency of individual members' answers.

Did group members agree with our definition of what makes a 'good' community group? At the end of each visit, we asked groups for their own definitions. Their immediate responses focused on the commitment and motivation of group members:

'... the people in it, doggedness and stubbornness.'

'... common enemies, anger as motivators.'

'... tenacity to nibble away at the council's backside all the time.'

'... can't turn round at the first disappointment, can't be disillusioned at the first knock back.'

'100% commitment.'

'Being bloody-minded.'

In addition, the groups understood, and acknowledged the importance of, the other aspects of the groups' functioning. In discussions with them, they articulated these in their own terms and in relation to their own experience. The four sets of criteria made sense to the groups and were relevant to them, as illustrated by what people said in response to the quizzes (see Table 6.4).

Table 6.4: The groups' views on what does and does not make an effective community group

Shared vision	• "There was always a problem with people on the committee who didn't share the big vision"
	• "The way forward is well defined … any residents' group needs an objective"
	• "The excitement of what it is going to be like in the future"
	• "Everyone has been asked to contribute ideas on how to raise income"
	• "We always try and compromise and take ideas on board"
	• "Lots of projects in our head …"
	• The group does things by "trial and error", and if it doesn't work "we ask why"
The group	• "I'm the boss, I'm a bit more strict but I try not to be a dragon"
	• They try to come to "unanimous decisions more or less. There's no 'I'm the boss', there's no gaffers here … we're no better than [X] who comes in and cleans the toilet"
	• "If you're involved in activities going on, you get a sense of achievement, for example the children's week, we've been knocked for it, but I saw the end result – happy kids"
	• "Any disputes tend to be over quite minor things …"
The community	• "We don't realise how known we are until we go out and people approach us"
	• "Some of the school kids think we're a waste of time … because we're not open more hours"
	• "Within 10 minutes of opening, we hadn't even got the kettle on, we had our first customer"
	• "You'd go round and all you'd get was [shrugs shoulders] … you go to all this effort and what do you get …. they thought there must be a catch because they were free"
External environment	• The borough council has "been good, they will try and work with us"
	• Talking about their biggest fan, one of the county councillors, "he knows what we've been doing"
	• "We're not in total control … [area initiatives are] using us"
	• "Local press have been supportive of the project … trying to breathe in as much good news as they can"
	• "We're lucky, we had incredibly supportive funders"

Summary

The groups are small informal associations that create their own working practices and structures to operate in response to a local need. The majority of community groups in the study were not legally incorporated, and nearly all operated solely with volunteers. The groups were not within formal systems of accountability or regulation. In order for the groups to operate effectively they had to organise themselves into a functioning team and create their own vision for their work, organisational ethos and approach, organisational systems, structures and working practices.

Our definition of a 'good' community group covered the following criteria:

- a shared vision and clear ethos, flexibility and the ability to adapt, a forward-looking entrepreneurial approach
- good teamwork, inclusivity and internal communication, with highly self-motivated volunteers
- active and positive relationships to the wider community
- well-made external links, ability to get outside help and plugged into the 'bigger picture'.

We designed practical assessment tools to see how far community groups met the criteria for our definition of a 'good' group. When piloted, groups found these true to life, and useful for generating discussion. Our definition came from synthesising material from the groups, good practice material, academic literature and resource materials designed for community groups.

There were many excellent examples of groups that did match these criteria. Successful groups had developed small self-managing teams, good teamwork, strong leadership and vision, flexible systems capable of growth, a risk-taking, entrepreneurial outlook, shared information and a customer focus. This is the exact blueprint for a 'high performance organisation' as outlined by many management 'gurus', although the groups were not familiar with this management literature. Not all of the groups met these criteria all of the time. Any organisation, whatever its size, and regardless of sector, can be vulnerable to common management problems. The areas where there were most problems with the groups were:

- poor internal communication
- conflicts over power and leadership roles
- unequal division of labour in the team
- high turnover of members
- financial mismanagement
- dilemmas over the degree to which the organisations systemised their work.

Good team working was often based on friendship and shared values between group members. The teams had to absorb difficult people and accommodate the idiosyncrasies of volunteers. They had to make all members feel part of the organisation and they had a valuable role to play.

Leadership roles had to be won, not given or appointed. Inspirational leaders helped to persuade people to join a group. Secretive or domineering leaders contributed to members leaving a group. The leaders of the groups had to use good negotiating and delegating skills to retain their team. Leadership roles were generally extremely difficult positions. Positive strong leadership models were also inclusive and equitable, and many of the groups were advocates for what is sometimes called 'open book management'.

Groups with dictatorial leaders, internal fragmentation and poor internal communication could still achieve results. This might suggest that team working was not important, provided there was strong leadership. However, an emphasis on delivery above all else can obscure the other costs that poor team working places on these groups, such as a high turnover of members, which adversely affects a group's ability to operate in the longer term. A strong team is likely to make a group more sustainable, even if it is not essential to achieve results in the shorter term.

The groups faced problems with a lack of continuity of members and high turnover of volunteers. Some groups maintained relationships with lapsed members in order to have a wider pool of supporters to draw on when they needed extra help. The volunteers' self-motivation was paramount. To stay involved they had to be motivated, the work had to be fun and worthwhile, and they had to be able to use their skills. Residents' groups had to keep up 'staff morale' otherwise their volunteer workers would simply not turn up for 'work'.

Vital factors for the groups' continued survival were their shared vision and joint goals. The groups needed clear goals about working in the community to exist, otherwise their members would have started asking 'why are we bothering?' and 'what are we doing here?'. There were some internal debates in the groups over their purpose and approach. The ability to debate was important in helping groups come to shared understandings and assumptions about what they were doing.

The groups aspired to be proactive, entrepreneurial, outward- and forward-looking organisations that could learn and adapt. They felt these were organisational attributes that contributed to a successful group. It also helped to increase the chances of success with their projects, thereby helping to retain and recruit members. The projects had to conserve cash out of necessity. They prided themselves on their ability to be cost saving. Nearly all of the groups had raised significant help in kind. Some generated income. They were inventive in the ways they equipped and resourced projects. They had the incentive and flexibility to use second-hand equipment, get help in kind and make do.

Day-to-day they had developed systems to help them implement their work. The projects illustrated the principle of 'best fit', that is, their organisational structures needed to fit with the type of work and the environment they were working in.

The groups' small size and voluntary nature also meant that they exhibited a high level of concern about financial probity and transparent accounting. Their concern for financial openness and control meant the groups only occasionally fell victim to fraud or had misplaced their trust in members. They strove to have high standards in terms of health and safety, or training of volunteers, and general regulation and legal matters, partly in order to show that they were 'voluntary but not amateur'. There were markedly varying approaches to internal systems and structures. One approach was to keep the working of the organisation on an informal basis with relatively few internal systems. Other groups developed more formal systems to help them maintain the teamwork and communication they valued. Some of the larger organisations had developed more formal organisational structures and started to systematise procedures as a result of growth, bigger funding and taking on staff.

The success of community self-help is dependent on the participation of the wider local community, through taking part in the activities organised by the group or helping to run those activities. Like any business or institution, a community group is not sustainable if there is little or no demand for its services. This means that the groups had to have good intelligence gathering, and were forced to be close to the 'customer'. The projects that worked best took a proactive approach to reaching residents, and relied on face-to-face contact.

SEVEN

What gives residents the right to take charge

'[We have] always been a very small committee and poorly supported by the residents. They've only started supporting us since we opened the advice shop – now they know our faces. Now people who've had help tell their neighbours. People worried [that we'd be] a bunch of do-gooders and loads of leaflets and nowt else. [But] we've gone far beyond what we thought we would in two months.' (resident, Derbyshire)

It would seem a legitimate activity for the groups in the study to have taken it on themselves to organise, for example, a social evening of music and supper for people in the neighbourhood. It would have been clear from the number of tickets sold, and attendance levels at the event, whether other residents felt this was a legitimate endeavour for those organisers. If other residents were not interested, then nothing much more than a booking fee would have been lost.

But often the legitimacy of community action is more controversial than this. What if this group was then used by a landlord as the only consultation mechanism for plans to demolish homes, or close the neighbourhood housing office? Does attracting people to a social evening qualify the organisers to speak on other residents' behalf on important decisions? If not, then what would give them a mandate as community representatives? What if they wanted to take over ownership of a local asset, like a building, for year-round community discos? Why should they be given an asset rather than anyone else? What if they applied for charitable or government funding for a social events coordinator? This illustrates a central question hanging over community self-help and involvement: what legitimacy do community groups actually have?

Community self-help is about people putting their heads above the parapet in order to help their neighbours, neighbourhoods, themselves and their own families. As we saw in Chapter Five, people had good intentions. They wanted to help other residents and to represent their views to service providers. But good intentions by themselves were not enough. In order for the groups to have taken on wider roles effectively they needed legitimacy and credibility in the eyes of both other residents and the agencies working in the neighbourhood.

The standing of community groups in the local community is an extremely controversial issue in nearly all areas, particularly when they are arguing with other agencies for change. From all corners there come doubts and questions about whether community volunteers and their organisations are adequately representative, but no common understanding of what being representative might mean in practice (see, for example, Hastings et al, 1996; Taylor, 2000; Aspden and Birch, 2005; Barnes, 2005).

In the study the groups' relationships with their neighbours were not always easy. Other residents may not have even been aware of the groups' activities. The groups' members were self-selecting and not necessarily statistically representative of the area's population – they held elections for committee positions but this was often more of an internal process. When public or charitable resources were being given to groups to provide facilities and activities, it was essential that the groups had wider community backing. The worst case scenario in any neighbourhood was that a tiny group of self-selected people tried to impose unwanted decisions on behalf of other residents without their consent. The Gatsby Project grant award process therefore had wider community backing as a key criteria.

In this chapter, we look at:

- why so many people are so concerned about the representativeness of community groups and community volunteers
- what relationships the groups had with the wider community, and what methods they used to create and enhance these relationships
- the groups' attitudes to external scrutiny and their attempts to implement equal opportunities
- the complexities of community groups' accountability to the wider community and how this differs within the community sector
- different forms of democracy, local leadership and how they interrelate.

Controversy over the representativeness of volunteers

There is a widespread concern about the degree to which community volunteers are representative, for example worries about: 'small unrepresentative cliques dominating' (Aspden and Birch, 2005, p 64). So why is the representativeness of community volunteers so controversial?

The first reason is that it genuinely matters. It matters particularly if other bodies are to take seriously what people tell them. It matters if other bodies are to share power and responsibility with local people. The implications of getting it wrong are potentially serious for decision makers and people in control of resources.

Secondly, in some cases there can be an element of politicking involved. Throwing the legitimacy of community opinion into doubt can also be part of not taking people seriously, and refusing to share power and responsibility with local residents. Some have pointed out that the representativeness of community groups is questioned more when people disagree with their views (Taylor, 2005a).

Thirdly, debate in the UK tends to suffer from a one-dimensional understanding of democratic representativeness. Being representative is usually taken to mean having a mandate through the political process. In practical terms, this means people voted for in local or national elections. More sophisticated debates add the dimension of statistical representativeness, that is, people reflect the make-up of the local population. The local government White Paper (DCLG, 2006) reinforces the democratic mandate as 'the' definition of representativeness. One example of the focus on a single type of legitimacy is who sits on local strategic decision-making bodies such as local strategic partnerships (LSPs):

> However, there have been tensions between community representatives and the council, particularly on the issue of community representation. Councillors, having been elected to represent and deliver services to their communities, see themselves as legitimate and accountable community leaders and representatives. They are concerned that this role is not fully recognised by government in relation to LSPs. There were also concerns about the extent to which community representatives represented, and could make decisions on behalf of, their communities: a particular issue for London, given the highly diverse nature of its communities. It is not only local authorities that consider this to be an issue: many statutory sector partners voiced the same concerns: 'Community members feel that they represent "the community", however it is clear that the leaders of the community are actually the professional leaders of the community and not representatives from small groups.' (ALG and GLE, 2003, p 19)

We put forward our own definition and criteria for representativeness later in this chapter.

Fourthly, things can and do go wrong in community representation. Some of the problems people have identified include:

* community leaders 'pulling up the ladder behind them' once into positions of influence and excluding others;
* the emergence of 'community aristocrats' (ESRC, 2007) as a result of the high level of knowledge and sophistication required to participate in partnership structures and decision-making processes. This 'inevitably excludes many residents' (ESRC, 2007, p 7) and privileges those with previous experience;
* that those who shout the loudest get heard while the views of quieter people are not heard;
* that community groups can be cliques that exclude certain sections of the population, for example along racial lines;
* that people who put themselves forward can be 'the mad, bad and the sad'.

Box 7.1, devised by one writer on community development, shows some ways in which community dynamics can be anti-democratic.

Box 7.1: Worse alternatives to democracy

Community groups are not all democratic but are expected to work democratically. Experiences of elected democracy may be frustrating but democracy is bigger than that. Here are some worse alternatives:

Oligarchy –	where a few people control things the way they like.
Theocracy –	where a religious group decides on God's behalf how things will be.
Bureaucracy –	where the accountants and form fillers make all the decisions.
Patriarchy –	where the men tell everyone what to do, or we do what Dad says.
Matriarchy –	where the women are in charge, or we do what Mam says.
Apartheid –	where the white people decide the lives of black people.
Dictatorship –	where one person decides.
Social disability –	where a person's impairment is the excuse for others to decide how they will live.
Monarchy –	where one family has control year after year.
Conspiracy –	where a secret group decides how power works.
Hegemony –	where a series of organisations use their power to control.
Tyranny –	where people are frightened by violence.

Source: Jonathan Roberts, lecturer at the University of Teeside, unpublished teaching material for National Occupational Standards in Community Work.

The groups' relationships with other community organisations

Tables 7.1 and 7.2 summarise the comments the interviewees made about relationships between community leaders and community organisations – their own and others – and the wider population. We collected 311 references on this subject in total, the second highest number of comments for a single topic. This was a highly relevant issue for the groups we talked to, who were keen to discuss the detail of how their accountability structures worked in practice. Other research has found that the voluntary and community sectors take issues of accountability seriously (Taylor, 2005a).

We look first at what relationships the groups and others had, then at what methods the groups used to create and enhance these relationships.

Competition with other community groups

The groups were critical of some other community leaders, community organisations, and methods of consultation (18 comments, ranked 1st; see Table 7.2). The groups' criticisms indicate their understanding of what they considered to be adequate systems of accountability. For example, they pointed to meeting

Table 7.1: Relationships between community organisations and the wider community – positive comments

Comment	No. of comments	Rank
Relate via project work	67	1
Newsletters/media	52	2
Informal relationships	32	3
Public meetings/open days	31	4
Social events/door knocking	30	5
Surveys/questionnaires	20	6
Involve users	13	7
Use elections	12	8
Relate via children/schools	10	9
Group not criticised	7	10
Block representative system	5	11
Total	**279**	

Table 7.2: Relationships between community organisations and the wider community – negative comments

Comment	No. of comments	Rank
Critical of other community leaders/organisations	18	1
Self-criticism/poor relationships	14	2
Total	**32**	

structures that did not encourage discussion or include quieter members. They were unhappy with groups that operated selective membership policies.

In one neighbourhood in North Wales, 10 years ago, there was a group called the Ratepayers' Association that non-ratepayers could not join. The community worker managed to convince them that people on benefit were ratepayers. There was a "splinter group" in the area called Residents Against Crime: "They select who they invite to their meetings" (resident). This other group blamed certain groups of residents for the problems of the neighbourhood, for example the "doleys", that is, the people living in the flats and houses of multiple occupation.

And some groups could be suspicious of other organisations' statistical data and methods of consultation.

In Derbyshire people were paid £10 to come to an original consultation meeting, which the group felt was not the right way to encourage people. After a while, fewer people started coming to meetings, because they were not fully on board.

In Warrington the residents' association helped to complete an estate survey that was then analysed by another organisation. A housing developer had promised £64,000 for play facilities and the survey was to see how to spend the money:

> 'When we got the figures back, there was only one for football, but we know that loads wanted it because we asked them. They don't want to know, they say, You're just a residents' association. They only want tenants to know what they want them to know. They don't consult like on the roofs versus the central heating. The council's committee decides.' (resident, Warrington)

Some groups had friendly rivalries with other associations, such as between a tenants' and residents' association and a community association in a neighbourhood. Indeed, the history of tenant organising (see Grayson, 1996) shows that in the interwar period some local authorities like Liverpool set up community associations as challengers to the tenants' groups of the 1920s because tenants' groups were seen as too oppositional to the council (Grayson, 1996). This fermented tensions and rivalry, which still lingered some 80 years later, as the example below from Liverpool, and many others in the study, illustrated:

> 'We both used to run tenants' associations in block 1 and block 3. [In one block] ... it was a tenants' association, and kept it to that. [In the other block] ... we did community too. We were a tenants' association but the community could come in, there's a difference to the other tenants' associations. All the people from the houses used to come. Before, the two tenants' associations, we both had rooms, but never the twain. It was West Side Story! We had to come together because of the demolition. We still fight! But we don't bear grudges.' (resident, Liverpool)

The interviewees felt that some charities working in their areas were 'do-gooders' with the wrong approach to the community. Or at least the groups had had to overcome this initial suspicion.

In North Yorkshire the Methodist church did youth work in the town. They were "Ministers with attitude!". At first, the residents were suspicious of the church's motivation: "what are they after?" and for the church, the youth worker said: "it took a while for us to get used to the, umm, 'direct' style of the residents!". Now residents do not think they need to mind their P's and Q's in front of the vicar. And, "the Church just wants to say, We're here as friends if you need us. If you are interested in the faith side as well then great, but if not fine" (church worker).

Lack of credibility in other organisations

Some felt that other community organisations, both local and wider area umbrella groups, lacked credibility or were not operating in the interests of the whole community.

A tenant-led organisation in Birmingham had considered joining a national umbrella group, but did not because there were "too many arguments, personality clashes. We didn't feel they could do training as well as existing agencies, they aren't as bothered with policy decision changes with [government], and there is a credibility problem" (resident):

> 'We're not actively involved because the community fed[eration] isn't as effective as it could be.' (resident, Liverpool)

> 'We don't work with [the tenants' federation], we went to one meeting and it was a closed shop. [The tenants' association said the federation people were] … all full of it when [they] came down, but when we went, we didn't even get introduced over three meetings.' (resident, Lancashire)

In West Yorkshire there was also an Asian Women's Centre that used to do a crèche and other activities, but "over the years it became one-sided, focused on Pakistani women" (community worker). This resulted in the Bangladeshi community feeling left out. The history of conflict between Bangladesh and Pakistan in 1972 is still "recent" for some of the generations so it still "affects people" and their relationships. The local Iman – "he's a man! He blocks things for religious reasons but that isn't the real issue. He has lots of say in the community" (headteacher), so there are some things they do not try to do, for example Saturday classes for Religious Education instead of going to the mosque.

In Humberside there used to be a tenants' federation: "it fell through. I didn't like the man who ran it. It was a bit council run. Nobody fancied that, why should they look at your accounts when they don't fund you?" (resident). The people involved "call themselves political activists" but the resident described them as "political agitators", for example, "the demolitions at [X estate] – not all the tenants want it".

A tenants' federation in Nottinghamshire was not seen as representative, so the community worker set up another 10 groups but tried to keep them away from the federation because the new tenants' associations had a different, more positive and cooperative attitude: "let's work with the council" (community worker). So all the new tenants' associations went to the federation's annual general meeting as a whole group and "took over", "it was a coup". That night, some of the old members threatened to firebomb the community worker's house.

The groups' relationship with the wider community

Self-assessment

Alongside their criticisms of other community organisations, the groups were also self-critical and self-aware, for example when their relationship with the wider community had apparently broken down or was difficult (14 comments, ranked 2nd; see Table 7.2). It was a major worry for the groups if the community seemed to be rejecting them, as this was their main constituency.

The groups used common sense indicators to gauge how the wider population felt about their work. A good example of a sign they used to assess levels of support was damage to property, and whether this could be interpreted as malicious or not. In Wolverhampton, for example, the minor problem residents had so far with the building was that someone had "nicked the security lights! But we've done well considering the rate of burglary" in the area.

And in Wrexham:

> 'There's been some vandalism to the tennis nets. Once I believe because some people were camping and they got cold so they made a fire with them. And once for pea nets – squares cut out exactly 8" by 3"!' (resident, Wrexham)

Some damage to a church building in the Stoke area where the youth club was had been accidental. One of the sinks in the toilets came off the wall because the girls sat on it to chat. A mirror got broken because some of the children were fooling around but it was not malicious: "But some is deliberate to get attention" (resident), for example letting off the fire extinguishers.

Non-responsiveness of residents

We tried to include a tour of the estate and projects during all the visits/interviews. The lack of deliberate damage to the groups' work was striking, particularly when compared to our observation of damage and vandalism to some regeneration work led by mainstream agencies in other places. But the groups did find their relationships with fellow residents difficult on occasion. They used indicators such as usage or take-up of services as a measure.

In Lincolnshire some residents thought that the general population would probably say that the project, a cafe for young people, "was a waste of time and money, especially if you told them it was £90,000". The local authority, district council and Development Trust "grudgingly acknowledge the project because it's in existence now". "Some young people, yes, think it's a waste of time" because of the lack of a pool table etc, and "the hours of opening aren't conducive to young people". But, "it's like any market, it takes time for people to decide to come through the door, for word to get round".

A group in Leyland had opened a community house that was being well used by public services and agencies such as social services and a job club for timetabled sessions with residents. However, other residents were "a bit suspicious of coming – you say it's free, maybe they think we want something out of them". Some residents were waiting to see "how long it's going to last" and were "waiting till it looks like we're here to stay", especially because of the collapse of previous projects. Some were confused about what a 'community house' was, for example they thought it was where people lived, like a hostel. Things were "slow" for the first two months, "no one came down except the officials" (resident).

A residents' association in Rhyl agreed with the Prince's Trust to do a greening scheme, but there was almost zero response to the questionnaires. So the group went door knocking: "We took Carter Seeds brochures, to show what shrubs you could have, it was arm and leg aching" (resident). Even this was "very difficult", "it took arm-twisting, you'd go round and all you'd get was [shrugs shoulders]. They thought there must be a catch because they were free".

Criticisms

There were examples of where the groups had been directly criticised by other residents:

> 'People think we TRA [the tenants' and residents' association] are keeping secrets, they keep asking what's going on but we don't know either.' (resident, Wolverhampton)

A businessman in Rhyl who owned a cafe was always concerned about a group's advice shop and tea bar because "this place would take his business. But he forgets, he opened opposite a cafe" (resident). This group felt that there was a lack of support from local businesses because they saw the people they helped as "dropouts. They think we're harbouring alcoholics".

Interestingly, it was often those people who had an active relationship with the groups who were criticising them. A good example of this ambivalent relationship was from County Durham: "Three years ago people thought the residents' association would throw people off the estate if they took drugs". At first families were worried that the residents' association would be "a witch hunt". Initially they were seen as "whistleblowers", for example: "[it's seen as our] fault if there are police raids, people think we brought them in". People were scared that the group would tell police about other illegal activity such as illegal cigarette smuggling, or minor things such as not paying television licences, neither of which the group were bothered about. However, the people who were suspicious of them had since attended events they organised, like a seaside trip where 145 people went. And the same people "who criticise still come to have their problems solved". They gave a few examples, like someone who had criticised them coming to ask to borrow one of the group member's ladders and tools:

'These people were giraffes in their last lives, because they've got to have a lot of neck to do what they do!' (resident, County Durham)

Winning respect slowly

Groups, such as in the examples above and below, took time to earn other residents' trust and worked hard to win respect. They saw the process of building relationships as taking time, and one that was based on the groups' actions as well as its words. The quote at the beginning of this chapter illustrates this well. That group has now built up trust by offering practical help to residents on issues that matter to people in the neighbourhood, for example covering issues like a dangerous power pylon running near someone's house:

'It's not just repairs, we wouldn't have thought our first welfare case was an eviction.' (resident, Derbyshire)

'... until [the community house] gets established it gets cliquey then a bit more settled. You are never going to get more than 10% of the population using it. People need it at different times for different things. Some pop in once to ask something. Some people moan because it's here. At the beginning it was the fear of the unknown – they criticise and are hostile. People are used to it now. There are people who use it and people who don't even know it exists.' (resident, Kent)

Evidence of community backing for the groups

Despite the rather gloomy portrayal of ambivalent and conflictual relationships with the wider community shown above, the positive signs of backing for the groups were also very much in evidence. The weakest form of this was an absence of criticism (7 examples, ranked 10th; see Table 7.1).

In Kent, residents felt that the group added to life on the estate by helping to create and maintain "community spirit". One of the houses had never suffered any vandalism and the group felt this showed that they were supported by the other residents.

'What we tried to do all the way along is get the kids involved – the main ones. They painted it green at the front. So far, hopefully ... [there's been no vandalism]. For example, the shed at the back. If it's theirs, they'll look after it. We've stored the pool tables in there for a while and we had no lock. They knew it was open and they didn't try to steal anything.' (resident, Bedford)

It may seem like an evasion to say that an absence of criticism was a good sign, but this is a significant point. Only a minority of the population of the neighbourhoods were actively involved, and only a relatively small number were users of services or attended activities. The majority of the wider population were in a more passive position in relation to the groups' work. The groups described themselves as being "cushioned" by passive support from the wider community. It was an important form of backing for the groups.

But whether people were providing passive support, rather than being indifferent or unaware, was extremely difficult to discern, and partly explains why the groups tried to use other signals such as lack of vandalism (described above) to assess levels of support. Stronger signs that the groups had backing were that other residents sought out help from the groups' members. We collected 32 examples (ranked 3rd; see Table 7.1) of these informal face-to-face relationships between groups' members and other residents:

'We can't walk down [X] Road without being stopped. You could be in the Post Office, anywhere. I was in Marks and Spencer and got stopped.' (resident, Rhyl)

'We're social workers, everything, I've been shopping this morning [for an elderly resident], we give lifts to the hairdressers.' (resident, Liverpool)

In County Durham group members got requests to help the pensioners with their gardens and brambles, or to fix things: "The number of people who 'phone or come here, even though we've got [a] housing office at the top of the village, the police office and the Town Hall, they still come here first" (resident).

'People would knock on us doors – housing problems, neighbour problems, we did everything from the bottom of the stairs.' (resident, Derbyshire)

Where possible during our visits to the neighbourhoods we gathered examples of these very loose informal relationships. For example, people coming to call unexpectedly while we were interviewing in people's homes, or group members greeting passers-by as we did a tour of the estate, or members getting stopped by residents as we walked round.

Not just all talk

But by far the biggest single piece of evidence of backing for the groups was their project work. This was also the most frequently mentioned method used by the groups to make a relationship with the wider community. We collected 67 examples of this (ranked 1st).

In Leeds, "A few women came together who felt there was a need for services for Chinese women" (community worker). They started off by organising activities such as day trips out and they used to do a jumble sale once a year to fundraise for activities, raising around £200. Running activities was very important before they got a base: "if you don't run activities people don't know you exist". They used the Chinese supplementary school as a base and ran sessions like sewing, knitting, welfare benefits and advice.

Many groups used converted properties as a community venue. A physical base was useful for organising activities and as a drop-in.

In Warrington, "When you're kept up all night with the kids, the council can say, Put it in writing, but it won't change unless they live on here (resident). They knew about this because "people come with complaints through the coffee shop" that the resident ran as a volunteer.

A housing office in Liverpool got an average of 20-25 callers a week. They had had 30-40 one week: "People come in with enquiries. We get more if there's something" (housing officer), for example, a couple of houses on the estate had opened as a children's home and it was a bit of a problem. One resident said: "We opened the boardroom" for people to meet and discuss the problem.

In Rhyl, "The idea of the drop-in was because it's very difficult to get people to come to formal meetings, so it's not just about providing services" (community worker), but also the idea that the advice centre would act as informal community consultation. "People can express their views and opinions, and it's proved to be so by the number of volunteers using it, people who previously didn't come to meetings" (community worker).

The groups gathered complaints about neighbourhood issues through their contact with residents via the activities and services they provided. Other evidence of support for groups was residents helping to fundraise for or give financial backing to the groups in small ways.

A group in Warrington did regular car boot sales: "Tenants give us stuff. We put a notice on the boards and flyers out. We raised £80-£90" (resident). They ran a tombola and made around the same amount. They did raffles, selling tickets door to door: "A tenant gave us a microwave from his own pocket" as a prize. They made £81 on the last one.

A local social club in Liverpool had a fundraising night to raise money for the two play schemes on the estate. They raised £1,500 to get tents and camping equipment and sent the children on trips. They had done this in previous years, for example one year they raised £8,000 and took the children to Disneyworld. They took 50 children on a trip every year. The centre had a lot of support locally: "This estate, if people win money at the social club they always donate it to the centre" (play worker).

And the parents of the children that attended an after-school club in North London offered help to the club, such as by providing free pencils from their offices and free photocopying.

Organising activities to give the groups legitimacy

Whether a group could generate reasonable levels of usage of facilities or attendance at events was a good 'ready reckoner' of their credibility and organisational ability. For example, other residents needed to be at least partly assured that the group was trustworthy and capable before they would consider booking and paying for a seat in advance on a coach trip.

There are obviously some grey areas, however. For example, the groups themselves commented on the casual approach of some parents of young people they worked with, where parents had not thoroughly checked the group before allowing their children to attend play schemes or youth events. And, admittedly, it was more difficult to argue the case that buying toast from the community cafe was an indication of trust. However, repeat usage at regularly run events was another positive indication.

While usage of services or facilities did not automatically entail a mandate for groups per se, it did show that they had correctly estimated people's needs or wants for those things. More importantly, where groups' sole role was to provide activities or facilities (rather than be representatives), the major test of their legitimacy was whether they persuaded people to use the services or attend meetings. The groups attributed the success of activities to good promotion. For these small-scale events a common method of advertising was word of mouth. This also indicated both local connections the groups had and a certain level of popularity.

To get a service or event set up, the group had to have some level of organisational ability. Organising activities also usually involved winning backing from local stakeholders, getting favours and possibly convincing a funding body that you were worthy of money. This was also an indication of the groups' togetherness.

The residents' groups also tried to be actively representative by reaching out to the wider community and making links outwards in different ways. We list the more traditional routes – newsletters and surveys – below. But the need to reach out to the wider community also explains why the groups' dual role as community organisers as well as community representatives was so crucial. Their community organising gave them links to other residents that enabled them to be actively representative, for example by gathering views and getting backing. Their small-scale community self-help activities were demonstrable forms of proof that they had some legitimacy and standing in the wider community. This was by virtue of the local endorsement by users, as well as the ability needed to galvanise enough backing to get a service up and running in the first place.

More traditional ways of relating to the wider community

The remaining ways groups had of reaching out to the wider community were more traditional information and consultation methods:

- newsletters, local press, flyers, posters and letters (52 examples, ranked 2nd)
- public meetings/open days (31 examples, ranked 4th)
- questionnaires/surveys (20 examples, ranked 6th)
- social events, door knocking, outreach (30 examples, ranked 5th)
- contact via schools and own children (10 examples, ranked 9th).

The methods that seemed to be most effective at reaching 'hard-to-reach' groups, or at promoting less immediately popular ideas such as environmentalism, were:

- contacting people directly face-to-face, for example by door knocking
- social events
- outreach work such as chatting to people while they were using local facilities, for example at the shops.

Newsletters helping to make outward connections

Of all these information and consultation methods, the most open to criticism was newsletters, local media and other forms of one-way information. It was difficult to judge whether people saw the information, took the information on board, or felt positively about what they read and heard. To argue that a newsletter was a significant link between a community organisation and the wider population sounds possibly dubious. Many bits of paper through the letterbox are thrown away and not read. However, a crucial point to emerge from a number of the examples was how big a role was played by information about the groups in building links to the wider community. The interviewees said that getting information to put into a newsletter forced a group to find out what was happening in their areas, giving a two-way information flow between different local organisations in the locality. The other key advantage of written information and other forms of publicity was that it was a basis for generating more involvement, thereby making organisations more representative as a result. One group from Stoke explained how radio appearances generated new volunteers for their youth cafe. One member joined the youth project because she had heard the leader speak in the meeting: "I thought, she can't half talk! She was full of ideas" (resident). Another member also joined after being inspired by the group's leader: "I heard [the group's leader] on the radio and wanted to work with her because of her enthusiasm".

A resident explained how the newsletter helped generate interest from volunteers. The group from Liverpool had always prioritised doing the newsletter "because people get involved if they're informed and they want to. So, you have to get the information out, even when you're a small group" (resident).

The groups' attitudes to external scrutiny and efforts to promote diversity

Other relevant measures of the legitimacy of an organisation could be that it was scrutinised and regulated by an external body, like the Charity Commission does for registered charities, or the Audit Commission does for local government. However, nearly all of the groups were not subject to any form of external regulation. For constituted tenants' and residents' associations recognised by the local authority, the recognition criteria were understandably basic but not the same as regulation or scrutiny.[1] For two thirds of the groups, the Gatsby Project grant was their first grant (other than running costs from the local authority of usually not more than a few hundred pounds) or first grant of that size. This meant that they had not been monitored by other grant funders. Even for the groups that had been awarded grant funding prior to the Gatsby Project grant, nearly all felt that the monitoring had not been thoroughgoing. We were the only external monitoring organisation of any kind that had visited for at least half of the groups, for understandable and wholly appropriate reasons.

One indicator we used of the groups' scrupulousness, genuineness and openness was their *attitudes* to external scrutiny. Obviously this was relatively difficult to gauge on a general level because of the absence of any common inspection framework for these very small-scale groups. Most groups welcomed the LSE Housing monitoring visit. The majority of the responses about the visit were extremely positive, and appeared thoughtfully given. The comments about the LSE Housing visit included positive comments without prompting, with residents saying they were pleased we had come down to see them face-to-face:

'It's nicer than filling in evaluation forms, it's nicer really. A lot of them, it's just filling in forms. They just want the receipts. They're just interested in what we spent the money on and nothing else. Apart from the [X] trust. He's been really interested and he comes to see us. It's nicer doing it like this, it's much more personal, you can't get things across on a form.' (resident, Bedford)

We discussed the difference between genuinely active community representatives and others, and how you got a sense of whether projects had that 'feel-good factor' or not: "You know if people are for real. You get to tell. You must know with your job" (resident, Liverpool).

> 'I don't mind people asking personal details – after all, no one's going to be attracted to the project if you're not friendly. You want to know what sort of person you're giving your money to – I know I would!' (director of a voluntary organisation, Exeter)

> 'Do you visit everyone? Yes? That's good. You go all round, then you can tell what sort of people we are.' (resident, Wrexham)

Five groups were indifferent or puzzled in response to the monitoring and research visits. This was either because of a change of group membership to someone who was unaware of the Gatsby Project, or in one case because the group had returned their grant cheque, or a last-minute change of interviewee. In addition, many groups said that they "didn't know what to expect" before the visit.

Overall, however, the groups commented enthusiastically about the visits. A common theme was that they had not received attention in that way before. They appreciated the opportunity to have their work scrutinised, display their achievements and get external feedback and validation where deserved.

An interview in Wrexham had been going full steam for a few hours when one of the residents apologised for giving too much information: "We talk too much because no one ever asks us to brag, but we like what we do and we're proud of what we do and where we live".

And in another example from Walsall:

> 'Your last visit was hard work. It was like pulling teeth! There's still things we haven't mentioned yet! It's a shame you don't have all day. When you come next time.... You're the only nosy person we've had! No seriously, it's nice to see that someone's interested in everything we've done. It's like a pat on the back.' (resident, Walsall)

This reflected the groups' perception that there was generally a lack of recognition of their efforts from others. The groups were keen to be externally scrutinised and recognised as part of their desire to be seen as performing a legitimate function.

Promoting diversity

Finally, we used groups' efforts in promoting tolerance and diversity as another gauge of their 'representativeness' and legitimacy. The groups' stances on equal opportunities issues in their work are an important aspect of their credibility. Neighbourhood-based community groups were sometimes reproached because they could not be trusted to represent the diversity of local populations (Morrison, 2003). The groups' legitimacy was seen as wanting because it was argued that they failed to reflect the full diversity of an area, particularly minority ethnic groups, as well as gay, lesbian or disabled groups (Purdue et al, 2000). Attempts to promote diversity and tolerance was largely an externally imposed criterion, and one that the Gatsby Project used as part of its assessment for awarding grants for groups in ethnically mixed areas. Equality was also one of the core principles of community work (PAULO, 2003).

BACK YARD GARDENING FOR WOMEN
WORKSHOPS ARE TO BEGIN ON WEDNESDAY 20TH MAY
FROM 1.30pm TO 3.00pm
AT THE PRESTON MUSLIM FORUM

The groups promoted diversity in their work, and tried to include people from all backgrounds and cultures.

On the whole, in the same way as we found in Chapter Three that people were proud where there was racial and ethnic tolerance, overall we found that the groups were concerned to include all 'races' and cultures in their work where it was immediately relevant, or where there was a significant minority ethnic population. Diversity was certainly an issue for groups in racially mixed neighbourhoods, and there were seven examples of tension or anxiety around 'race' issues in relation to the groups' own work. For example, a newer member with more formal education had joined a group in north London but was going too fast developing a particular project for the rest of the group: "He'd written six pages of job descriptions! He wanted to go fast and we felt left behind. The Turkish and Somalis turned up, they didn't know what was going on" (resident). Three of the original group members, who were all white, fell out with this newer volunteer: "He told us we weren't ready to administer a pint of milk. Then the split and divide came". Another group member working on this project happened to be from a minority ethnic background. So when there was a fall out about the project "we got accused of being racist". All in all, "things started going wrong. We could never pinpoint any specific moment. He was accusing us of racism – we weren't – but it created a bad atmosphere ... the college worker and tenants on the estate were saying, Well, if he's saying it [it must be true].'

There were six examples of proactive work by the groups to promote diversity. For example, groups organised celebration days with food from different cultures, or successful attempts to achieve a mix among the groups' users or volunteers. The first example below was from the group discussed above, who managed to resolve tensions over 'race' through joint work with minority ethnic communities.

There were some good things that came out of the accusations of racism against the group. The person making the accusations had persuaded the local college to use some of their community training budget to train up the tenants' association's members and other residents. Fifteen people did two days a week at college for four weeks. The course was IT and ESOL (English for speakers of other languages). Eight of the 15 were the Somali women mostly doing ESOL, and the other were the white residents doing IT. The groups "weren't afraid to sit together" and they did talk together, but "it was difficult" because of language barriers, although they had a "laugh" (resident).

In Manchester in one group there was a good mix of people from different ethnic backgrounds, in terms of the staff and children who attended the play scheme, partly because black parents saw the mix of staff and felt okay about bringing their children. They felt that they had got an ethnic mix because "we were open, and because we recruited local people and mixed the staff – it's an attitude thing" (community worker).

There were a further nine examples of targeted work to support specific minority groups, for example support for groups of Asian women, or young African Caribbean musicians or older Chinese women.

Part of a group's aim from Oldham was to promote African Caribbean culture, via music and events. They used dance, music, arts generally, for example street performance, and food to do this. They also wanted to promote an image of the variety within African Caribbean culture: "This community is not about rice, peas, and curried goat!" (resident). The common features of African Caribbean culture they wanted to promote were: "warmth, unity between people; an atmosphere of openness and tolerance; creative heritage and a rich history in the arts like rap, poetry, dress; pride in one's own culture" (community worker). The group themselves were into roots and roots/reggae music, but were breaking down barriers between different types of music, for example calypso, swing, soca, etc. Young people coming up were into soul, garage and R&B so they tried to accommodate and mix.

Different forms of accountability

In this book we tend to use the term 'community volunteers' rather than 'community representatives' because of the complexities around the question of representativeness. There are many different possible ways that groups could or should be accountable that partly depend on the size and nature of the groups.

So far in this chapter we have used different ways to judge how accountable and legitimate the small informal groups in the study were. The first set of measures was about the groups' direct or informal relationships with other people in their neighbourhoods. The second set of measures was about the groups' relationships with external bodies or externally imposed criteria. These are summarised in Box 7.2.

Box 7.2: Ways to judge the legitimacy of small informal groups

The groups' relationship with the wider community:

- The groups organised activities, and people used the services the groups provided
- Residents sought out help and advice from the groups' members informally
- Residents helped to fundraise for or gave financial backing to the groups
- Lack of vandalism of the groups' projects
- An absence of criticism
- The groups reached out to the wider community using information and consultation

The groups' relationship with external bodies:

- They were open to scrutiny
- The groups had positive approaches to promoting diversity

Wrong ways to hold community volunteers accountable

Absent from the lists above are other criteria sometimes used to indicate that groups are representative. One of these is the election of group members at a group's annual general meeting. While this is an important way of safeguarding internal accountability, it does not usually guarantee accountability to the neighbourhood at large, mostly because most people do not turn up to the meeting. Even the excellent National Framework for Tenant Participation Compacts does not specify much further than the basic recognition criteria for tenants' groups (as described previously in this chapter), an equal opportunities policy, newsletter to residents and regular meetings including an annual general meeting as the criteria to show they are 'democratically elected' and accountable to their communities, although the Framework also says that tenants' groups should have an active membership, 'determined by the council and tenants', to be defined as accountable (ODPM, 2005b).

Some have suggested that other sorts of elections for community volunteers would resolve the issue of representativeness. Some commentators have pointed to successes in New Deal for Communities elections for community board members as a way forward (Shaw and Davidson, 2002), although promising initial turnouts in the early stages were followed by disappointing results overall (Rallings and Thrasher, 2002). Some of the groups in the study had faced elections, for example for a tenant management organisation to take over management responsibility of homes. Tenant management organisations were pleased to be able to use turnout figures and positive votes as a demonstration of their representativeness and community support.

Elections for community organisations are useful when significant one-off neighbourhood decisions are at stake, such as tenants taking over management of homes, or who decides how £50 million is spent. These issues also tend to generate good turnouts. However, elections as a solution to the everyday, run-of-the-mill issues of community legitimacy are not necessarily the right answer for two reasons. First, because it is likely that turnouts would be low, so they would not work. Second, neighbourhood-wide elections would be too close for comfort to the system of elections for local councillors. It could place community volunteers in very negative direct competition with elected members, and the advantages of having a mix of elected representatives and community 'representatives' would be lost. We look at the relationships between different forms of democracy below.

Other definitions of 'representativeness'

Here we use the idea that to be worth taking seriously or listened to, the groups needed to be able to demonstrate a positive relationship with the wider population in one or more of the ways listed above. The groups had control over these things. Our concept of 'representation' is that the volunteers had a constituency, and could therefore say '*we* think that ...' and be reasonably confident. We see this as the responsibility of the groups.

A cross-section of the population

There are other reasons people might be worth listening to (Barnes et al, 2003). We see the following other methods of getting 'representativeness' as the responsibility of other organisations, rather than the groups.

One of interest is the idea that people are statistically representative, that is, they reflect the make-up of the local population. So, for example, take an area that is mixed in terms of 'race', ages and tenure, with lots of young families. A panel of 20 'representatives' for this area might have mostly parents of younger children, some of them would be from a minority ethnic background, some of them would own their own homes, some would rent and so on. With this sort of legitimacy the individuals involved may not be held accountable to the local population at all. A government overview of citizen engagement in neighbourhoods and public services found that women and black and minority ethnic groups were better represented on the boards of tenant management organisations than among elected members of local authorities (Aspden and Birch, 2005). Social housing tenants were more likely to be single women, members of certain minority ethnic groups, not working, or in low-paid or part-time work, disabled or with a long-term health problem. The profile of tenant activists in the UK tends to be similar to that of social tenants as a whole and is therefore representative of traditionally under-represented groups.

Unless large numbers of people are involved it is difficult to argue that people are truly statistically representative; instead they are a rough cross-section of the population (Barnes et al, 2003). When consulting most people would want to get a solid mix of types of people with different experiences, personal circumstances and needs. In our other research we found that the presence of people from different sectors and groups changed the nature of a discussion, for instance having a community volunteer present in a debate between policy makers about community engagement. This is another option for creating 'representativeness', and a useful one in some circumstances.

But is this something that the community volunteers should be responsible for? We would argue that if this method of ensuring representativeness is being used, then it is up to the organisation doing the listening to go out and find the cross-section. The responsibility for ensuring adequate representation must be on the organisation doing the consulting.

From the horse's mouth

However, as one writer points out:

> ... demographic factors remain popular in ensuring a balance of gender, age, ethnicity, class and so on. Nevertheless, there may be situations when we are more interested in securing the participation of people who are knowledgeable and interested in a topic than in achieving a demographically representative sample of disinterested and ill-informed citizens. (Burton, 2004, p 194)

A person just by virtue of the fact of their gender or ethnicity or disability does not know what other women or people with disabilities think. Community volunteers can be advocates for young people, people with disabilities or people from minority ethnic backgrounds even if they themselves are, say, white men over the age of 50, if they have a commitment to promoting diversity and if they have listened to what young people or Asian women or whoever has tried to tell them. However, what the young person or Asian woman herself can offer that the well-meaning white male volunteer cannot is their personal experience.

Direct grass-roots experience can bring an issue to life, and help people to understand what it is like for the person experiencing something. 'From the horse's mouth' is a powerful and convincing way to get a message over. We have combined broad ideas about a cross-sectional mix, together with people's ability to offer personal experience as selection criteria in our other policy development research (see Richardson and Hills, 2000; Bennett with Roberts, 2004; Richardson, 2004). The organisation Business in the Community uses this technique with senior business leaders with their Seeing is Believing Programme of trips to deprived areas and other settings to see how projects are trying to find solutions.

Where direct experience is the grounds for someone being listened to, there are likely to be other criteria that are not usually made explicit. The person needs to be able to tell their personal story in a powerful, convincing and memorable way. They need to be confident at speaking in public, and to people from different backgrounds including 'high-status' professionals. There is no reason why this specification could not be openly advertised, for example as a 'job description' to advertise a representative position to make the process open to all. Open advertisement for community positions generally has been used in some neighbourhood management projects. Of course, open competition tends to attract confident people with a particular set of views they want to get across. Therefore, there is an argument that 'representatives' offering powerful personal experiences to illuminate policy decisions could be sought out and nurtured – not coached in *what* to say, but hand-held in being confident to speak in open forums to decision makers.

Again, the responsibility for recruiting and nurturing people to share their experiences is the responsibility of agencies that want or need to listen. The role of community volunteers could be to offer their personal experience where appropriate.

Methods of accountability within the community sector

As we saw in Chapter Two, the groups in the study were small, with modest average annual cash turnovers, no paid staff and no legal status as organisations. We will see in Chapter Eight that the groups felt inexperienced and lacked confidence. As discussed in this chapter, their relationship to the wider community was informal, immediate and a lot to do with trust. There are many grey areas – for example, buying toast from the community cafe cannot be considered automatically an indication of trust. Nevertheless, their accountability could be summed up as 'accountability through tea and toast', as this suggests the nature of the face-to-face friendly relationship.

In contrast, some larger organisations in the community sector such as community development trusts have turnovers of over £100,000 per year, are set up with legal structures such as a limited company with a charitable arm, may have paid staff and aim to have skilled and experienced boards of directors. Their relationships to the wider community are more complex, probably with greater distance between the organisation and the population. People might relate to the organisation primarily as service users. The committees running the organisation might be composed of a mix of elected residents plus co-opted (that is, unelected) experts and advisers, and residents might even be in the minority overall, such as with a third–third–third structure (one third residents, one third public sector partners and one third private and independent partners). The organisation may be multilayered and cover a wide area, with most active residents only directly involved in their particular neighbourhood through a sub-group or local forum. The challenges faced by Manor and Castle Development Trust in Sheffield illustrate these issues. Their ex-chief executive described how in the early days they wrestled with decisions about what form of organisation was best suited to their needs, and what could best guarantee community control. Now 10 years on, the issue is still ongoing especially as the Development Trust has grown in size. The trust acknowledged the dangers they faced: becoming overly hierarchical; distant from the community; and overly business-driven rather than values-driven. They resolved these in part by creating a federal structure, with the Development Trust as the incubator organisation, then a series of spin-off businesses/social enterprises with their own boards, bank accounts, etc, which also contributed to sustainability (Clarson, 2005).

Accountability to the wider community for larger more complex community organisations would need to be judged according to different criteria than those laid out here, measures that better suited the nature of those organisations. The Development Trust Association defines 'community-based, owned and managed' in the following way, which also includes the activities they organise, which are the same as our criteria for the smaller groups:

> Development trusts are driven by and accountable to their community in various ways. Some have boards elected by a ballot of all those in the area, others have a membership base from which elections can be made. Others have a structure in which community groups, the local authority, local businesses, and others are represented. Others have arrangements to safeguard balance between sectors, or interest groups. Others involve a mix of people through co-options. Many derive their community legitimacy not only through constitutional arrangements but also from day-to-day practice – the ways in which they involve local people in their work. (www.dta.org.uk)

Different forms of democracy

In this chapter so far we have looked at the question of the groups' legitimacy in relation to their own role in isolation. Here we examine the groups' role in relation to other forms of representation. The groups followed a model of participatory democracy – small organisations with direct active involvement and largely self-selecting members. They operated alongside other forms of local democracy, in particular the structures of local representative democracy. How did they relate to locally elected members? How did the groups fit into other democratic structures?

Community volunteers and local politicians: sometimes one and the same

Tenant and community group members can be both 'volunteers' in a traditional sense and also political activists – many local councillors in the UK started out as tenants' representatives (Beckford et al, 2003). Many local councillors are involved in neighbourhood bodies; for example, in the same period as our research in 2001 60% of councillors were school governors, 42% involved with other public bodies and 57% involved in voluntary work (LGA, 2001a).

Occasionally poor relationships between community groups and local councillors

Despite the overlaps between local politicians and community volunteers, there were sometimes poor relationships between the community groups and local councillors. These groups were broadly supportive of the principle of majority representative democracy. However, in practice, there was an underlying tension between the groups and local councillors that filtered through in the discussions. Local representative democracy has a chequered history of hard-fought and sometimes underhand battles.

Nationally there is evidence of cynicism towards local elected members. Fifty-five per cent of respondents agreed with the statement that elected members 'tend to lose touch with people pretty quickly' in the local government module of the British Social Attitudes Survey 1998 (Chivite-Matthews and Teal, 2001). Cynicism about local democracy got worse between 1994 and 1998, with the percentage of people agreeing that councillors lose touch up from 47% to 55%, and more people agreeing with the statement 'councillors don't care much what people like me think', up to 40% from 36% (Rao and Young, 1995, 1999, quoted in Chivite-Matthews and Teal, 2001). Sixty-three per cent said that they would trust councillors 'only some of the time'/'almost never' to make important decisions (Chivite-Matthews and Teal, 2001). Eighty-eight per cent agreed with the statement 'local councils would make better decisions if they made more effort to find out what local people want', with only 7% who felt that 'local councillors should just get on and make the important decisions themselves. After all, that's what we elected them for' (Chivite-Matthews and Teal, 2001).

The public are unclear about what councillors' roles are, and do not see councillors as representative (White et al, 2006). There is still a dislocation between local elected representatives and their constituencies. As decision-making structures in local government have changed some councillors have felt pushed out (Gains, 2006). One writer has described these councillors as '"wounded lions", their powers might be draining away but it [isn't] advisable to try and take them on' (Taylor, 2005b).

There were 17 clear examples of the remoteness of local elected members and the failure of local elections to provide an adequate mechanism for local accountability in practice. The groups that commented on this saw local members as unrepresentative and occasionally patronising. They identified conflicts of interest between local councillors and community groups.

In North Wales, one resident said, "You see [local elected members] at strategy meetings but that's the last you see of them. They don't get involved at the grass roots. They've been voted in unopposed". They're "unapproachable". The chair of the residents' association was very supportive of local elected members, her brother was one and her uncle was also a local councillor. But she said: "When they're presented with a strategy, half the councillors say, What more do these tenants want?!". Members "don't know what happens on the ground". Councillors see a conflict of interest between themselves and residents' associations: "We do the same job as them, we tread on their toes, now we've got access to council officers we don't use [councillors] really".

Severe antagonism between groups and councillors

Although two groups specifically mentioned that they had developed friendly relationships with local councillors as a pragmatic measure, in some neighbourhoods there were antagonistic relations between community organisations and local councillors.

For one group in Nottinghamshire in the past the tenants' federation had an overly confrontational approach: "It was all intimidatory, nasty; I want to kick the council to death" (community worker). Now the federation and council worked closely together, although "we don't always agree". But still, not all the tenants' and residents' associations or the local councillors were equally as supportive of these new cooperative relationships: "There are varying degrees of support. Some [residents' groups] have the same old attitude, like 'the only good councillor is a dead one.'"

For another group in North Wales, "In the 50s and 60s a lot of councillors owned [homes in the area], they were giving themselves permission to change the houses. Rachman got jailed for what he did, and [our local councillor] is still going" (resident). The local councillor who rented flats out has "some big boys" who will physically threaten or hurt people who "upset" him, "you can get kneecapped. He supplies a social need but he also preyed on it".

One community worker described the local views about one local councillor who, despite having been recognised for her community work, was not well liked:

> '[X], she stood for councillor and she got an MBE for work on this estate. [But] the RSPCA did her for animal cruelty. The kids still bark at her now. So she was ostracised by the community. There was lots of things [she did] – harassment at work, calling people fat cow. You can't do that.' (community worker, North East)

A vacuum in local community leadership

The service failure issues discussed earlier in Chapter Three, such as poor management and maintenance of homes, or rude customer care, also highlight the ineffectiveness of locally elected members in ensuring local authority accountability. The community organisations making these criticisms were themselves self-selecting, but they felt justified in criticising local members because the groups felt that councillors were unrepresentative by their own definition, and therefore open to challenge by groups who did not profess to achieve the same standards or criteria. Local councillors spoke on a platform of local accountability that the residents felt was not genuine due to the low turnouts for local elections.

Low turnouts for local elections are well documented, and range from 32.8% in the 2002 English local elections to a slightly higher figure of 36.5% in 2006, still only around a third of all registered voters (Electoral Commission, 2006). There has also been an issue of uncontested seats, for example, 800 seats went uncontested in the 1999 local elections (6% of seats), although this dropped to under 1% overall in the 2000 local elections (figures taken from the Local Government Chronicle Elections Centre, University of Plymouth). One group from Wakefield discussed the issues. There was only around a 20% turnout in local elections in the area:"The three parish councils think they know what the community wants" (resident). The councils and councillors "feel threatened" by community involvement. One group member was a local councillor and stood unopposed.

The resulting vacuum in local leadership opens up space for competition between community members and councillors for a community leadership role. The poor quality of local elected democracy does not help to attract people to the position.

The alternative 'ideal' scenario for local democracy

Democracy is more than representative democracy and voting, and there are several different forms of accountability and legitimacy in local decision making. The modernisation agenda for local government (DETR, 1998) established new approaches to local decision making (ODPM, 1999; DCLG, 2006). The cabinet or executive committee system at local authority level offers a strong centralised executive, made up of a small number of elected members. This is designed to strengthen the accountability of local government across all departments and services in an authority. Alongside this, some authorities are devolving decision making with local members in a lead role at ward or neighbourhood level. This is seen as a way of reviving representative democracy and local electoral accountability. The community groups in the study represent a model of participatory democracy which operates at neighbourhood level that offers another potentially complementary contribution to local accountability and democracy. Multiple forms of democracy and accountability are a necessary part of a healthy democracy.

Starting from street-level democracy

The residents' participatory democracy model tries to devolve down to the lowest level. Four of the groups specifically described changing their structures to provide a block representative system that pushed representation to the unit of the individual street:

> 'When we expanded we got new people on the committee. It was okay at first, for two or three meetings. Then they drifted off, so it was the same people doing the work for a larger area. So, we reorganised into streets, so each road looks after itself. But so we don't get too cliquey we've got the community association for the whole area. All streets have reps. It works much better. It means we can cover the wider area, we can't do it all by ourselves.' (resident, Liverpool)

Direct participation is an ancient form of democracy going back to ancient Greece. Anglo-Saxon England had a tradition of local participatory democracy in the 'moot' or meeting. Street-level democracy can provide a ground-level infrastructure for citizenship. It needs to be complemented by majority democracy.

New structures for local accountability

There are many experiments happening in local authorities to create new models of local democracy and local leadership. There has been interest in devolving down to area or neighbourhood level, as we saw in our visits:

> 'Previously we had sub-committees for the council. Two years ago the Local Government Act devolved to area committees. So, we have monthly meetings with the councillors for the area. It makes democracy clear to everyone. They have opportunities to feed in. People can see how we're performing on your behalf. This is a major breakthrough.' (council officer, Humberside)

Local authorities are trying out decentralisation strategies such as area committees or forums like those described above. They identify the potential they have for strengthening the elected councillor community leadership role, and for linking small area and strategic priorities, but continue to find it difficult to implement this and to make it work in practice (Sullivan et al, 2001). There is still a long way to go to make local structures genuinely effective (White et al, 2006). At the time of our visit in the example above:

> '... attendance [at area committees] has unfortunately been very poor. There are small community groups. Half a dozen people with specific interests is better than a few reps, because they're serving the whole

community, not being quasi-councillors. Tenants' associations act as a conduit between the local authority and the group – it doesn't matter how small the group is. [The council] has worked hard to push the decentralisation agenda.' (council officer, Humberside)

Chief executives of local authorities themselves admit that they will have to develop and use new skills, alongside major cultural change within authorities, if they are to play a community leadership role successfully (LGA, 2001b).

Resolving the relationship between participatory and representative democracy

Community organisations, citizen engagement and direct protests are all signs of a healthy democracy. However, they cannot substitute for more stable forms of majority rule and local and national representation. They do not substitute for the operation of local politics. The groups in the study were markedly not big-P political. Their causes, while ideological in many senses, did not have a strong overt political bent. Deliberative engagement was not organised around political parties.

The agendas of community leaders, local political leaders and other local strategic bodies are potentially complementary but different. Community leaders' focus is on local priorities. Strategic bodies such as LSPs have their focus on strategic priorities for the area in a regional context. Local elected members' focus is on reconciling local and strategic priorities. But work needs to be done to make this happen.

Direct participatory democracy has a localised focus that allows people to engage on matters of immediate concern to them. This is also a sign of healthy local accountability, and can guard against the distortions of representative democracy. This should be within a strong representative democracy to balance local priorities in a fair way, and to balance against the distortions of direct democracy. Local strategic bodies give a forward- and outward-looking perspective.

However, the reality in many localities is that the roles of local elected members in relation to forms of direct participation are not fully worked through. This is potentially very damaging to local democracy in all its forms if energy is wasted in battles for supremacy, for example between resident volunteers and councillors, rather than working together to tackle local issues.

The 2006 local government White Paper (DCLG, 2006) strengthened local councillors' community and local leadership role based on their 'democratic accountability' and mandate through local elections. The risk is that this ultimate authority devalues the role of community participation. The local democratic mandate has been portrayed as the local authority being 'first among equals'. But if local people feel their views are second place, they are even less likely to get involved. This is a serious and real point, and this tension continues to be played out in some neighbourhoods with injurious results (White et al, 2006).

Instead, there must be a recognition of the different forms of accountability and legitimacy that not only local politicians and residents but also officers and professionals can offer. We need to revisit our understanding of what we mean by 'accountability'. Table 7.3 shows what happens when different groups' legitimacy and mandates are not respected, and what could happen if they were.

Central government's mandate is clear through national democratic elections. As already discussed, the basis of legitimacy of local residents is based on their direct or first-hand experience. In addition, they have status as service users and council tax payers. The basis of accountability of local members is their ward-level democratic mandate through local elections, their local knowledge and links upwards to wider local government structures. In the UK we also have a tradition of using political parties as ways of organising local politics, which some feel adds to accountability – as we can easily find out what policies politicians stand for. Officers and professionals are ultimately accountable to their local politicians. However, in reality they play a role in decision making, for example offering guidance on options. This role needs to be made explicit and recognised. Paid staff arguably also have their own form of legitimacy as professionals. The basis of legitimacy of officers and professionals is through the 'evidence base' and objectivity they offer based on knowledge as well as their value base – the public service ethos.

When different groups' mandates are not respected, they tend to feel disempowered and frustrated, and do not play an effective role. When residents' legitimacy is not respected, they feel not listened to, think that they have no control over decisions and therefore are less likely to engage, and will feel unsatisfied, with agencies and politicians. Similarly, when ward councillors' democratic electoral mandate is not respected, they too feel not listened to, think they have little control over decisions, and therefore do not play an effective community leadership role. When officers and professionals' basis of accountability is not respected, they can have concerns about a lack of effective or equitable service delivery, and do not have sufficient incentives to problem solve.

If the stakeholders' different forms of accountability and legitimacy are respected, they can be empowered to contribute. Residents can engage and contribute to local democracy, and can start co-producing. They are more likely to be encouraged to make self-help inputs to their own quality of life. Local politicians could be better stimulated to play an effective community leadership role and contribute to local democracy. Local workers and other professionals could be encouraged to problem solve at the front line. They could add professional expertise and feed in evidence to guide options for local action to raise the quality of the decision-making process.

Each set of stakeholders in a neighbourhood has criticisms and suspicions of the others, but a common theme is that each suspects the others of being sectional and acting in their own interests. Other groups accuse residents of being captured by sectional interests, argue that the basis for their accountability is too narrow and say that they act in own interests. Politicians are criticised for being party political,

Table 7.3: Reconciling different forms of accountability and legitimacy

Stakeholder	Central government	Local residents[a]	Local politicians	Officers/professionals[b]
Basis of accountability or legitimacy	National-level democratic mandate through national elections	Direct/first-hand experience Status as service consumers/council tax payers	Ward-level democratic mandate through local elections Local knowledge	'Evidence-based' objectivity through knowledge base Officials' public service ethos
If legitimacy/mandate not respected (disempowered)	• More difficult to deliver policy • Mistrust of localities • Reluctance to relinquish central control over decision making	• Do not feel listened to • Feel have no control over decisions • Do not engage • Feel unsatisfied with agencies	• Do not feel listened to • Feel have insufficient control over decisions and resources • Do not play effective community leadership role	• Concern about lack of effective delivery on efficiency and equity grounds • Lack of incentive to problem solve
If legitimacy/mandate respected (empowered to exercise agency ie problem solving)	• Can deliver on election promises • Can devolve decision making to appropriate level (subsidiarity)	• Can engage and contribute to local democracy • Can start co-producing • Can make self-help inputs to own quality of life	• Can play effective community leadership role • Can contribute to local democracy	• Problem solving at the front line • Can add professional expertise, feed in evidence to guide options and raise quality of decision-making process

Stakeholder	Central government	Local residents[a]	Local politicians	Officers/professionals[b]
Criticisms from outsiders	• Lack of understanding of local conditions • 'One-size-fits-all' solutions • Over-regulation and loss of local flexibility • Pass on responsibility without power/resources	• Capture by sectional interests • Accountability too narrow • Act in own interests • Lack longer-term vision • Lack understanding of resource constraints	• Party political • Accountability not broad enough base • Act in own interests • Uneven or inefficient allocation of resources	• Lack of local knowledge/ direct experience • 'Producer mentality' • Act in own interests • Uneven or inefficient allocation of resources

Therefore, neighbourhood engagement structures should:
• Hold competing claims for accountability in check
• Respect different stakeholders, empower them and maximise opportunities for their exercise of agency, ie problem solving
• Have appropriate neighbourhood- and strategic-level governance structures
• High opportunity costs if not in place

Stakeholder				
Overall outcomes	Reduced conflict between stakeholders Better decision making More efficient, effective and equitable decisions Stronger national and local democracy Better quality of life, better services			

Notes: [a] 'Local residents' here does not include local councillors, although many local councillors are also residents of the neighbourhoods they represent.
[b] Officers in local authorities are accountable to local elected members, but in reality also play a role in decision making, and arguably have their own form of legitimacy as professionals.

that their accountability does not have a broad enough base and that they act in their own interests. Workers and professionals are criticised for their lack of local knowledge and direct experience, and their 'producer mentality' that means that they act in their own interests. And none of the groups of stakeholders trusts the others with decisions about resources.

If the different forms of accountability are respected, then all groups can be empowered to contribute positively. Placing frontline councillors in a lead role does not resolve the problem. Seeing all forms of accountability together means that each group can hold the others in check, self-interest can be balanced out, competing claims can be examined fairly and everyone will be empowered to contribute.

Summary

The legitimacy of community action, groups and volunteers was, and still is, extremely controversial across the UK, more so when other people disagree with community volunteers. There is no common understanding of what being representative might mean in practice.

The groups' relationships with their neighbours were not always easy. Some of the groups were criticised by fellow residents, while still being asked for help by the same people. They had to work hard to win the trust of other residents and negotiated sometimes ambivalent relationships with their neighbours. The majority of the wider population were in a passive position in relation to the groups' work, neither actively involved nor users. The groups had passive support from the wider community. The minority provided benefits for the majority. The groups' members were self-selecting and not necessarily statistically representative of the area's population.

Despite sometimes ambivalent and conflictual relationships with the wider community, the positive signs of backing for the groups were also very much in evidence. The groups used common sense indicators to gauge how the wider population felt about their work. The weakest form of this was an absence of criticism. There were two sets of measures of the accountability and legitimacy of the groups. The first was about the groups' direct or informal relationships with other people in their neighbourhoods: services the groups provided; informal advice; help with fundraising; lack of vandalism; lack of criticism; and consultation.

The second set of measures was about the groups' relationships with external bodies or externally imposed criteria: they were open to scrutiny; and the groups had positive approaches to promoting diversity. The ways that the groups engaged with their wider communities suited their small size, their informal nature and their modest and practical goals.

Establishing informal activities was a way of establishing links, demonstrating credibility and gaining experience of implementation. The groups' community self-help activities were demonstrable forms of proof that they had some legitimacy and standing in the wider community. Reasonable usage of facilities or attendance at events was a good 'ready reckoner' of the groups' credibility and organisational ability. Usage of services or facilities did not automatically entail a mandate for groups per se, but it showed that the groups were not just all talk. The groups also needed to be actively representative by reaching out to the wider community and makings links outwards. Newsletters were a two-way information flow between community organisations and the wider population. Door knocking and social events were effective at reaching 'hard-to-reach' groups. The groups were keen to be externally scrutinised and recognised as part of their desire to be seen as performing a legitimate function.

Neighbourhood-based community groups were sometimes not trusted by professionals to represent the full diversity of local populations. Community groups were sometimes felt to exclude minority groups. Overall we found that the groups were concerned to include all 'races' and cultures in their work where it was immediately relevant, or where there was a significant minority ethnic population. The groups that welcomed diversity were all successful.

Elections for community organisations were useful when significant one-off neighbourhood decisions were at stake, like tenants taking over management of homes, or who decided how £50 million was to be spent. These issues also tended to generate good turnouts. However, neighbourhood elections were not necessarily a good solution to the everyday, run-of-the-mill issues of community legitimacy because it was likely that turnouts would be low, and could place community volunteers in very negative direct competition with elected members.

The groups were worth listening to because they had had relationships with the wider community through their activities. Building these relationships was the responsibility of the groups. Other methods of getting technical 'representativeness' were the responsibility of higher-level organisations doing the consulting, rather than the groups – the consultees. These other methods of getting 'representativeness' included statistical representativeness.

'From the horse's mouth' with direct representation is a powerful and convincing way to get a message over. Representatives and community members offering powerful personal experiences to illuminate policy decisions could be sought out and nurtured.

Methods of accountability vary within the community sector by size of organisation. Small-scale groups, like the ones in the study, make up over half of the voluntary sector. Their accountability could be summed up as 'accountability through tea and toast'. Larger, more complex community organisations could face the challenge of becoming too distant from the community.

The groups were critical of some other community leaders, community organisations and methods of consultation. There were some friendly rivalries with other local associations, and some charities working in their areas were seen as 'do-gooders'. Some felt umbrella groups lacked credibility or were not operating in the interests of the whole community. These groups were broadly supportive of the principle of majority representative democracy. However, in practice there was also competition between the community organisations and local councillors for the local leadership role, partly because of democratic deficits and vacuums in local political leadership.

Democracy is more than representative democracy and voting. There are several different forms of accountability and legitimacy in local decision making. The community groups in the study represent a model of participatory democracy which operates at neighbourhood level that offers another potentially complementary contribution to local accountability and democracy. Multiple forms of democracy and accountability are a necessary part of a healthy democracy. Direct participatory democracy has a localised focus that allows people to engage on matters of immediate concern to them and can guard against the distortions of representative democracy. However, lack of respect of the legitimacy of different stakeholders means people are disempowered from problem solving. If the different forms of accountability are respected, then all groups can be empowered to contribute positively.

Note

[1] Typical recognition criteria are: adoption of a constitution that includes an outline of committee positions; holding an annual general meeting where committee members are elected or re-elected; and having an independently checked bank account.

EIGHT

Obstacles and limits, supports and potential

'We spent more than a year trying to get funding because we were shown an expensive newsletter. The workers kept bringing us examples of rather grand publications that had plainly been printed professionally at some expense. But no one ever came up with suggestions for sources of funding that we could implement ourselves. It was a revelation when we got to Trafford Hall and saw examples of other newsletters from other community groups. They were all exactly like ours! We were not poor relations. This realisation came as a huge relief. The best thing is to learn by experience. When we went to Trafford Hall we were already doing it but it told us we were doing the right thing, it gave us lots of confidence.' (resident, Wakefield)

As we have seen, organising community self-help evolved out of people's concern for their communities and neighbourhoods, as well as their personal interests. It was a task that people volunteered for, and required a high level of self-motivation and organisational management to sustain. Community volunteers and the groups they belonged to contended with many obstacles and downsides to their community-organising work that made their task more difficult. In this chapter we look at how the 'thankless task' of volunteering made the volunteers feel frustrated, guilty and stressed at times.

One key obstacle identified by volunteers was that of 'apathy', or lack of widespread participation of the wider community. Did this seeming lack of interest undermine the case for community organisations? How many residents did actively get involved? Were other people just apathetic, and did it matter that they did not seem to bother? How should we see the minority who did bother – as 'the usual suspects' or as 'gold dust'?

Another key barrier identified by the groups for their own project work was that of resources. The simplest answer would be to give community groups more money and let them get on with things. But was it simply a question of the groups being short of cash, or did other obstacles get in the way? And not all cash is equal. Much of the available charitable funding for the groups, including our own, was one-off grant funding for new projects, rather than for long-term core costs or to keep existing projects going. What sort of funding did the groups find most useful? The groups also identified organisational weaknesses, shortage of suitable premises and barriers put up by external organisations. What kind of resources would have helped?

Given the lack of appreciation for community volunteers' work, the large burden on the shoulders of the few, and the severity of the issues the groups dealt with, how could volunteers be better recognised and rewarded? Should 'volunteers' be paid?

Some resource support for groups was 'in kind' in the form of a community development worker. How many of the groups accessed workers, and what were levels of provision of support? What did community workers do for groups, and did the groups appreciate it? The Gatsby Project was another form of support that the groups received. We give the results of the programme here, and describe what the groups thought about the training and grant programmes.

Community volunteers paid the personal costs of volunteering, but the costs of community capacity building were usually paid by an outside body. What were the costs of capacity building in the Gatsby Project? Experience shows that responsibility for financing involvement often falls between stools, meaning groups lose out. Does spending more produce better community engagement? Whose pocket should resources come out of?

In this chapter we look first at the obstacles and barriers the groups faced, focusing on the organisation and activities of the project. We look at the personal costs and downsides for volunteers, and how the volunteers could be rewarded. We then look at forms of support the groups used to assist them in overcoming obstacles and how the groups rated their supports. We look at an attempt in our own work to speed up and bulk up the groups' work, before turning to a more successful example of developmental work with groups – the Gatsby Project. We then look at the costs of community capacity building.

Obstacles and barriers

Table 8.1 shows the top five barriers to groups' work, identified by the groups themselves, based on a total of 289 comments about obstacles to groups' work that were collected in the face-to-face interviews, plus 1,554 barriers identified in written feedback from a bigger group of 888 people that attended Gatsby training courses. The top five barriers were the same in both cases, only ranked in a different order:

- lack of appropriate skills
- lack of funding and resources, and the issue of financial sustainability
- the 'apathy' or lack of active involvement of other residents, lack of local support and volunteers
- problems getting suitable premises
- barriers and external obstructions from local authorities and landlords.

Table 8.1: Obstacles to the groups' work

Comment	Rank from interviews	Rank from written feedback
Lack of appropriate skills	1	3
Financial sustainability	2	1
Lack of involvement of other residents	3	2
Lack of suitable premises	4	5
External obstructions	5	4

Organisational weaknesses

In discussions with the interview groups, lack of skills and experience was ranked first as a barrier to developing community self-help work (48 comments). This included lack of administrative, accounting and presentation skills, sometimes just called 'paperwork', and lack of experience and project development skills. Lack of skills and experience ranked third (232 comments) in the list of barriers from the larger pool of groups:

> 'It's taken over my life in the last 18 months. I still have trouble coping with the paperwork – like I have to do all the thank you letters. At the moment we are trying to get money for a new computer.' (resident, Wrexham)

Lack of administrative skills, and 'paperwork' were a major headache for the groups.

'We were total amateurs, wanting something doing but didn't know what.' (resident, Wakefield)

Funding problems

Both the written feedback from the 888 people that attended training and the in-depth interviews with the groups showed how important funding shortages were to the groups. But beyond a crude message that there was not enough money, the feedback shows a more complex situation. There were at least four distinct issues about financial sustainability:

- inability to get access to money that was available, because of inexperience, or ineligibility
- lack of available funding to sustain basic running costs and continue existing projects
- lack of one-off funding for capital costs
- precariousness of income-generating activities.

Difficulties getting access to funding

The examples above about problems with 'paperwork' give a fuller picture of the difficulties residents experienced in fundraising due to lack of skill, confidence or experience. This suggests that the issue was not always about the availability of funding but groups' ability to access it, particularly for new projects. The groups' lack of confidence, and lack of experience in project development, also held them back from successful fundraising. We will see this point very clearly later in this chapter when we look at the low grant application rates in the Gatsby Project:

'We would have asked for a lot more but we didn't know ... the Lottery was very new and none of us had applied for that kind of money before ... we thought, We can't ask for all that [eg new roof, kitchen, central heating for the community building]!' (resident, Wrexham)

According to residents and a community worker in Lancashire, the Single Regeneration Budget was oversubscribed and needed people to "fall off the edge", so they pushed people a bit to see how they would respond, and get the least confident to back out. This group did not take forward its application for an arts and music centre.

Other than lack of appropriate skills, the groups also mentioned ineligibility for charitable funding and lack of time to make applications as problems in raising money.

Long-term funding for core revenue costs

Regardless of the groups' ability to get their hands on funding that was available, the most common issue was the lack of available funding to sustain basic running costs and to continue existing projects. As discussed later in this chapter, with the costs of capacity building, responsibility for covering the costs of keeping small projects going often fell between stools.

In Bristol, revenue costs for a play scheme "are a big problem. We do get grants but they've gone down and down" (resident). They had "exactly the same outgoing and more kids", but less money. Only the higher profile projects were getting local funding, for example through the community safety work. A local action group was setting up new projects but they "forget existing projects" and did not support them long term.

And in another example from Nottinghamshire:

'No one wants to fund the basics, they all want to fund specific projects, so you just make the basics into little projects for them to fund. There's no statutory funding. So we make up mini programmes on the specifics so you can get money to do the photocopying.' (resident, Nottinghamshire)

Precarious income generation

The groups were working in deprived areas, with clients without the means to pay for services, with low-skilled staff and volunteers, providing services that other organisations did not. This made their financial viability hard work:

'My highs and lows are all the time and run together. I knew from the first hour I got involved that it would be difficult. Salaries is our major headache. Starting a business with no money, which doesn't generate money, with the long-term unemployed, in the most deprived ward, with no experience.... Until I've got sustainability, I've got nothing.' (development manager of a voluntary organisation, West Midlands)

'Domestic recycling is very labour intensive to collect, to sort and has a negligible resale value. A commercial operator puts a skip down, charges people. They pull out the timber and metal – just what they can make money from, stuff there's a market for. They work on a bulk scale, and put the rest to landfill. The focus is different.' (manager of an environmental voluntary organisation, West Midlands)

Financial sustainability and generating private income

The groups had small annual financial turnovers mostly of under £5,000. Many (although by no means all) of their activities were done at a relatively cheap cost, or funded through small-scale fundraising. They relied heavily on the availability and willingness of volunteers rather than on major amounts of funding. While both large- and small-scale funding for community organising are important issues, there are clearly two aspects to the sustainability of these micro-organisations: financial and organisational sustainability.

In terms of financial sustainability, community-led organisations with an asset base and clear revenue stream were the most likely to be financially sustainable in the longer term (Hart, 2005). Other larger community regeneration organisations, such as community development trusts, settlements and some intermediate labour market organisations developed good financial stability via endowments and trading (Thake, 1995; Ward and Watson, 1997).

Five of the Gatsby groups were tenant management organisations. Tenant management organisations do not take over ownership of capital assets and they remain agents of the local authority that owns the homes they manage. But the formalised responsibilities and budgets that they assume provide them with other kinds of assets. These give the organisations power, legitimacy and sustainability that most other community organisations do not have. These assets can then act as a base for developing activities beyond housing management. Only a tiny number of them have ever ceased operation, all with the agreement of the residents involved.

Of the remainder of the Gatsby groups, none had either an asset base or substantial income-generating activities. Instead, they relied mostly on a mix of some discretionary public money (for example, running costs for residents' associations from the local authority or landlord) and on grants from charities. A few, for example, the cafes, generated some private income, but usually on top of a subsidy. This made the position of the smaller organisations more financially precarious, but not unsustainable.

Generating income through the private market does not guarantee sustainability; there still has to be sufficient demand for whatever product or service you provide. Being dependent on discretionary grants meant the organisations were also operating in a market of a different sort. As long as the groups could continue to sell themselves to funders, they could generate income. The smaller groups all worked in this way; for example out of 20 Gatsby groups which received time-limited revenue funding for specific pieces of work, 15 had been able to continue their work after the end of the grant. Three of the groups that did not continue their projects felt happy that it had been a one-off piece of work. Of the projects that continued, two groups received grants of over £70,000 from other funders to continue the work they had piloted with the initial 'at-risk' investment of under £5,000.

Financial sustainability based on grant funding is obviously dependent on charitable trusts and public bodies continuing to fund bread-and-butter projects. The groups' financial sustainability was therefore dependent on a very uncertain basis. It was unclear whether public or private charitable sources would continue to carry the burden of funding this type of work.

The second aspect of sustainability is about organisational sustainability, which we now turn to.

Lack of active helpers

In comments about barriers to the groups' work in the interviews, the apathy of other residents ranked third on the list of issues (36 comments). This is also the barrier ranked second in the written feedback from the larger pool of community groups (see Table 8.1):

> 'Trying to get people to do the committee is one of the hardest things.' (resident, Warrington)

> 'There was five of us, we struggled on, it was hard but we struggled on.' (resident, Bedford)

Levels of active involvement

In the main, active participation was confined to a small minority of the population in the areas we visited. In the study areas, a rough average was a 1% regular active involvement rate in community-led and neighbourhood-focused activities: that is, around one in every hundred residents who would regularly turn out for partnership meetings, hold keys for meeting rooms, open up, buy and make refreshments and clear away, take charge of weekly youth nights, write funding bids, dig and weed green areas, or whatever other tasks had to be done for community-run activity to take place. If the less active committee members and other volunteers were added, the estimated active participation rate for the areas would rise to around 3%-5%.

High expectations for involvement

Many of the groups desperately wanted more people to get involved, and felt people ought to be helping more than they did:

> 'Getting volunteers is like getting blood out a stone. People don't seem to bother. They live their own little lives unless something upsets it. [Leafleting the estate has] been talked about but nobody's done it. It's one of the things people suggest but they sit back and wait for

someone else to do. The biggest problem is getting people to do more than moan. There's me, and ... there's ... me.' (resident, Derbyshire)

'[Following low response to the free plants scheme, one volunteer] was going to leave, you go to all this effort and what do you get? It's apathy.' (resident, Rhyl)

As we said in Chapter One, policy now encourages people to get involved in lots of different ways, from volunteering, to community projects, to making an input to decisions by local authorities and public services. There is a high demand for people to be involved from lots of different groups, committees, panels and local projects.

Consistently low figures for participation

We found 3%-5% active participation in the areas, with only 1% taking responsibility for running groups and activities. How did levels of activity in the areas compare to other areas across the country? Overall, the picture nationally was that the areas were broadly in line with low rates of community participation found in other deprived areas. The study areas were also in line with evidence that poorer people, people with fewer formal educational qualifications or those in manual work were less likely to get involved generally. Therefore because the areas reflected the average, this made the community volunteers we talked to distinctly un-average. The volunteers were unusual for both their areas and for people from those backgrounds in that they were active.

Detailed evidence about levels of participation in community organising nationally that we can use to compare our areas comes from several sources. There has been a welcome boost to the amount and quality of statistics and analysed data on different forms of social and political participation in the UK and internationally, particularly since 2000. Over the period when the groups were interviewed, there were not such good sources of evidence to compare the study areas with.

The National Survey of Volunteering in 1991 and 1997 showed that around half of the adult population did engage in formal voluntary activity (Davis Smith, 1998). These were reassuring solid figures for those who believe in the value of voluntary activity. Surveys of citizenship by the Home Office showed slightly lower overall levels of formal volunteering, starting at 39% in 2001 but increasing to 44% in 2005 (Kitchen et al, 2006a). However, formal volunteering covers a wide range of activities, only a small fraction of which includes the kind of neighbourhood-focused community volunteering and community engagement, organised around community-orientated associations (Parry et al, 1992), and done by less well-off people in less well-off areas as in the study.

To try to compensate for this, we found several estimates from community umbrella organisations for community volunteers involved in local neighbourhood issue groups. For example, one body for community organisations said that there was at least one community association in 85 of the 88 designated Neighbourhood Renewal areas in England. They stated that there were over 4,000 community associations in total in England and Wales with more than 50,000 volunteers (Community Matters, 2002), a substantial amount of activity overall, but still an indication of low active participation rates at the time.

In the late 1990s, the Community Development Foundation estimated that there were around three community organisations for every 1,000 adults in the UK. If those organisations had a typical core membership of around 5-10 people, then their estimate of active participation rates was similar to ours at around 1%-3%. Recent research has also settled on a 1% active participation figure as a realistic level (Skidmore et al, 2006).

A more optimistic figure was offered by the General Household Survey in 2000, which found that 13% had been actively involved in at least one local organisation in the three years prior to 2000, but there was variation by type of area. In the most deprived wards, 7% had been actively involved in a local organisation, as opposed to 18% of those in the least deprived wards (Coulthard et al, 2002).

In terms of levels of participation by different groups of people, there was already a wealth of evidence that there had been class, income and educational differences in social and political participation since the 1950s that continued into the 1990s (Hall, 1999; Johnston and Jowell, 2002). Indeed, there was evidence that between 1991 and 1998 differences got worse, with the odds of being a 'joiner' decreasing for those on lower incomes, in lower-skill jobs, or with fewer formal educational qualifications (Warde et al, 2003). Middle-class people were more likely to volunteer, be members of all sorts of groups and take part in other semi-structured social activities (Davis Smith, 1998). Only mutual aid – informal help to friends and relatives – showed higher rates of participation by less well-off people, with around three quarters of the population in lower-income areas doing favours for friends, acquaintances and relatives around 2000 (Coulthard et al, 2002; Attwood et al, 2003). Because statistically, white British, better-off, better-educated people are more likely to be involved there are many government efforts to target volunteering initiatives on 'individuals at risk of social exclusion' (Richardson, 2005a), including Public Service Agreement No 6 (Home Office, 2005b). The Home Office Citizenship Survey in 2001 found that those in the most deprived areas were the least likely to participate in civic affairs, be involved socially in groups or clubs, or volunteer either formally or informally (note that 'informal volunteering' excludes favours to relatives) (Prime et al, 2002).

Interestingly, new evidence from the government's 2005 Citizenship Survey shows that, unlike most other participation activities except informal help to friends and relatives (mutual aid), there was no significant association between levels of deprivation of an area, or the characteristics of an area, and levels of 'civic activism' (that is, involvement in local decision making, taking on responsibilities in the community, as distinct from contacting politicians, signing petitions and so on) or levels of involvement in 'civic consultation' (that is, whether people had taken part in consultation about local services or problems in the local area). 'High-rise hardship' (11%) and 'inner-city adversity' (10%) areas were nearly as likely to participate in civic activism as 'wealthy executives' (13%) or 'prosperous professionals' (10%) (Kitchen et al, 2006a). Unfortunately this question was not asked in previous years, but one possible explanation is that policy drives in recent years to promote involvement in decision making by service providers in less well-off areas (Richardson, 2005a) were having an impact. However, only 9% in England had participated in civic activism in the 12 months before the survey, which again is a minority. Nineteen per cent of the 9% were involved in tenants' committees, a total of just under 2%, which is in line with the levels of involvement we also found.

Whether the amount of active involvement in neighbourhood-focused organisations is 1%, 2%, 7% or even 11%, this is still only a minority. And while this issue clearly bothered the groups, these other estimates and figures do suggest that this is a fact of life. One group pointed to the comments of a well-known writer on radicalism and citizen organising:

> 'Saul Alinsky said it was 1 in 400 – 0.25%! You only ever get a minority – and that's OK. It's reassuring to know…. [The group was] cushioned by passive support [from the wider community].' (resident, south London)

Gap between expectation and reality

The groups wanted more people to come and help, but did not get the help and support. In many other areas across the country, people were disappointed about low levels of involvement (Burton et al, 2004). Disappointment was made worse by the fact that when we asked people if they would like to get involved, a respectable number said yes. For example, in one local authority 20% of residents said they would like to have more say in how their local services were run (quoted in Burton et al, 2004), but when we investigated deeper, it turned out that most of these people did not want to go to meetings. Instead those who wanted to be more involved were offering to complete postal surveys rather than come out to events or meetings.

Another survey in a different area found that 82% of respondents were in favour of extended community partnerships to other parts of the borough; 26% of those in support said they would personally be interested in getting involved. The level of actual involvement was 2% of eligible residents (Page, 2005).

The gulf between expectations, people's general desire to influence local decisions and real levels of involvement led to many problems. Those volunteers who were involved felt deserted and ground down by the 'apathy' of others. People who did bother to get involved were blamed for being 'the usual suspects' rather than thanked for coming along when so many others did not (Anastacio et al, 2000; Blakey, 2004). People did not accept the low levels of participation (Burton et al, 2004; Skidmore et al, 2006).

Blaming 'apathy'

Many groups blamed other residents' lack of active involvement on their willingness or motivation, such as being 'lazy' or not caring:

> 'With two or three people it's hard work, like doing the extras and the discos [for children of residents]. I feel it's "out of sight, out of mind", they just honestly can't be bothered. People only ever come to complain, they're lazy, they don't want to get involved. The only time we see the parents is the day before a trip when they haven't booked, and they're shouting at me, I live here ... why can't my kid go?. If there's a BBQ, or a fun day, or a freebie then they come.' (resident, west London)

Groups referred to 'apathy', suggesting not only that a majority of people *should* have wanted to become community volunteers, but also that they did not because they 'couldn't be bothered'.

One group did point to a possible alternative explanation for the lack of wider involvement based on people's mistrust in the possibility of change, suggesting that it was possible to activate increased levels of participation for example through showing a clear feedback loop between involvement and positive action results:

> 'There is apathy, but apathy through experience. If one landlord won't do anything....' (resident, Wakefield)

There is consensus on this point among practitioners, who agree that people can be demotivated to get involved if they feel that their input will not make or has not made a difference (Blakey, 2004). There is also evidence from research that the degree of responsiveness of institutions to involvement is a factor in whether people get involved (Barnes et al, 2003a). People become 'apathetic' if they try to create change and nothing happens. A common problem, sometimes called 'consultation fatigue', is where there are several rounds of similar consultation in a neighbourhood which do not result in visible change, but which do create cynicism about the value of getting involved. One writer has described this situation in some areas leading to attempts to do consultation 'result[ing] for the most part in reactions that ranged from indifference to outright hostility' (Ashworth, 2000, p 256).

There are several additional reasons why apathy is not a useful term and fails to capture a true sense of non-active people's motivations and experiences. The idea that people *should* want to get involved is debatable in the first place, but it turns out that most people do care about their neighbourhood and communities, as we saw in Chapter Three, and are interested in local affairs and even national politics, and say that they would in theory like to get involved although in practice they choose to do other things. Generally, people want the chance to participate even if they do not use the opportunity. People like to be kept in the know, but the majority do not have a huge enthusiasm to get more involved (Burton et al, 2004). National surveys show that most people 'just vote' (Parry et al, 1992; Docherty et al, 2001).

The idea that most people do not get involved because they lack interest is therefore inaccurate. It is well known that the most common forms of engagement, such as meetings or events, do not match the preferences of the majority to be contacted by door knocking or other forms of outreach (Page, 2005).

Another group found that just making their need for volunteers clear was enough to encourage people to come forward, and others had positive experiences with new volunteers coming forward. Others have argued that the creation of opportunities is important in getting people to come forward (Lowndes and Wilson, 2001; Birchall and Simmons, 2002).

In County Durham, they persuaded some new people to volunteer by sending a "blackmail letter. [It said] we're suffering from a lack of support, we've come this far, do you want to see it fold? I need help" (resident). The group was "amazed" that they got four new members, including young mothers and couples, plus three other people who said they could not be on the committee but could help out. They got a total of seven new people.

Accepting others may not want to help

Some groups felt that it was acceptable for other people to have different motivations and interests, which meant that those people did not get involved. This acceptance of other people's choices can also be found in other interviews with active volunteers (Devine, 2003):

> 'People are prepared to let us get on and do it, but if anything happened people would come forward.' (resident, Wrexham)

Although one group felt that there was a problem with getting other residents involved, they accepted that there was a divide between "the ones who do, and the ones who receive, and that's OK" (resident, Walsall). Their community workers were concerned about the problem of getting new volunteers involved but the group were "happy" with the situation because they accepted that only a minority would come forward:

> 'We're open to criticism, but if you say, You come and do it, then they never do. Some time we get a bit fed up but never to the point of packing it in. If we don't, no one else will.' (residents, Wrexham)

We have described how the groups are informal associations, often based on friendship and relying on relationships between group members to hold together. This suggests there may be a 'natural' upper limit to any one group's size that puts a cap on growth.

The problem of 'apathy' further reinforces the need for those who are involved to make efforts to keep up links to the wider community. From an insider's perspective, for the handful of people who do volunteer, their position may feel isolated and exposed.

'The usual suspects' or 'gold dust'

We have looked at the evidence about the numbers involved in communities and found that active participation in organising local community activity has been universally low, despite hopes that masses of people will get involved. We have found that this has led to disappointment and frustration for both residents and others doing community engagement. We have seen how the focus of attention has often been more on the people who do not get involved than those who do. Worse than that, the people who were actively involved as volunteers were sometimes criticised as 'the usual suspects'. Another approach would be to see those who did get involved as unique and special contributors to be valued. An alternative term for 'the usual suspects' could be 'gold dust'.

Shortage of suitable premises

Ranked 4th (27 examples from interviews, 147 comments from written feedback) on the groups' list of barriers were problems finding and securing suitable premises from which to operate. One example forcefully illustrates this. The original project was for people to bring in aluminium cans to a central point for recycling, and to get a few pence for them:

> 'Initially we thought we'd run it from [a local recycling project]. But then, [the project] felt that they couldn't do it. So it fell through. Then, it was a shopping centre, in a vacant unit owned by the city council. We applied for planning permission, and were flatly refused. So, by now we've had two goes. Our 3rd go, was with [another organisation]. But although they were interested, they need commercial rent in their business plan, so they can't do it. It's one step forward and two back all the time. The commitment is there. We've been close on three occasions. We haven't given up. If [the funders] are willing to be patient we will get there.' (director of a voluntary organisation, West Midlands)

There were many more mundane examples of problems with venues, such as:

- opening times, rules about usage (for example no young people), high rents or inadequate facilities in existing venues
- physical problems with available or potential venues, for example leaking roofs, damp.

Initially a group in Hastings decided to run a homework club at the local community centre but "they kept putting the rent up and it was always cold, the heating was never on" (resident). Also, you could not make tea and coffee, which was "no good, because some are excluded pupils and we wanted [the homework club] to be informal".

Groups were helped by:

- specially tailored office spaces for voluntary groups
- help from landlords in offering empty properties for conversion
- funding to rent or hire premises
- innovative thinking about space, for example choosing lower-cost options like refurbished Portakabins, or using containers to run a (mainly outdoor) play scheme from.

The government's review of capacity building for community groups also recommends that the infrastructure for groups should include a meeting space or a base which is available, welcoming and accessible to all (Home Office, 2004b).

Local authorities 'being difficult'

The fifth barrier raised by groups (26 examples) was obstacles presented to them by outside bodies, such as the local authority. This also ranked 4th in the barriers identified in written feedback from the larger pool of groups.

Particularly where groups were lobbying for change by others or where they were involved in decision making by agencies, a key issue was the responsiveness of those agencies to resident input. Other studies have shown that responsiveness of authorities has improved in recent years (Lowndes et al, 2001), but there is still a way to go for public agencies to create a climate where community activity can flourish. These examples are from an earlier time before local authorities were more open to community-led activity, but they give a flavour of the challenges the groups were battling against.

It was sometimes difficult to tell whether these obstacles were a genuine inability to help, deliberate obstructions or unavoidable delays in negotiating agreement or providing information for groups, as in the example below.

A group in North Yorkshire had been in development for a tenant management organisation for several years. They were about to go to ballot, but they were delayed because the local authority said that it was having difficulty calculating a local budget for the estate. The council then offered the group a package including an estate agreement and a generous set of local budgets if they did not go to ballot for a tenant management organisation:

> 'It'd be better than we could have if we were a TMO [tenant management organisation]. It's funny we spent ages asking them for budgets for the estate and they couldn't do it, but then all of a sudden they can get them when they want them.' (resident, North Yorkshire)

There were several examples of different approaches to risk management, with residents feeling held back by what they saw as unnecessary health and safety measures, but agencies wanted to do things by the book to prevent accidents.

A lunch club in Wrexham started by getting fish and chips on Fridays. "Then, [X] suggested, Instead of fish and chips, why not do stew and dumplings?" (resident). X is the oldest resident in the block at 86. "We were cooking in our flats then bringing it down here." The new warden told them they had to stop. The community worker explained: "They were carrying down from each flat big pans of potatoes, and if you don't mind me saying, they're these dothery old ladies!". But undeterred, the ladies decided to upgrade the communal kitchen downstairs so they could carry on making food and eating together:

> 'I rang [the landlord]. They came armed with health and safety and an environmental health exercise, purely to put us off. They said we needed a health and safety certificate. So, we did one! It was three and a half days, we did it at the library with the college.' (resident, Wrexham)

Extreme cases of sabotage

But other examples were more clear-cut cases of the groups being blocked, in many cases where the groups had tried to take over management of their homes. The example below was from a period where some local authorities, or at least some of their elected members, were fundamentally against tenant management. There was fierce opposition on political grounds to any form of transfer of the management and ownership of council housing out of council control, even to community hands.

At the time these tenants from Merseyside wanted "to stop that waste" of public funds by the council housing department so they decided to go for an estate management board where they managed their own homes. But, the old Labour administration was very anti-tenant management because they considered it to be a form of privatisation of council housing. The group became "the subject of a hate campaign, a barrage. On the day of the final ballot every house on the estate got a four-page newsletter with a picture of the grim reaper on the front" (resident). They showed a copy of the newsletter that also contained malicious accusations and misinformation. "They wanted to smash the EMB [estate management board]." The group said that some local councillors and the local MP were involved. Overall, the group got a "severe kicking. It was terrible, so disheartening". But they have now decided to "go for it all over again". The new ballot will be in the next six months. Political control of the local authority has now changed and the council is "very supportive. That's all history now, the administration has changed in our favour. Now, we have significant support for the EMB" (residents).

Downsides of the groups' work

We have already looked at the positive aspects and motivators of volunteering in Chapter Five. Understandably, in the interviews the groups did not dwell on the negative aspects of their involvement for them personally. These personal downsides were directly related to the problems of apathy, the gaps and ambivalent relationships between these active volunteers and the wider community, and obstacles to groups' work described above. Table 8.2 shows the negative personal effects on volunteers.

Table 8.2: Personal downsides of volunteering

Comment	No. of comments	Rank
Frustration, guilt and stress	28	1
Others hold you responsible	15	2
Personally threatened or accused	9	3
Vandalism/damage to work	4	=4
Project failure	4	=4
Fraud	3	6
Total	**63**	

Frustration, stress, guilt and overwork

The most quoted negative feelings were of frustration, guilt or stress (28 comments, ranked 1st), particularly where they hit obstacles or projects did not work. Overwork for community volunteers was a common problem for lots of groups generally (Joseph Rowntree Foundation, 2003). Residents felt stressed and tired because of their heavy workloads, which also had a negative impact on their home and family lives:

'You get people knocking at two in the morning – it never stops.' (resident, Rhyl)

Her husband told me later: 'I never see her – she's out at meetings all the time.'

At one low point for a group, the committee was not getting enough support from other people: "I don't know how we kept going, when you look back, it's quite soul destroying" (resident, Derbyshire).

> '[After some serious problems] everyone wanted to go home, all the heartbreak caused, we were gutted, absolutely gutted.' (resident, North Wales)

A thankless task

Ranked second on the downsides of groups' work (15 comments) were comments about the lack of appreciation from other residents for their work and of the position they were in as volunteers. Because groups took responsibility for trying to improve services, people sometimes held them responsible for the failures of other organisations. Being a representative could occasionally be a thankless task. One of the trainers on the Gatsby courses at Trafford Hall summed up the issues in a way that resonated with community volunteers:

> 'Everyone thinks you're on the take. It's a thankless task sometimes. They see you as responsible for everything that goes wrong.' (trainer, A Sense of Place, at Trafford Hall)

> 'People knock on the door about this and that. I'm sick of it. They treat you like the council.' (resident, Warrington)

> '[People] come to expect the play scheme, especially because it's free. Accountability [to the wider community] can feel like being stabbed in the back! But I'm putting something in instead of whinging and whining, they don't realise, if they got on board and helped you, it would help.' (resident, Rhyl)

Personal attack

The downside ranked third (9 comments) was personal criticism, or worse, of volunteers by other residents. This ranged from threats of physical violence to accusations of fraud. On one estate in the West Midlands, a resident said that there had been some intimidation – one member had a stone thrown through his window with a note on it saying 'grass'.

And in North Wales:

> 'I got a new car and people accuse me of lifting from the tuck shop.' (resident, North Wales)

One volunteer in County Durham had her windows put through by children because she was involved in the committee. All the committee had had eggs thrown at their windows.

Support for the groups

In contrast to the disheartening picture of blocks and frustrations just outlined, the groups also received a great deal of external support. In total, 75 of the 82 grant award groups (91%) had received at least one form of external community development support (other than from Gatsby Project or grant funding by itself). Sixty-two per cent of respondents to the follow-up survey of over 450 groups said their group had a support worker. Many had more than one form of help from more than one source.

The relatively high number of groups getting support is perhaps surprising given the national picture. The estimates are of 20,000 full-time equivalent professional workers across the UK carrying out community capacity building, with 40% on short-term contracts (Taylor, P., 2006).

Who got help and where from

Fifty-two groups from the total of 82 community groups had access to time from a dedicated external community worker or workers. This included groups getting help from a mix of tenant participation workers, community development workers, health development workers and community safety workers. These local community support staff were employed by different departments within the local authority, as well as by the landlord, health authority and by regeneration initiatives such as Sure Start, the Single Regeneration Budget and others. The picture nationally is very similar with a wide mix of local organisations offering help. A study of professional community development workers in 2004 found that as many as six different types of agencies employ workers with a major community capacity building remit (Taylor, P., 2006).

Another nine groups had community workers as part of their group either in a voluntary capacity or as part of their jobs. Ten groups specifically mentioned using local advice and support from organisations such as volunteer bureaux, centres for voluntary services and local business support organisations. Twenty had received consultancy help, for example on specialist pieces of feasibility work, or on developing tenant management. Sixteen had accessed advice and help from national community support organisations and five groups were supported by a parent body such as a church or development trust.

The general point made by the groups was that they used a mix of support agencies as appropriate. They appreciated the fact that support came from lots of different places. Other consultation with community groups indicates that groups felt that a range of organisations helped creativity (Home Office, 2004a).

'We have a range of advisers, and we use them all appropriately. For example, when we want to know what's happening in the wider world – we go to Community Action Network. When we want to know about setting up community businesses, or need advice about asset development we go to the Development Trust Association. When we need to know about health and safety legislation we go to Community Matters.' (resident, South London)

'There is no one form of support.' (member of a mental health support group, Cheshire)

'Sometimes we deal with so many people we don't know who they are!' (resident, Bedford)

But the number of different sources of help, different in each area, could occasionally be confusing for residents, as other evidence has backed up (Home Office, 2004a). In other research it has also been clear that no single body had a comprehensive overview of all the community capacity building taking place in an area (Glen et al, 2004). This might be particularly important for the overall amount of help available in different locations. It is recognised by government that the infrastructure for the community sector has come together in an ad hoc fashion, and overall coverage is variable in quality and fragile (Home Office, 2004a).

Types of help the groups received

Fifty-seven of the groups received general ongoing support, which was wide-ranging and covered things such as:

- help with funding applications
- help developing projects
- ideas, inspiration and case studies/study visits
- administrative help such as free copying and the equipment to write correspondence
- help with accounts, business planning and cash flow
- technical and legal advice
- recruiting volunteers
- designing and producing publicity.

A quarter of the groups had more hands-on help with direct project implementation along the same lines. Forty-one had been helped to set up by external community support workers. Some groups credited their existence to the trigger factor of having someone there at a point they had decided to do something.

A common pattern was an intensive input in the initial stages, then gradual scaling down of the high level of support as the group became more able to operate independently. The transfer of responsibilities to the group was a delicate process, but one that groups could understand the need for.

A local community development agency in Nottinghamshire did a tailored training programme for a group on committee skills, presentation skills, newsletters, etc. The tenants' federation "liked the idea of training, because we're all volunteers, so we need training" (resident). Now the residents were expected to do more and take on a heavier workload, which they felt was "for our betterment really".

The community development workers employed by a landlord in Liverpool put a lot of time into the group at the beginning, but now they were going so well "they really are falling away from us now because we cope, so we only see [the community worker] once a month" (resident).

And in Leyland:

> '[The community worker] was the main one [who helped the group set up]. He's slacked off a bit now. He said, Stand on your own two feet, make your own decisions now you've got the idea of how to do things. He's backed off, he's working on another area, now he's a "community adviser" – he puts us on the right track and helps with funding.' (resident, Leyland)

Varied quality of local community development support

The 75 groups that did receive support did not value and rate all the help they got equally highly. There was relatively little middle ground – groups either rated help as extremely good or as bad.

One reason for the patchy nature of the quality of help could be the way that community development is structured. The profession is not highly paid, jobs are often casual and insecure, with women more likely to be in the worse jobs (Glen et al, 2004). The experience and qualifications required for community development work posts vary considerably. Many workers find it difficult to get training and good management back-up (Glen et al, 2004). People in the field are aware of the need to raise the status, standards and consistency of the community development profession. There are currently attempts to do this, such as through developing national frameworks specifying elements of effective community development and engagement (PAULO, 2003; Barr and Taylor, 2007).

Valued support: the groups did form very close bonds and loyalties with workers and organisations when they felt they had been of use:

> 'Having a paid worker makes all the difference.' (resident, Wrexham)

The main support for this group used to be the community agency that no longer existed. The group "miss them terribly. We're suffering from them not being there any more" (resident), even for things like copying. There was a worker for the community strategy, but she only worked on the strategy and was not for group development. What she did is "not the same as what [X] used to do – come in and help the group" (resident).

A community development worker in Liverpool employed by the landlord was one group's main support: "[They] definitely helped us, we wouldn't have got through without them" (resident).

A local community development agency in Rhyl were "our stalwarts. This really should be called the [residents' association] and [X] community agency project because they've done 90% of what we've achieved" (resident).

And a group in Oldham had strong links with the African Caribbean project, which was an umbrella for lots of different local projects. A worker from the project helped them on things like fundraising and he was called "Jedi Bid master!" (resident).

Poor quality help

But the groups also experienced what they felt had been some poor quality forms of help. There were 19 specific examples of this that fell under the following categories:

- bad advice on grant applications, project development, costings and business planning
- lack of support and selective supports
- unusable or inappropriate forms of help.

Bad advice on grant applications, project development, costings and business planning: the group in the quote at the beginning of this chapter are a case in point. They had been advised by the publicity officer for the local regeneration scheme that their newsletter needed to be professional and 'glossy':

> 'Our every effort fell down at the point where could we get some finance to get the project off the ground. This complete lack of funds and perhaps lack of specific knowledge on the part of those trying to help us led to the complete waste of a year. No one ever came up with suggestions which we could implement ourselves such as giving us addresses of funding sources or contacts with similar groups which had started out without funding.' (resident, Wakefield)

The group then decided to go for a low-cost basic newsletter instead to get things off the ground and now distribute 750 copies of a popular quarterly newsletter that has lots of local information, and *Private Eye*-style local gossip about developments and politics in the area.

Other groups had similar bad experiences with poor quality advice. The equipment list in one grant application written by a previous community worker in Derbyshire "looks like someone's Xmas list!" (resident).

And in Merseyside:

> 'We cut back [on rates of pay]. We asked why they wanted the job and the applicants said I live here, etc, etc, but at the end they all said that the money was marvellous! The salary we have now discovered is too high. [The economic development officer's] costings were all in good faith but they were wrong.' (resident, Merseyside)

One economic development department in a council in the Greater Manchester area wrote a business plan for a community project with predictions of £2,000 income. The residents said: "it's a bit extortionate, you can't work to that". Their income at the time was £40-£50 a month.

In the East Midlands:

> '[The worker] took the form away, we didn't realise, he told us we couldn't [apply for revenue costs]. There was no mention in the application about running costs really [they] hadn't read the application properly. I've learnt my lesson − I'm not doing that again. We were embarrassed in front of [the funder].' (resident, East Midlands)

Lack of support and selective supports:

> 'Previously our relationship to community development was harrowing. They were seen as empire building, living in ivory towers, with their pet projects. The members said it and a lot of community groups thought so too. Now, we're more on the same wavelength. [The community development manager's] on the top of my invite list now, before it was garlic and crosses! [Previously] we did everything through education and social services. The one department of the council we didn't have a relationship with was community development − it's funny because that's the one you would expect.' (resident, Merseyside)

Unusable or inappropriate forms of help: a group asked the tenant participation unit of the local authority about what insurance they needed, what they were liable for and so on, but the group said that the unit did not know, and did not offer to find out for them. In another example: "[the worker] was reading it off an official document ... she lasted half an hour, it was all, You must get 25% of the quorum ... and that was the end of that" (housing officer, West Midlands).

The availability and quality of help could depend on the area. In West Yorkshire community development in the area was seen as "dire", although, the local council for voluntary services was "very proactive, good". But generally, there were "lots of meetings" but not much action. "There are all sorts of weird and wonderful community posts" but they tend to only be for a year at a time "by the time you meet them, they're gone" (teacher).

Paying volunteers

One controversial form of support not yet discussed is payment for volunteers. There has been a vocal lobby for payment for volunteers, over and above payment for expenses or lost wages (for example see www.urbanforum.org. uk/valuingvolunteers.html). Campaigns have focused on community volunteers who sit on boards or partnership structures guiding large-scale regeneration programmes spending many millions of pounds. Part of the campaign case was that members of boards and trusts were routinely paid for the time and effort they put in, but not resident members.

Payment for volunteers was seen as a way of offering direct support to people, and as a sign of the value of the role. Payment would be a reward for the time and effort people put in. Some felt it could overcome the problems of 'apathy' and low levels of involvement described earlier.

It is understandable that this argument has arisen give the important work that community volunteers do. There are two sets of arguments against, and the first is practical. Even those in support only targeted certain types of volunteering where it was practical to argue for payment. It is difficult to see how payments would be funded. Volunteers who sit on the boards of large regeneration organisations, at the request of those organisations, could try to get payment from the boards. But in most cases of the groups' work there is not a board to ask for payment, and no official body has requested that the groups perform their jobs.

The second set of objections is more fundamental. The issue of payment for volunteers is still highly controversial with community volunteers themselves, and unpalatable to many. We saw in Chapter Five how people felt there was a cultural difference between them and paid workers, precisely because one group were paid and the other was not. The groups appreciated the independence that being a volunteer gave them, particularly when lobbying for change. None of the groups raised the issue of payment despite the long conversations we had about lack of involvement, heavy workloads landing on a few shoulders and other pressures as already described.

The types of rewards and support the volunteers talked about were the pleasure they got from fun and friendships, as described in Chapter Five, and the feeling of doing something for their communities, rather than financial reward. People were pleased and proud to be performing a socially useful activity, and derived a sense of self-worth from being useful in some way in wider society. As discussed in Chapter Seven, volunteers wanted recognition for their efforts, and recognition of their legitimacy, but not through payment. The Gatsby volunteers were wary of the idea of personal reward as they felt it would undermine their position in the eyes of the community. They felt vulnerable to criticisms of their work that sometimes took the form of accusations of personal reward, and did not want to leave themselves open to these accusations. The people that attended training valued the courses as a form of recognition. We had annual celebration events – the Gatsby Party – as a reward for volunteers' efforts.

Payment for certain types of altruistic activity might even be counterproductive and have the opposite effect. This idea was originally put forward by academic Richard Titmuss in *The gift relationship* (Titmuss, 1970), who argued that monetary compensation for donating blood might reduce the supply of blood donors. He argued that paying for blood donations would undermine cherished social values and would therefore reduce or totally destroy people's willingness to donate blood.

This idea is often referred to as 'crowding out', that is, people's altruistic motivations are 'crowded out' by financial incentives. This theory suggests that economic incentives may sometimes backfire. An example from Israel was the decision to fine parents who dropped their children off late at nursery (Halpern et al, 2004). In contrast to reducing lateness parents subsequently felt entitled to drop their children off late since they were now paying for it. There is also evidence from other fields such as adult learning that shows when people are paid to attend adult literacy classes they are less likely to attend. This fits with the idea that their own inner motivation to go was pushed out by the payment involved.

Accelerating growth in the community sector: the Gatsby Pioneers programme

Overall, the Gatsby Training and Small Grant Project programmes were successful in facilitating self-help, but not all of the support offered by the Gatsby Project was equally successful. Indeed, it was a positive feature of the Project that different approaches were tried, and many aspects of the programmes were changed, as a result of our 'real-time' developmental research. Towards the end of the five-year pilot period we tried out the Pioneers programme. This evolved out of our experience of working with the Gatsby groups – some of them for four years – and seeing them develop over time.

The Pioneers programme was an advanced-level residential training plus consultancy package. It was designed for community groups who already had a track record in developing small-scale community activity, and who wanted to do more. We wanted to see if we could work with the groups to scale up what they did and to work in more structured and targeted ways, with public sector partners, with more clearly defined outcomes, to achieve more effective solutions.

We advertised for groups to apply for the programme, and selected five groups based on their applications. There were some great elements of the programme. It pushed the groups to set clear goals and milestones for progress. The training and consultancy support stretched groups beyond their current levels of activity, as was hoped, and the groups valued their status as Pioneers. For some it legitimated their role as a player in regeneration with external partners. They were successful in drawing in public services and others as partners and formed new organisation structures. At least two partnerships went from having vague, overly ambitious plans to having realistic action lists with deadlines, for example, the group we had funded to take young people on fishing trips, where our original 'fishing trips problem' came from. Through Pioneers they developed a plan to scale up their youth work into a youth and community centre. They developed a fully costed action plan for setting up the building and running it for three years. They used lateral thinking to get a construction option that overcame their shortage of land and the need to get off the ground quickly.

However, only two of the original five groups went on to develop full proposals and started to work to deliver them. The proposals were a significant scaling-up of the groups' work but did not achieve the goals we had imagined, such as projects targeting educational attainment specifically. There was a high drop-out rate from the programme. One dropped out before the training started because they could not agree the terms of the partnership. The other group came together for the purposes of the pilot and never properly bonded as an action group. A third group could not settle on a doable idea – the problems were too overwhelming for them. As well as this, their work was sabotaged by the local authority officer put in place to help them.

Groups were far keener on just doing more self-help than on fulfilling our initial aims of them leading regeneration activity, or trying to persuade public bodies to do more. It was unrealistic to have expected groups to achieve more without agencies helping to lead from the beginning. We found that more input could not necessarily make progress on the ground any faster – it is not a short-cut; there was also a gap between the community agenda, community capabilities and wider regeneration and policy agendas. More input from the Gatsby Project, regardless of how much the groups valued it, could not bridge the gap between the groups' capacity, and delivering on very tough outcomes.

The results of the Gatsby Project described below show that there is much that can be done to help groups grow and develop. But growth is relative to the groups' starting capacity, and the overall direction is ultimately dictated by the groups' own agendas. The basic premise that community groups' growth is organic and does not follow a straight one-way path has been outlined by other writers. For example, John Pearce, in *Social enterprise in Anytown*, describes a hypothetical estate, and shows how community self-help and social enterprise blossoms organically over a period of time (Pearce, 2003).

There is intensifying interest across political parties and from central and local government in whether the so-called 'third sector' – community and voluntary organisations and social enterprises – can take over the delivery of mainstream public services (DTI, 2002, 2003; HM Treasury, 2002, 2004; Home Office and Office of Government Commerce, 2004; ODPM and Home Office, 2005; SJPG, 2006). The idea is that existing voluntary groups in a particular locality could be grown to take on this role, and that they would be happy to take on a role defined by someone else. The Pioneers programme suggests that this 'indigenous growth' model is misinformed in many cases. There is evidence from the community and voluntary sector elsewhere that this is not true (Kumar and Nunan, 2002; Chapman et al, 2006).

Other writers working in the social enterprise field have also questioned the assumptions in the 'indigenous growth' model. One writer has argued that for the delivery of public services we should focus growth on social enterprises that are up for the task, wherever they happen to be based. This would produce an 'accelerator' model in contrast to the 'indigenous growth' model (Young, 2006). Other 'enterprise accelerator' programmes are in line with our evidence (www.dta. org.uk). The idea of the accelerator model is that existing social enterprises could franchise their operations away from the home base. This is seen in some parts as controversial because it means organisations going into an area that is not their 'local' area, and possibly being in competition with home-grown organisations. However, an accelerator model could result in benefits to local groups from others bringing in new expertise.

Potential for growth in the community sector

The question of whether we can significantly accelerate growth in the community sector is important in two ways. First, it is positive that policy makers want the sector to do more, and the sector should have a collective interest in making sure there is capacity available to take on public service delivery. The accelerator model outlined above could offer a realistic way forward to grow additional capacity.

However, the growth agenda is not relevant or appropriate to the vast majority of the community and voluntary sector. Very few of the groups, most with annual turnovers of under £10,000, were in a position to take on major contracts, even though they had an appetite to scale up and do more. The groups had the desire, but not the capacity.

They differed from larger voluntary organisations, many of which had neither the capacity nor the desire to compete for public service contracts. For example, one study in the North East (Chapman et al, 2006) found that only 11% were currently raising earned income, half saw grants as their main income source in two years' time, and 17% rejected the idea of delivering contracts because it clashed with their mission and values. Another study (Cairns et al, 2006) also found that people in the sector were unhappy about moves to contracts. Half said their independence had been compromised. Medium- and larger-sized voluntary organisations wanted to hold on to their role as an additional source of provision from the private and public sectors, rather than be seen as merely 'an alternative provider of statutory services' (NCVO, 2006b, p 3).

There is a danger that the value of what informal community groups can offer would be lost in a discussion purely about growth to take on public services. Small groups make up the majority of the community sector, and at least half of the voluntary and community sector is made up of small groups such as those in the study (Chanan, 2004).

Most of the groups were not big enough to be registered charities, but even for charities, the majority were of a small size. There has been a significant expansion (NCVO, 2006a) in the number of charities in recent years – their number (of active general charities) increased by over one-and-a-half times from 1991 to 2004. Over half of those new charities had annual incomes of less than £10,000. Organisations with incomes of under £10,000 per year made up 56% of the voluntary sector in 2006 (NCVO, 2006a), and small charities amounted to just over 100,000 of the 188,000 organisations.

Charities of all sizes are thought to account for around one third of the not-for-profit sector as a whole. There are estimated to be 600,000 organisations in the not-for-profit sector (Cabinet Office, 2002), of which 188,000 are registered charities. Between 180,000 and 360,000 of the 600,000 are community-level organisations with small amounts of income not registered as a charity, like our groups (Cabinet Office, 2002). This equates to between three and six community-level organisations per 1,000 people.

Income generation in the community and voluntary sectors is extremely concentrated, with 2% of the voluntary sector generating two thirds of the total sector income in 2003/04 (NCVO, 2006a).

Although significant growth is not applicable for the majority of the sector, the work groups do is itself of incalculable value, as discussed in Chapter Four. Next, we show that it was possible to facilitate the groups in their work.

Results of the Gatsby Training and Small Grant Project

All of the groups in the study had participated in the Gatsby Project. As seen, the Gatsby Project was only one form of support the groups had received. But had it worked?

As described in Chapter Two, the Gatsby Project was a five-year experimental national programme to stimulate and facilitate community self-help action in low-income neighbourhoods. The pilot ran between 1996 and 2001 and cost £1.25 million, sponsored by the Gatsby Charitable Foundation, one of the Sainsbury Family Charitable Trusts. The model used in the project combined intensive residential training for community organisations on community organising and action planning, with a small grant fund to help participants put ideas into practice in their own areas. We detailed the community training courses, and types of projects funded, through the small grants programmes in Chapter Two. Here we look at the thinking behind the project, and its results.

The Gatsby Training and Small Grant Project approach

The cost of £1.25 million is a significant investment. However, it could easily have been absorbed by the costs of building and running just one or two community facilities, and the amount is tiny in comparison to mainstream spending. We chose to try to spread the investment as widely as possible. We wanted to complement all the work already happening in neighbourhoods and areas and we had to provide maximum value. We knew that we needed to develop the strengths of poor areas from within. Our approach had to be sensitive enough not to crush the abilities and potential capacity that poor communities had. We wanted to see practical results. We offered three simple things that most people would find useful when they wanted to set up a project or do an activity – whether that was organising a trip to the cinema, or organising a supplementary school for Afro-Caribbean children: an idea and a plan for doing the idea, a bit of help along the way and a bit of cash.

We decided not to use screening procedures for groups before they went into the programmes. Instead we wanted to 'cast bread on the water' to see how many small, relatively untested community groups would respond.

An example of how the project worked in practice

We wanted to tap into community groups' own thirst for learning, as seen, for example, with 'Bob' and his onions, the community allotment group in Stockport we met in Chapters Four, Five and Six. The allotment had been in operation for a year but "last year was experimental. Last year we only collected the onions and the lettuce" (resident). None of the group were gardeners before the project: "I've never read a book since I left school, except the Highway Code, now I read all the garden news"; "We read books, magazines, ask around and watch gardening programmes on the TV".

The group were keen to learn about gardening. The council gave them information about the 'Growing Ideas for Your Environment' training course running at Trafford Hall in October 1998. They went on the course and found out how to tackle the earworms and leatherjackets that had destroyed part of their crop. They came back to their neighbourhood, built raised beds with a polythene lining to stop the earworms, and then applied for a Gatsby small grant for a polytunnel. We visited them after they had grown their second crop in the polytunnel, their plant sales were going well and the group were planning to grow more difficult vegetables the following year.

Evaluation of the project

We used several measures at different levels of evaluation. We did a mix of developmental evaluation (checking if we were delivering in the right way), output evaluation (whether we helped people through training), and outcomes evaluation (seeing what happened as a result). Figure 8.1 shows the structure of the Gatsby evaluation.

Figure 8.1: Structure of the Gatsby evaluation

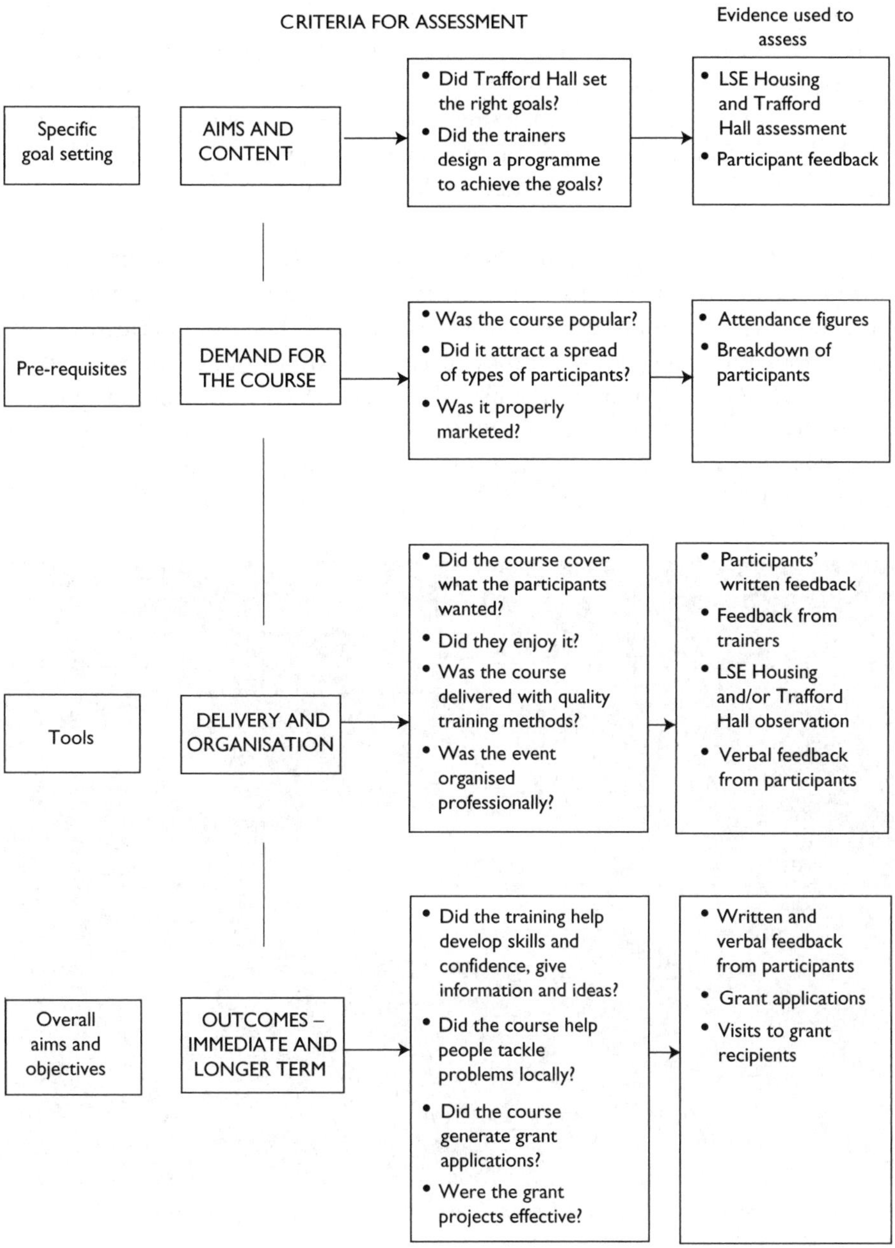

CRITERIA FOR ASSESSMENT   Evidence used to
                                            assess

| Specific goal setting | AIMS AND CONTENT | • Did Trafford Hall set the right goals?
• Did the trainers design a programme to achieve the goals? | • LSE Housing and Trafford Hall assessment
• Participant feedback |

| Pre-requisites | DEMAND FOR THE COURSE | • Was the course popular?
• Did it attract a spread of types of participants?
• Was it properly marketed? | • Attendance figures
• Breakdown of participants |

| Tools | DELIVERY AND ORGANISATION | • Did the course cover what the participants wanted?
• Did they enjoy it?
• Was the course delivered with quality training methods?
• Was the event organised professionally? | • Participants' written feedback
• Feedback from trainers
• LSE Housing and/or Trafford Hall observation
• Verbal feedback from participants |

| Overall aims and objectives | OUTCOMES – IMMEDIATE AND LONGER TERM | • Did the training help develop skills and confidence, give information and ideas?
• Did the course help people tackle problems locally?
• Did the course generate grant applications?
• Were the grant projects effective? | • Written and verbal feedback from participants
• Grant applications
• Visits to grant recipients |

Results

Action results: the training courses helped community groups to take local action. We have already seen many examples of the groups' work in Chapter Four.

Three out of five groups took specific follow-up action on an issue or problem. Most of the rest planned to act. Two thirds specifically attributed part of their success in those follow-up actions to the training and 90% found the training generally useful for all of their local community work.

Two out of five groups engaged in small practical actions but did not apply for small grant funding from the project. The actions included liaising with landlords, police and others, organising one-off events, lobbying for changes in local services and developing feasibility plans for projects. They needed know-how and confidence rather than cash to do these things.

Small grant applications: just under one in five (17%) of the 700 groups that attended training applied for small grants. Many people presume that grant programmes for community groups will automatically be oversubscribed. Lots of grant programmes are, but the most experienced and confident are more likely to apply. The Gatsby groups were more likely not to have experience of applying for grants, even small amounts of £5,000 and under, for example for two thirds of the successful grant groups, the Gatsby Project fund was the first significant grant that they had applied for.

Groups appreciated small amounts of funding. The Gatsby Project 'training first' model combined training and support with funding.

There are other facts that point to lack of experience, lack of confidence and need for support and development as reasons why the rate of application was relatively low. Groups spent on average nine months developing their projects to grant application stage. Applications to Trafford Hall went through several revisions following visits, telephone calls and sometimes follow-on training. A quarter took over a year to make an application. Two fifths of the grant applicants attended more than one training course before they applied. Overall, 17% of all the 700 groups attended two or more courses. This also reinforces our decision to go for the 'training first' model.

The grant fund was flexible, with open criteria, a straightforward application system and personal contact. People could send draft applications and make changes after advice (we look at our 'hand-holding' approach to small grants below). Yet only one in five applied. Groups were modest in their requests – there was no 'padding' of applications. People applied for amounts to the penny. Some applied for only a few hundred pounds out of the maximum of £5,000. The average request was for £3,400, well under the maximum amount of £5,000, indicating that the main problem was not an insufficient amount of funding on offer.

Groups with good problem-solving, organisational and leadership skills were more able to draw on their training for follow-up action. These skills were not necessarily linked to the type of group, length of operation or age and experience of volunteers. Individual personality and group dynamics played a big role in how people used the training and took action. Recruiting local leaders to the training programme was very important. Both the quality of training and the nature and experiences of groups influence outcomes.

Training benefits: at a basic level, 88% of participants were satisfied or very satisfied with the training courses and 80% found the training to be at the right level. The courses met expectations for 80% of participants and 3% said that they did not feel they had benefited from the course, while 17% felt that some ideas had not been relevant to them. Participants found it easier to learn with a variety of training methods and strongly disliked didactic training styles, that is, chalk-and-talk style 'telling'. They liked participatory, active, 'doing' sessions, practical examples and a hands-on approach. We found that learning based on people's own experience was effective (Kolb and Fry, 1976). Getting people to reflect on their own experience, and reinforcing what people already know, works. The training courses did this by bringing people together from different parts of the country and through the participatory training techniques used.

Most training participants were looking for applicable solutions to live problems. They enjoyed meeting other people with similar problems and sharing experiences.

Being away from home and at Trafford Hall gave them a chance to think afresh, see the broader picture, realise they were not alone and gain new energy. Nearly all of the people involved in the groups were volunteers and were not paid to organise and run groups. Residents' groups had to keep up 'staff morale' for their volunteer workers, and the courses helped keep people motivated, confident and upbeat. Community activists felt valued. The Gatsby Project programmes were seen as a form of recognition and reward. They found Trafford Hall a relaxed,

Residents enjoyed the tranquil environment for learning at Trafford Hall. The organic garden offered inspiration for environmental projects.

peaceful, resident-friendly atmosphere and liked the old historic Georgian house and organic gardens.

Participants identified five key benefits of the courses:

- *Information:* 85% said the courses had given them new information. Nearly all the participants who responded to a follow-up survey had retained relevant facts after the training.
- *Ripple effect:* 81% of respondents told us that they had fed back information about the training to others in their neighbourhoods after they returned home.
- *Motivation and confidence:* 77% told us the training had made them more determined to take forward an existing idea and 67% said the course had boosted their confidence in their ability to make a difference.
- *Practical ideas for projects:* 73% told us immediately after the event that the training had given them new project ideas or new solutions to area problems; 60% said the training had made them reassess their existing ways of doing things; people had gained new action planning skills.
- *Developing networks:* the central benefit from the courses was meeting others and sharing experience, feeling that 'we are not alone'. For many, this benefit was sustained after they got home – 42% of respondents in the follow-up survey had kept in touch with people they met on the course after the event.

One example of how the courses helped groups is that of the Wakefield residents who wanted to produce a newsletter (described on pages 185 and 204), who were initially advised to produce a higher-cost, professionally printed publication. After reluctantly making their decision to scale down their plans and go for a basic newsletter at lower cost, they were reassured that it had been a good thing to do by going to Trafford Hall. As one resident said, "It was a revelation when we got to Trafford Hall" and saw examples of other newsletters from other community groups:

> '… they were all exactly like ours! It was a bolt from the blue. All we'd previously been shown were commercial standard. We didn't know that this [black and white on normal paper etc] was normal. We were not poor relations, nor did we have to look for funding for some grander professionally printed version. What we thought was not good enough was not dissimilar to most of the newsletters. This realisation came as a huge relief. [The Trafford Hall course told us] what to do and what not to do. [It gave us] a huge sense of proportion. The best thing is to learn by experience. When we went to Trafford Hall we were already doing it but it told us we were doing the right thing, it gave us lots of confidence. The course tutor looked at our constitution and suggested some changes might help us the next time we applied for funding. We have made these changes.' (resident, Wakefield)

Based on feedback from participants after courses, and the follow-up survey completed two months after groups returned home, training delivers both immediate and longer-lasting benefits. Motivation and belief in the possibility of change that result from the courses are key to sustaining voluntary community activity. The underlying message from participants is that training validates what they are trying to do, offers a reward and recognition for their efforts and is a source of practical ideas. It helps people to overcome community isolation, reinforcing people's common need for practical help when tackling difficult problems.

Groups do not always grow in a straight line

One sign that training has worked is if participants set up new related projects immediately after the courses, for example a community gardens course led to gardens that were not there before. However, projects rarely go straight from an idea to implementation. Instead, projects go through many stages of development before they start up and they need help after they have started. Groups came on Gatsby training at all of the different stages looking for support. Projects could run into difficulties at any stage that meant people could decide to change their plans or stop. If projects needed to be rethought at any point they might need to go back to a previous stage, for example back to feasibility or consultation on changes to the original idea. Some never made it all the way to implementation.

This is why our measure of the action impacts of training was not simply the number of new projects created, or the number of grants awarded; this is why we wanted to offer training as well as grants. Figure 8.2 shows the stages of project development.

Figure 8.2: Stages of project development

STAGE	DESCRIPTION
I	Generating interest and investigating ideas. Decide to develop or stop ↓
2	More serious feasibility and/or broader consultation. Decide to take to next stage, re-design or stop ↓
3	Fleshing out plans, getting partners and organisational development. Decide to keep going, change plans or stop ↓
4	Grant applications and/or starting small actions. More consultation. Redefining plans. Decide to keep going, stop or do something different ↓
5	Project implementation – early stages. Decide to keep going, rethink or stop ↓
6	Project implementation – ongoing work/ongoing evaluation and reassessment. Decide to continue in same way, or develop, or expand or stop ↓
7	Project development and/or expansion – back to stage I. Or closure/finish. Or new small project – back to stage I

The fact that community groups do not always grow in a straight line has also been shown by other research (Kumar and Nunan, 2002). We call this the 'linear fallacy', by which we mean that it is not true that all groups want to keep growing, or that growth is in one direction from small to big without ups and downs along the way. Some people presumed that the groups came to the Gatsby Project as newly created groups without a track record. Many of the groups and volunteers were new, but not all were. Training and project support are suitable for groups and volunteers at all stages.

For example just under half of the Gatsby grant-funded projects were run by new groups just starting out, but another 30 of the grants were given to groups that were between three and seven years old. Another 10 of the grants were to organisations that had been set up between 1980 and 1990, up to 16 years before the project started. Even so, the Gatsby grant was the first grant, or grant of that size, for two thirds of the projects funded.

On the training courses around one third of the 1,800 participants were new to volunteering and had been involved for less than a year. But, at the other end, another third were experienced community volunteers and had been involved for over four years in community activity. Just over half of the 700 groups that sent people to Trafford Hall had been set up for over four years, and just under half of the groups were younger organisations that had been going for under four years.

We had a similar experience to one research project, which found that:

> ... whether consciously or not, the Project found a tendency for the Charity Commission, funders and local development agencies to make three assumptions about groups and organisations. These were that: (a) they were new; (b) they wanted to grow; and (c) their development needed to follow a linear path. These assumptions are flawed. (Kumar and Nunan, 2002, p 17)

In practice, most of the community groups that came on courses were already active in some way but they wanted to learn, get new ideas, develop their work and meet other people with similar problems. Over half of the grant applicants attended several courses before applying. Some people on courses already had a project under way, but wanted help to adapt or expand. One of our measures of effectiveness was that groups were more motivated to take forward an idea they already had before going on training. Another of our measures was if training had made them reassess their existing ways of doing things.

Groups used training courses for both new and older members. Both new and established groups could develop new project activity at different points in their development. The Gatsby Project appealed to newly created community organisations, as well as organisations with a longer track record, which suggests that more mature organisations still value learning, particularly where they are looking at expanding activity into new areas.

Barriers to going away for training

We introduced a limited travel fund in 1999, and there was a small take-up of this fund from under 10% of participants. Travel barriers are as much to do with fear, health problems and organisational problems as with cost. However, the fund was kept in place to help ensure equal access for people coming from a long distance and unfunded groups.

Trafford Hall had a crèche on site and provided childcare costs for children to be looked after at home. The potential for abuse of the fund, the difficulties in checking claims and the unclear lines between family help and paid help made childcare grants contentious, but still important for participants. Take-up of both the crèche and childcare costs was low – less than 1% of participants – in spite of the programmes attracting many women with children. Parents enjoyed a break away from home without children, and concentrating on learning uninterrupted. Most often, friends and family helped out, removing the need for expensive childcare. This was usually the only way parents felt happy to leave their children overnight. A small allowance was paid for this and Trafford Hall has kept the fund on other programmes to ensure access by parents.

Reduced rejection rates

LSE Housing and Trafford Hall together assessed grant applications at regular meetings based on simple criteria, a personal visit by the grant assessor and carefully spelt-out conditions. One of our conditions was whether the group and project had a 'feel-good factor'. Figure 8.3 shows the Gatsby small grant fund criteria.

Applicants could contact the Gatsby workers if they needed help before submitting their application. People could discuss ideas for grant applications with the Gatsby workers during courses or over the telephone afterwards. Figure 8.4 shows the 'hand-holding' application process.

The hand-holding process resulted in fewer applications being rejected. Unsuitable applications were less likely to go through to the final stage, but applicants were encouraged to come back to the project when they were ready to try again. This meant that groups did not spend time doing an application at risk before they got an indication of whether they would be successful. The contact between the grant worker and the applicants made sure their applications were completed and had all the necessary information, and that any concerns about the project could be addressed.

The project rejected 25% of applications, compared to 41% of applications rejected by large national funders.[1] Fifteen per cent of the large national funders' rejections were due to lack of information, and 9.5% due to 'planning and management concerns'. The visit by the Gatsby grant assessor helped to give groups a chance who were not skilled at the grant application 'game':

> 'The problem is writing it down, I can't get it across, its OK when I talk.' (resident, Hastings)

The special approach of the Gatsby Project

When we started the Gatsby Project, our approach was special in several ways.

The 'training first' model: this used residential training as the starting point for problem solving and community organisation, with a follow-up small grant fund. It was different to most community training that did not offer follow-up grants, and was different to most small grant funds that did not offer initial help with project development. The small grant programme only came into play after the

Figure 8.3: Criteria for Gatsby small grant fund

Group	
Area	
Date visited	
Training course attended	
Application for	
Grant amount requested	
Grant recommended	
Number of group members	
Pitfalls	
Strengths	

CRITERIA

- A project that residents organise
- The group has a shared goal and works together
- The activity is of benefit to their community
- The intended beneficiaries support the idea
- The activity is replicable or helps us to learn about community action
- The activity is ongoing and/or has development potential
- There is an ongoing plan for funding
- There has been some training
- There is local support and backing for the idea
- There is good quality leadership
- The activity is new or is a clear development of existing activity
- The group has a constitution or democratic decision-making structure and a bank account with two signatories

CHECKLIST

Constitution	Bank account	Committee	Application relates to training	Figures correct and reasonable	Not replacing withdrawn funding	Group know what they are doing	Group is united	Group is stable	Beneficiaries represented on committee	Action plan filled in	Sustainable	Financial situation okay	It is needed	Feel-good factor

COMMENTS

participants fed back on what they could realistically do. Linking pump-priming grants directly into training underlined the connection between learning and doing. It put a premium on capacity building and it valued many different kinds of action, some of which required little or no cash.

Community self-help relies on uncovering and accessing local resources, inspiring others and thinking creatively, and implementing and managing action over time. But community groups face many barriers to action. The training strengthened the skills, confidence and motivation of residents to make a critical contribution to their communities.

Solving neighbourhood problems often relies as much on the ability to negotiate between residents and with other agencies as on actual cash. Training helps develop these skills. Groups and individuals rated training highly and often used the skills they acquired for community development rather than project development.

Figure 8.4: The Gatsby small grant application process

Support and advice on site
↓
Ideas clarified and developed during training, including information session on grants
↓
Simple, short form given out during the course
↓
On the return home draft applications can be faxed or posted for comment
↓
Informal telephone discussions throughout the process
↓
Flexibility to change, develop ideas or put an application on hold
↓
Incomplete applications – more information requested, not rejected
↓
Personal visit to grant applicants to assess application
↓
Quick decisions made on grants
↓
Follow-up evaluation and monitoring visit by LSE Housing researcher nine months into project
↓
Contact maintained with groups across life of project; regular progress reports

Source: Beck and Richardson (2004)

Developing training courses for community volunteers: the market for community action training was not well developed and we designed nearly all of the courses in the first three years from scratch, together with trainers. The training was clearly action orientated, with courses tackling practical problems and organising practical actions. We had to work hard to tweak the courses to make them more hands-on and practical. New trainers, new courses and new techniques emerged during the programme. Once a successful residential training package existed, we ran it as long as there was demand. Residents developed action plans at the end of each course and then fed back to LSE six weeks later on what they had done. The project welcomed paid workers, such as tenant liaison workers. They could attend together with the community groups they were helping. Paid workers received some financial help on a discretionary basis. Some courses were aimed specifically at workers' needs; these were self-funding.

A broad focus on all forms of DIY community action: the emphasis was on small local self-help action on a scale that would be overlooked by many bigger charities. A wide range of local activities – family work, youth work, community enterprise, environmental action, crime prevention and community venues – emerged because these were what residents asked for help with. The community action programme was not restricted to particular fields, unlike many programmes focused on particular types of activity. Crime, young people, community cafes and community buildings were some examples of popular programmes. All the courses were 'how to' courses about how to deliver practical activities.

The 'can do' principle: we needed to overcome professional resistance to handing over some control to communities to make some of the courses useful. We found that we needed to promote the first principle that communities 'can do', that they can do things to help themselves. For example, our first 'tackling drugs' course did not work because the trainers told residents that helping drug users was a job for specialists. The residents came away more 'aware' of the different drug types, their effects and sources of professional help. But they also came away feeling impotent. The trainers for the 'tackling crime' course were rightly concerned not to give a false message that residents could wipe out crime by themselves. We agreed. The trainers responded very positively to our request that they emphasise what residents could do, rather than what they could not. The courses promoted this message responsibly, informing residents about the limits of their activity and emphasising the useful role that professionals could play.

Going away for training and learning – a national programme: bringing residents together to share experiences made people feel part of something bigger. This raised energy and ambition to act. It also raised the profile and status of community action training more generally. The national programme stimulated and enhanced local training.

A national focus and central organising base gave the project and its training programmes coherence and recognition. A central organising body anchored accumulated experience and know-how. It made it easier to ensure quality, to place demands on trainers and to tap into a range of skills in a national centre rather than in local one-off courses.

Costs of community capacity building

The Gatsby Project costs

Around a third of the project's total spending went on training. Another third was invested in projects through small grants. A final third was on hand-holding support, development and evaluation. We provide an extremely crude guide to the costs of the project below. It is difficult to assign development costs to different outputs from the programmes because development costs paid for the staff time, office costs and the marketing needed to develop and run the project as a whole. Grants flow from training courses, so it is difficult to assign separate overhead costs to the organisation of the grant fund and organisation of the training programme.

We have divided the total costs of organising the programme across different outputs, as specified.

The guideline costs were:

Direct costs of training not including total programme costs:

- average cost of a training place = £250
- average cost of a training course = £250 × 20 people = £5,000
- average training cost/spend per tenants' group where two to three people attend a course = £500 to £750

Costs of training including programme costs (excluding grant awards):

- average cost of a training place = £450
- therefore average training cost/spend per group = £900 to £1,350

One calculation we did was to simply average out the total cost of the Gatsby Project just across the grant-funded projects. This calculation is biased against the project because it assumes *no* benefits from training for the non-grant award groups. Even so, using this measure, the average investment per project was just £12,500. This figure includes the £5,000 grant award; £12,500 is a relatively small investment to deliver the community impacts described in Chapter Four.

More investment in capacity building to produce better results

There is mixed evidence on whether spending more produces better community engagement and action. One study found that there was a weak relationship between the amounts spent on tenant participation and outcomes (The Housing Corporation, 1999/2000). Clearly there are many other factors that influence whether tenant involvement in decisions by social landlords is effective. However, a different study found the opposite, that there was evidence of a strong relationship between the amount of money, staff and other resources allocated to tenant participation and its effectiveness:

> Those landlords spending a higher proportion of their income on tenant participation appeared to be doing a wider variety of different tenant participation activities, communicating better with tenants, involving a wider range of people, and being more effective at incorporating tenant participation as standard practice. Notably, these landlords recognised that tenant participation could not always be 'controlled' and that it would bring change to the organisation itself. The willingness to commit more resources may have arisen from the underlying trusting relationship with tenants. (JRF, 2003, p 3)

Paying for community capacity building

The community volunteers paid the personal costs of volunteering, but the costs of community capacity building were usually paid for by an outside body. We offered bursaries to unfunded groups for the costs of the training and accommodation: 80% of training participants received bursary funding and 20% of groups paid for themselves – usually through local authority or landlord funding. We asked people applying for a bursary about training and regeneration monies in their area. We offered to help groups ask official bodies for help towards costs. These funds were difficult to access for training and not usually orientated towards residential training and learning. Community groups found it difficult to afford the costs of community development, like training, themselves. There was no clear, simple, usable route for groups to get money to pay for learning and training.

We have already indicated that the most common issue for groups in funding problems was the lack of available funding to sustain basic running costs and continue existing projects. Responsibility for covering the costs of keeping small projects going often fell between stools. Despite this, we have shown that the groups managed to achieve some, albeit precarious, levels of financial sustainability through grant funding.

It is understandable that from a funder's point of view, it is more attractive to fund new projects rather than provide 'continuation' funding for small projects or just for groups to keep going, however worthwhile. Our own funding in the Gatsby Training and Small Grants Project also gave grants to new activities, and only gave second grants where there was a substantial development or expansion of the original project. We made this decision because we wanted to encourage groups to do things that they had not done before, and as many groups as possible to be supported within our relatively tiny budget. However, this focus on new over old had the negative effects of diverting groups' energy from their original purpose (Beckford et al, 2003), and also meant successful projects either needed to reinvent themselves unnecessarily, or pretend to be doing new work when they were not, or run the risk of stopping good work.

As a single funder, our aim to stimulate and facilitate new community activity was positive. We checked that groups had capacity to increase their activity if they already had other projects on the go. But the danger of a focus on new projects by funders on a grand scale is that overall there would not be a net gain in activity, as existing work was dropped in favour of new work.

A fund for organisational running costs rather than new project work would achieve different, longer-term goals. The project did not supply these costs. Resources for longer-term project support, training and development would lead to more follow-through. Research has shown that voluntary organisations devote large amounts of time and resources to dealing with funders and making grant applications which 'absorb[ed] organisational resources and [made] it chronically difficult to plan strategically' (JRF, 1999, p 1).

Charitable funders have the advantages of flexibility in what they fund, and can often 'fund the unfundable', and take more of a gamble in funding unusual, innovative or risky work than more small-c conservative government bodies spending public money.

In any case, charitable funds are dwarfed by the scale of mainstream public spending. In 2003/04, the biggest national charitable funders had budgets in the region of £25-£50 million per year, compared to central government spending on neighbourhood renewal of around £765 million that financial year, or local authority main programme spending of around £53.6 billion. The large charitable funders' budgets each amount to between 3%-6% of the 'special' money for improving deprived neighbourhoods. And that neighbourhood renewal money itself is less than 2% of mainstream spending on public services.

Therefore, there is a strong case that the priorities of (private, as opposed to semi-public charitable funds like the National Lottery) charitable trusts and foundations should be on new work and pump-priming, rather than on supporting activities over the long term. Central government has long had voluntary and community sector funding programmes across different departments. As with most government programmes, these wax and wane with policy changes. Local government support is patchy, and also changes according to political priorities.

This issue has been raised in other research. For example, one study found that deprived communities could find getting funding complex, difficult and slow. A particular problem was the lack of small-scale funding that was available quickly. This overview of capacity building funding argued that the major sources of funding for capacity building were problematic, with few sources of funding that were flexible, independent, quick and un-bureaucratic (Duncan and Thomas, 2000).

The independence of the project from central and local government allowed flexibility and gave community groups access to a simple, flexible, un-bureaucratic source of assistance. Independent funding for training was vital as residents' groups had very limited access to local budgets for training, even where these had been set up.

The question of who pays for community capacity building has not been resolved, meaning groups trying to do community action often lose out.

Summary

Community volunteers contended with many obstacles and downsides to their community organising work that made their task more difficult. The top five barriers were: lack of appropriate skills; lack of resources; the 'apathy' of other residents; problems getting suitable premises; and barriers from local authorities and landlords. Being a representative could occasionally be a thankless task. The volunteers felt frustrated, guilty and stressed at times. Overwork for community volunteers was a common problem for lots of groups generally.

Only a minority got actively involved in our areas – 'apathy' was a key obstacle identified by volunteers. Expectations for involvement were high but figures for participation were consistently low. There were similar experiences across the country. The gap between expectation and reality led to disappointment. 'Apathy' is the wrong word, however, because it is not true that most people did not get involved because they lacked interest – some groups accepted that other people did not get involved for their own reasons.

Attention has often been more on the people who did not get involved than those who did. Active volunteers felt deserted. People who did bother to get involved were blamed for being 'the usual suspects'. Another approach was to see active community volunteers as unique and special contributors. An alternative term for 'the usual suspects' could be 'gold dust'.

There was funding available, but the groups found it hard to access. The groups' lack of confidence and experience held them back from successful fundraising. Many of the community self-help activities were done at a relatively cheap cost, or funded through small-scale fundraising. They relied heavily on the availability and willingness of volunteers rather than on major amounts of funding. Few funding bodies would take responsibility for keeping small projects going. Despite this, we have shown that the groups managed to achieve some levels of financial sustainability through grant funding, albeit precarious. Resources for longer-term project support, training and development would lead to more follow-through.

The groups' lack of skills and experience included lack of administrative, accounting and presentation skills and project development and management. The groups had problems securing suitable premises. They were helped by things like help from landlords in offering empty properties, and innovative thinking about spaces.

The groups' work was hampered by outside bodies. People could be demotivated to get involved if they felt that their input would not or had not made a difference. There was still a way to go for public agencies to create a climate where community activity could flourish. In the project we needed to overcome professional resistance to handing over some control to communities. We had to promote the first principle that communities 'can do'.

The groups did receive a great deal of external support. They appreciated that community capacity building support came from lots of different places. However, no single body had a comprehensive overview of all the community capacity building taking place in an area. Community support was variable in quality and coverage. Groups receiving support either rated help as extremely good, or as bad. Quality issues were partly because of the way that community development was structured: jobs were often low paid and casual; requirements for the job varied considerably; and workers found it difficult to get training and back-up.

The issue of payment for volunteers was still highly controversial with community volunteers themselves, unpalatable to many, and possibly counterproductive. Instead, volunteers valued the rewards and pleasure of fun and friendships, and the feeling of doing something for their communities, rather than financial reward. We had annual celebration events – the Gatsby Party – as a reward for volunteers' efforts.

There was a gap between the community agenda and capabilities and wider agendas. It was difficult to bridge the gap between the groups' capacity and delivering on very tough social inclusion outcomes. It is a positive step that policy makers wanted the voluntary and community sectors to do more. There needs to be significant growth of voluntary and community organisations to create capacity to deliver public services. Growth should be focused on social enterprises that are up for the task, using an 'accelerator' model where existing social enterprises franchise their operations away from the home base. There is a danger that the value of what informal community groups can offer will be lost in a discussion purely about growth to take on public services. The results of the Gatsby Project show that there is much that can be done to help groups grow and develop. Growth is relative to the groups' starting capacity, and the overall direction is ultimately dictated by the groups' own agendas.

Although significant growth was not applicable for the majority of the sector, the work groups did was itself of incalculable value. The Gatsby Project worked with groups to develop their work. We did this through residential 'how to' training courses organised through Trafford Hall – home of the National Communities Resource Centre, and a follow-up small grant fund for community self-help projects. We spent £1.25 million over five years. We wanted to develop the strengths of poor areas from within. Our approach had to be sensitive enough not to crush the abilities and potential capacity that poor communities had. The emphasis was on small local self-help action on a scale that would be overlooked by many bigger charities.

We wanted to see practical results. We offered three simple things: ideas and action plans; hand-holding; and funding. We wanted to tap into community groups' own thirst for learning. The training courses helped community groups to take local action. Two thirds specifically attributed part of their success in those follow-up actions to the Gatsby training. Grant programmes for the least experienced and least confident community groups were not always oversubscribed. The Gatsby grant was the first significant grant for two thirds of the successful grant groups. The hand-holding grant application process resulted in fewer applications being rejected. The market for community action training was not well developed and we designed nearly all of the courses in the first three years from scratch, together with trainers.

Participants liked participatory, active, 'doing' sessions, practical examples and a hands-on approach. The training courses brought people together from different parts of the country. They enjoyed meeting other people with similar problems and sharing experiences. Being away from home and at Trafford Hall gave them a chance to think afresh, see the broader picture, realise they were not alone and to gain new energy. The Gatsby Project programmes were seen as a form of recognition and reward. They found Trafford Hall a resident-friendly venue. The training strengthened the skills, confidence and motivation of residents to make a critical contribution to their communities. People got new practical ideas from courses.

We created the 'training first' model. Linking pump-priming grants directly into training underlined the connection between learning and doing. It put a premium on capacity building and it valued many different kinds of action, some of which required little or no cash. The groups did not always grow in a straight line, which meant that training and project support were suitable for groups and volunteers at all stages.

Bringing residents together to share experiences made people feel part of something bigger. This raised the profile and status of community action training more generally. A national focus and central organising base gave the project and its training programmes coherence and recognition. A central organising body anchored accumulated experience and know-how.

The average training cost per tenants' group was between £900 to £1,350, including all organising and developing costs. A crude guide figure for the average investment per grant-funded project was just £12,500. The evidence is mixed, but there is research to show that spending more produces better community engagement and action. There is no clear, simple, usable route for groups to get money to pay for learning and training. Independent funding for training was vital as residents' groups had very limited access to local budgets for training, even where these had been set up.

There is a strong case that the priorities of charitable trusts and foundations should be on new work and pump-priming, rather than on supporting activities over the long term. The question of who pays for community capacity building has not been resolved, meaning groups trying to do community action often lose out.

Note
[1] Unpublished figure kindly supplied by Awards for All England. Figures exclude applications to Awards for All England that were rejected due to lack of funds.

NINE

Conclusions: championing community self-help

In this chapter we present our conclusions based on the findings from Chapters Two to Eight about what community self-help contributes to neighbourhoods and communities. We look at the links between tackling neighbourhood issues, tackling social exclusion and community building, and conclude with recommendations for how communities could be made more vibrant and further empowered.

We start with the story so far, and position the Gatsby research in the wider historical context. We then outline two key definitions of 'community' and 'social exclusion'. These theoretical underpinnings then help illustrate why and how community building is intrinsically linked to social inclusion and neighbourhood renewal.

We then put forward seven lessons that flow directly from our research and that of others, which are about the role of communities and community building and why it is worthwhile championing community self-help. We look at the role of communities, the role of self-help generally and the role of community or collective self-help. We also outline the grounds for supporting community groups.

We conclude by looking at how we can expand community action through a community building framework, and make recommendations for policy and practice based on the implications of the framework.

The story so far

Our study sits in a bigger historical context. The Gatsby Project aimed to help people take control of solving collective problems where they could, and where they wanted to. In the UK we are still renegotiating the relationship between the state, the individual and local communities to give back more responsibility to individuals and their families for their well-being and behaviour that the growth of the welfare state has threatened to overwhelm. For example, in 2000 half the population agreed with the statement 'The welfare state encourages people to stop looking after each other', up from a third of respondents in 1991 (Hills, 2004). This debate over the redrawing of lines of responsibility has been alive (in its current form) for most of the past century and continues into this one. We saw in Chapter Five how residents felt disempowered by too much dependency on outside bodies. The current focus on community self-help and social capital is partly the result of the most recent failures of large bureaucratic structures to perform appropriately and effectively some functions for individuals, families and neighbourhoods. The examples given by residents in the study in Chapter Three demonstrate some of the consequences of previous neglect of responsibility for neighbourhoods by large-scale institutions. In the study neighbourhoods, there had been job losses in Birmingham, for example, that were felt directly on one particular estate, and in Merseyside we saw how the impact of failing services spiralled into area abandonment, car crime and urban blight. How 'vertical' structures of mainstream institutions and society hit on the ground were all live questions for residents in the neighbourhoods.

Another theme running through this book is about the failure of representative democracy to ensure that public institutions are properly accountable to residents. This theme can be seen underlying the anger at misinformation and praise for greater transparency of agencies in Chapter Three, the lobbying work of service providers we saw in Chapter Four, and the arguments in favour of community involvement in decision making of mainstream services in Chapter Five. It is on these grounds that the relationships of residents and service users to mainstream institutions are being reconfigured.

And while we as citizens have relationships upwards to the 'vertical' structures of the state, democratic institutions and mainstream services, we also forge bonds and understandings about how we live sideways, between each other. 'Horizontal' structures in society sit somewhere between the individual, families, the market and the state. The neighbourhoods in the study clearly illustrated how horizontal structures worked or were destabilised; these structures are referred to as civil society (Marx, 1970; de Tocqueville, 2002; Centre for Civil Society, 2005) and include the sorts of community organisations and collective action based on shared values portrayed in this book. Civil society also refers to the systems of informal social relationships that we saw holding together and breaking down in Chapter Three, and that the groups tried to reinforce and maintain in Chapter Four. We saw some of the damaging consequences of some individuals and families not taking full responsibility for themselves and their neighbourhoods, and some hope giving examples of associational life being strengthened.

Civil society is also part of the debate about where lines of responsibility fall between people and the state and mainstream institutions. As we saw in Chapters Five and Eight, current policy is also moving towards offering scope for the organisations of civil society, like the groups in the study, to play a greater role. We discuss later in this chapter whether civil society welcomes these moves, and if they are ready to take on this role. It has been argued that strong associational life is also supportive of strong democracy (Almond and Verba, 1963) – where horizontal structures intersect with vertical structures. Based on the material and debate in Chapter Seven, we take a further look later in this chapter at how the groups' operation of participatory democracy might work in harmony with the structures of representative democracy and how this could be expanded.

A definition of 'community' and 'social exclusion'

Two key concepts underpin the arguments and evidence in this book – the idea of 'community' and the issue of 'social exclusion'. We now give brief definitions of these two concepts, which is in order to explain why the residents we talked to saw such a strong link between their community-building work, attempts to make their neighbourhoods better and to improve the lot of the people that lived there.

Definition of 'community' as people and place

This is a book about communities. The definition of 'community' that emerged from the research as described in Chapter Three encompassed both 'people' and 'place'. Our definition of community, or what we have called 'social infrastructure' (Richardson and Mumford, 2002), is that a community is firstly the physical environment of a neighbourhood, together with the services and facilities that contribute to creating and maintaining neighbourhood conditions. Secondly, a community is a set of social relationships and the social organisation within a small geographical location. It is crucial to note that the social organisation of a neighbourhood is not simply about the formal and less formal face-to-face relationships that residents have. It is also about the operation of informal social controls, and about the standards of behaviour that residents adhere to, aside from any face-to-face contact. Social organisation includes friendship networks and informal mutual aid, informal small voluntary groups, clubs and societies and informal social controls operated via a set of commonly agreed norms and rules.

'Community' does not always mean good

We do not imply an idealised concept of community as a result of this definition. Indeed, the eloquent comments about the downsides of community show that neither do the residents we talked to, and on whose thoughts and experiences we have based our definition. In Chapter Three the groups debated how community relations impacted negatively on people's lives. They explained about community divisions, insularity, claustrophobia, isolation of newcomers and a lack of privacy. This revealed how facile it is for commentators to dismiss residents' desire for successful 'communities' on the grounds that residents see community in a one-sided way as wholly wonderful. 'Community' as a shorthand term for social systems in a neighbourhood was shown to be an arena for tension and conflict as well as support. We saw that the flipside of closeness was the potential for greater division. Interestingly the more direct contact we have with our neighbours, the less inclined we are to feel trusting of them (Coulthard et al, 2002).

In any case, the notion of 'community', when understood as people and place as outlined, is unavoidable. It exists whether we like it or not, and has to be tolerated or made to work. The use of the term 'community' as a shorthand for geographical neighbourhoods does not presume that they are, or should be, the primary focus for residents' careers, leisure time or social lives. Instead, our definition acknowledges the importance of the quality of neighbourhoods and services on people's everyday lives, and the impacts of the behaviour of others in close proximity to us, whether we care about those people or not.

A definition of 'social exclusion'

We talk in this book about people facing aspects of social exclusion. We define 'social inclusion' as people's ability to participate in socially valued activities (Burchardt et al, 2002). In the definition of social exclusion we use here: 'an individual is socially excluded if he or she is unable to participate in the key activities of the society in which he or she lives'. When this definition was discussed with residents, they came up with an equivalent formulation that social exclusion was about 'not being able to play a part in the activities that others can' (Richardson and Le Grand, 2002, p 504).

The core element of the definition is that an individual's status is defined relative to other members of the society. It is about whether a person participates in the vertical structures, such as being in employment or voting, and about whether a person participates in horizontal structures, such as social networks. This is expressed in the definition as participation in socially valued activities. The definition includes four key socially valued activities:

- *Consumption:* adequate consumption of goods and services, for example being able to buy or access food, decent shelter, healthcare, transport and leisure.
- *Production:* opportunities to participate in productive activity, for example being in paid employment, training, caring for family or volunteering.
- *Political engagement:* the ability to have a voice or be politically engaged, for example being a member of a tenants' group, campaigning organisation or voting.
- *Social interaction:* access to social interaction and supports, for example having someone to call on in a crisis.

Some, including the current author and community volunteers, argue for a fifth element to the definition, that is, the consumption of public services and public goods and neighbourhood quality (Richardson and Le Grand, 2002).

Links between social inclusion, neighbourhood renewal and community building

The underlying aim of neighbourhood renewal and promoting social inclusion is ultimately to try and close the gaps in the integration of citizens at the bottom of the socio-economic scale with the rest of society. It highlights gaps where vertical structures intersect with neighbourhoods, such as in the case of inadequate service provision. Our focus in this book has been on community building as intrinsically linked to tackling social exclusion and to neighbourhood renewal. In summary the links between community building, neighbourhood viability and tackling social exclusion are as follows:

- Part of being socially included means having access to good quality goods, services and facilities. Neighbourhoods are places where some of the goods, services and facilities are delivered to achieve social inclusion, for example a clean physical environment is something that people expect to have access to in order to feel socially included. Run-down neighbourhoods, as seen in Chapter Three, make social exclusion worse.
- Run-down neighbourhoods and social exclusion are grounds for community building because part of our definition of 'community' comprises the physical environment of a neighbourhood, together with its services, facilities and residents. Therefore community building, in the sense of improving places and the services supplied to places, is clearly a way of renewing neighbourhoods and improving people's inclusion on the basis of adequate consumption of quality services.
- Relationships and behaviour in a neighbourhood form the other part of our definition of 'community'. Part of being socially included is to have social supports. The different types of social relationships and social systems that make up a 'community' provide social interaction and social support for people to be socially included. More importantly, when these go wrong, it leads to both neighbourhood decline, and to the exclusion of areas and individuals. Therefore community building, in the sense of increasing civic responsibility and strengthening social relationships, is the basis for tackling neighbourhood decline and social exclusion.
- 'Community', in the sense of civic engagement and the groups in the study, works both to link people in to decision-making structures, and to give people a small measure of control over decisions that affect their lives. Part of being socially included is to be 'politically engaged' in some way in this sense of control. Therefore community building, in the sense of community engagement and community self-help, also plays a part in tackling the political engagement aspects of social exclusion.
- As we saw in Chapters Three and Four, community engagement holds services and authorities accountable for decisions about a community in all its aspects. Therefore building 'community' in the sense of community engagement and community action also contributes to improving the quality of life in neighbourhoods.

We therefore cannot tackle social exclusion without creating viable neighbourhoods and services, and we cannot do either without community building. At the end of this chapter, we present our recommendations for a community-building strategy, based on a framework for community building.

Seven lessons about community building

We now turn to our seven lessons based on the Gatsby research, backed by wider evidence.

I Neighbourhood renewal and social inclusion are about more than just tackling poverty

One obvious alternative to a community self-help programme would be to either give people cash, or focus on economic and job growth instead. However, other dimensions of disadvantage than income and wealth, or the lack of it, are arguably as important (Atkinson, 1998). The concept of social exclusion that we use here is much broader than a simple focus on poverty. So, going back to the definition of social exclusion outlined above, clearly some aspects of social exclusion are about how much cash people have. For example, consumption, particularly of private goods, requires people to have money to pay. Participation in production, for the majority, is being in paid employment in order to get a wage. While the evidence presented in Chapter Eight shows that getting involved as a volunteer is less likely if you are on a low income (see also Richardson, 2005a), and having a thriving social life is harder to do on a low income (Kempson, 1996), people do not always need to have more money before they become more politically engaged or get better social interaction. In fact, we saw in Chapter Eight that people with better incomes actually prioritise getting involved more than people who are less well off, indicating that people with money agree that money is not the only important thing in their lives.

And unless people move, having more cash in your pocket does not mean that the publicly funded and provided services in your neighbourhood will get better. Individual economic success for those that stay cannot compensate for neighbourhood disorder. There is now a body of evidence suggesting that above a minimum level of income more economic growth and higher average incomes do not generate significantly greater happiness (Layard, 2005). In the UK, a study comparing people born in the 1960s with those born in the 1970s showed that despite greater material advantages the later generation was more likely to be unhappy with their quality of life (Bynner et al, 2002). Much of the explanation for these findings is to do with individuals comparing themselves unfavourably relative to other individuals in terms of status. These negative feelings despite greater economic success are related to the degree of security individuals experience about their labour market prospects.

There is a parallel process for an individual's feelings and experiences of their neighbourhoods. An unfavourable comparison of the place a person lives in relative to the general standard for neighbourhoods causes unhappiness despite greater individual economic achievement. This is strongly linked to the degree of security and safety people experience in their surroundings. So, while (some) people may have more individual consumer power, more gadgets, more spare time, they can still feel unhappy about their social relationships, and about their physical environments. Their improved individual quality of life does not compensate for a decline in the quality of life in the neighbourhood.

This all suggests that focusing on raising incomes to tackle social exclusion is insufficient. It reinforces the case for the links between community building and achieving social inclusion and neighbourhood renewal.

2 Neighbourhoods and communities matter to people

A more fundamental challenge to the case we present here is the idea that neighbourhoods and community do not matter to society, or do not matter to people. Neighbourhood problems like those amply described in Chapter Three were highly relevant to people in the study and nationally. We noted that neighbourhood concerns were shared by people across income groups in more densely populated areas. The social housing tenants in the research prioritised anti-social behaviour, inappropriate housing allocations policies and youth issues. They had a strong focus on controls over behaviour in public and shared spaces, like people nationally. These are all neighbourhood issues. As also noted in Chapter Three, there was a significant minority of residents dissatisfied with mainstream services. The interviewees represented the most disgruntled of these households, and may have been the most vocal faction of dissatisfied people in deprived areas.

Knowing the neighbours is an important part of what is commonly thought of as making a place into a community in its traditional sense. It is sometimes argued that these traditional notions of belonging and community are dead or dying. There have been significant changes to the way we interact with family and friends as more of us move further away from each other, and keep in touch by email and text messages, and there is debate and conflicting evidence about what the implications of these changes are for our sense and experience of community (SOCQUIT, 2004).

Another idea is that community is no longer relevant for people based on changes in what sorts of groups we identify with and feel part of. Some argue that people feel closer to people who like the same music or same football team or who drink in the same pub as them, than their neighbours. Some commentators make the case that our attachment to premier league football teams is more significant than our attachment to family members and friends who we attend matches with, or to the pub team or Sunday league side we play in.

Although the trends are towards more geographically disparate friendship networks, place-based social networks continued to be relevant for people in low-income neighbourhoods. This was spelt out clearly in Chapter Three. There are structures that people identify with more strongly than the communities where they live. But people rely on communities to support some of their basic needs – for security, for contact, to live peaceful lives. Physical proximity matters. It was not true to say that people's desire for human contact had been replaced by brand loyalty, consumer goods or electronic communication. This has also been demonstrated in other research on the relationship between ICT and communities (Katz et al, 2001; Hampton and Wellman, 2003).

The neighbourhoods in the study were close-knit, relatively stable communities, with extended family networks. These characteristics were shared by a surprisingly high proportion of other neighbourhoods nationally, as we saw in Chapter Three. People in the neighbourhoods placed a high value on the idea of community. Again, the surprise was that these views were shared by a broad range of households across the country. We talked to people who were like many others in their belief in community and in their actual experience of community.

Even where social relationships between people in a geographical area were more fragmented, people's desire was for more integration. This was true for better-off and less well-off people. Residents in low-income neighbourhoods expressed their desire for there to be more direct social interaction. As we have said, the concept and experience of being part of a community was not unproblematic, but, despite this, community mattered to residents. The evidence on the value people place on 'community' is durable and compelling.

3 Self-help in all forms is at the base of community building

So far we have argued the need for a community-building approach to deal with social exclusion and neighbourhood disorganisation. What role was played by the residents within those communities?

Residents in neighbourhoods were in a variety of roles in relation to community building. Self-help happened, whether policy makers wanted it to or not, as part of everyday life. People experienced neighbourhood problems, the pressures of living on a low income and the stresses of life in low-income areas. They did not experience these pressures passively, and had a variety of responses. Some of these responses were individual, some collective. The way that people actively respond to and create new circumstances is sometimes referred to as the exercise of human agency, both individual and collective. The classic model for how people respond to issues like neighbourhood disorganisation is that people will either stay put (loyalty), use their 'voice' to complain, or get out of the situation (exit) (Hirschman, 1970), adapted later on to include the response of neglect (Lowery et al, 1992; Stewart and Taylor, 1995).

A minority in the neighbourhoods had a neglect response. They responded in ways that had a damaging effect on other people, and often themselves, for example those people depicted in Chapter Three. The damage could be a consequence of not doing what is required, like not disposing of bulky rubbish properly, or not exercising adequate parental supervision and care in the face of severe family stresses. At the more extreme end, damaging effects were caused by actively doing wrong, such as vandalism or criminal activity. Neglect has been wrongly characterised as a passive response (Lyons and Lowery, 1986) when it could equally be seen as an active choice and an exercise of agency both to not do the 'right' thing and to do neglectful things. Wider society condemns this sort of behaviour, outsiders may see it as ultimately self-defeating and we can recognise the constraints on people's choices and responses. However, they were still responses, ways that people had chosen to 'benefit' themselves at others' expense.

For some, their response to extreme dissatisfaction with their neighbourhoods was to try and leave – to take the exit route. There were certainly many families in the low-income study neighbourhoods who would have liked to have left if they could. The number of requests from social housing tenants to move was routinely high in the least desirable places, and many poor neighbourhoods suffered from high turnover. But many of those who would like to have left were unable to realise their dreams to move and were left in the least desirable neighbourhoods. Generally mobility out of the social rented sector for many reasons was relatively low.

For those who stayed, whether through choice or not, most tried to make the best of things for themselves and their families in ways that were not damaging to other people. Staying put, through choice especially, could be categorised as a 'loyalty' response. 'Loyalty' is arguably a misnomer, as many cases of loyalty could equally be described as coping strategies. And as with neglect, loyalty is also sometimes portrayed wrongly as a passive response (Lyons and Lowery, 1986), rather than an active one. Many people in the study areas were still actively responding even in the 'loyalty' or coping mode, for example by making their own homes more secure with gates and spyholes, by mothers attempting to protect their children by increasing supervision of play, by parents trying to improve their own situations by going to work or college. Responses included people, especially mothers, reaching out and making informal social contacts as a way of feeling less wary of neighbours, and putting support networks in place.

A minority at the other end tried to make the best of things not only for themselves, but also for other residents. People in the deprived neighbourhoods in the study expressed their desire for both neighbourhoods that worked, and social relationships between people in those neighbourhoods that worked. They then took action themselves to try and make these things happen, as we saw portrayed in Chapter Four. They exercised a collective form of agency, in contrast to the mostly individual forms just described.

While some citizens neglected their responsibilities for themselves and to their neighbourhoods, others voluntarily took on responsibility for the collective, but were often derided for doing so. Their work indicated some of the ways a culture of civic responsibility could be reborn. The minority of residents who found positive collective solutions to neighbourhood problems exhibited a 'voice' response. We saw how vocal the groups were about lobbying others for neighbourhood change in Chapter Four, although again the classification as voice is slightly misleading. Some of the groups' work was about voicing concerns to authorities, but as we also saw, some of the groups' work was about quietly getting on and doing projects themselves.

An alternative way of explaining people's different responses in low-income neighbourhoods is to see human behaviour as a result of rationally choosing to do one thing, or another, by weighing up the different costs and benefits. Understood like that, the neglect response shows that some people saw the costs of helping out as too high for them, and the voice response shows where people placed a high weight on the value of their communities to them.

We focus in this book on low-income neighbourhoods, and responses to neighbourhood problems, but we noted in Chapter Eight that levels of community activity were higher in better-off areas than in poorer areas. For example, there is a long list of place-based community clubs and activities that are also associated with more middle-class areas, such as rambling clubs, cricket clubs, WRVS (Women's Royal Voluntary Service), the League of Friends, galas, fêtes and festivals, local history societies, book groups, craft fairs and artists networks, collectors clubs, Brownies, Guides and Scouts, classic car clubs, pub-based clubs and fundraising.

Better-off places may not have had community forums in quite the same way, but they have established town and parish councils, and have usually had higher turnouts in local elections. The rational choice of better-off people has historically been to invest time engaging in their communities. In reality, community engagement and self-help was something that wealthier people also chose for themselves in order to have fun, provide activities, maintain social links and protect good neighbourhood conditions. It was not a second-best solution for deprived people only.

People's choice of response can shift over time. People may be using a mix of strategies at any one time, or not be consistent in their responses. People's decisions about what approach to take are constrained by experience, understanding of the alternatives, their resources and their assessment of the risks, costs and benefits.

However, all of these varieties of response suggest that self-help is intrinsic to human survival, that people do respond to circumstance, that self-help is a form of self-preservation, and that human agency wins through. Our work has shown that people try to exert control in both smaller and larger ways over the effects their environment and circumstances have on them. But as we have also seen in this book, the context and environment that people operate in crucially affect their ability to respond, and their responses.

All of this strongly suggests that a community-building framework or structure is needed to enhance people's self-help capacity, or capacity to exercise their agency in all its forms, in order that more positive social and neighbourhood structures can be developed and maintained (Giddens, 1984, 1993).

4 Community self-help is a choice by the minority that produces benefits for the majority

Even within the most severely declining neighbourhoods, there were core groups of residents committed to their neighbourhood who stayed, and fought to challenge the downward spiral as a group (Richardson and Mumford, 2002). The residents in this study were among the minority that had chosen collective solutions to combat shared or communal problems. This is what we mean by *community* self-help. Community self-help solutions are positive human responses to difficult situations.

The active minority took a role as community volunteers to try to improve neighbourhood quality of life on behalf of other residents. Many forms of collective response to social conditions could be regarded as public goods, that is, it benefits those who do not subscribe to it, as well as those who do, or at least a communal resource (Harris, 2006). There is evidence from the US about the important factors influencing how much gets done and fixed in a neighbourhood. What was important was the quantity of community organisations in a neighbourhood rather than the total numbers of people actively involved (Sampson, 2004).

People that responded in this way amount to a tiny fraction of the population – between 1% and 7% in less well-off places – as discussed in Chapter Eight. We look below at how this created questions about their legitimacy.

Community self-help was a solution that some of the people experiencing social exclusion and neighbourhood disorder prescribed for themselves. In Chapter Five the community organisers pointed to some unique benefits that, under certain circumstances, resident volunteers alone could provide, such as high levels of commitment, space to be flexible and an insider's understanding. More importantly, the principle of communities helping themselves was seen as empowering. One potential advantage of community organising was to increase feelings of civic responsibility in a neighbourhood context where cynicism about change was high.

We heard some articulate opinions about why people had chosen to get involved and organised in Chapter Five. This generally went contrary to arguments that participation was unfair on residents, although there were some cases where residents did feel forced to help themselves. The residents' explanations of why they got involved also contradicted arguments that participation was mostly imposed from above, or was simply a way of manipulating residents away from the real issues. Although at its worst participation could be like this, and there are examples of this sort of cynical abuse of involvement, the residents in the study showed an alternative version of how participation could be.

The minority of residents who participate or organise in collective activity had already made a choice not to go it alone. They had already recognised the importance of inclusive and viable neighbourhoods in improving individual quality of life, and the role of collective action in getting this. We heard in Chapter Five, and saw from their actions in Chapter Four, that the residents felt that we have collective responsibility as a society both for including the most vulnerable, and to tackle shared problems. Their actions are in line with a belief that the problem of social exclusion implied a commitment to both social justice and social solidarity (Barry, 2002). Collective action like this implies a recognition that individual solutions may not be the most efficient for the majority who lack social and material resources, as expressed by one resident activist in a separate piece of research:

> We are still suffering from the 1980s – there is no such thing as society. It takes a long time to change cultures, cultures of individualism. Some are excluding themselves without knowing it because they try and go it alone but without the resources to look after themselves. (quoted in Richardson and Le Grand, 2002, p 510)

Because community organisations were trying to positively exert control over their surroundings in order to improve conditions, and because this impulse was a positive example of human beings taking control of their own lives, we set up the Gatsby Project to support community organising. This study was based on the groups that participated in the Gatsby Project. We described in Chapter Two how the programme combined intensive residential training with a small grant fund to give community organisations a springboard from which to take action back in their areas. The majority of participants in the programme came from social housing areas, and people came from across the UK, as detailed in Chapter Two. The programme invested £1.25 million.

Overall, the work of the community groups, where successful, was to make a solid contribution to community building in all of its senses. They promoted the idea of collective responsibility to overcome symptoms of 'malaise'. People helping themselves was fundamentally more empowering than being passive recipients of help only, as presented in Chapter Five. And while the existence of community organisations did not automatically mean there was a high level of social capital in an area, residents who were not actively involved saw informal groups as visible signs of 'community spirit' (Mumford and Power, 2003). Families in low-income neighbourhoods like those in Chapter Three felt that 'community spirit' mattered to bolster quality of life, provide social support, enhance their feelings of safety and contribute to tolerance of diversity.

5 Community self-help in poor communities provides triple benefits

Community self-help in poor communities provides a set of triple benefits in improving mainstream services, in generating neighbourhood renewal and reviving democracy. This threefold role was not championed widely enough by a range of stakeholders, especially given the complexity of this set of tasks.

We have seen some of the reasons why community self-help lacked sponsors, including fierce debate over its worth and usefulness in Chapter Four, the issue of the size of individual groups and small scale of operation in Chapter Six, and criticisms of its rightness and representativeness in Chapters Five and Seven.

The community groups in the study were an example of bottom–up approaches. The scale and complexity of the problems in deprived areas required action by mainstream institutions, and often targeted intensive interventions. Partnership working was highlighted in Chapters Four and Five as integral to the groups' work. The triple benefits of small community organisations complemented mainstream institutions and democratic processes.

First, the groups improved mainstream services. They did this by playing a liaison and brokering role between residents and services, characterised by the examples in Chapter Four. They helped residents to access services, for example helping links with police by being conduits for people to supply information anonymously. They helped signpost people to relevant agencies and helped them to cope with paperwork and forms. Residents' worm's-eye views provided invaluable information for mainstream service providers on how their services impacted on the ground – positively and negatively. Residents often showed a capacity for innovative thinking around problems that the professions did not take a lead on, partly because the former were less hidebound than the latter by the conventions of the profession, as argued in Chapter Four.

Second, the community groups contributed to neighbourhood renewal by organising small-scale projects and activities, like the youth groups, social nights and lunch clubs described in Chapter Four. These projects and activities added in small ways to the total stock of facilities in the neighbourhood. Informal citizen organising and mutual aid were ways of developing and maintaining social capital and other forms of informal social controls that underlay the viability of neighbourhoods. This was through things such as face-to-face social interaction between residents, the improvement of aspects of the neighbourhood that sent out signals of its desirability or otherwise, and the containment and education of young people, again as seen in Chapter Four.

Third, small-scale organisations helped to underpin democracy, as we outlined in Chapter Seven. The organisations recreated civic engagement in decision making in micro-ways, as well as opportunities to increase a sense of individual and civic responsibility. The progressive alienation of citizens from the structures of representative democracy is well documented and lamented (Richardson, 2005a). Given this, these forms of participatory democracy were valuable steps in trying to re-engage people at the bottom, particularly in areas that were the most vulnerable to residents questioning authorities. Direct democracy operates at a small group level. The small size of the community groups, and their informal nature and ways of operating, shown from the inside in Chapter Six, were essential in generating this sense of control. But more importantly it was their relationships with the wider community, detailed in Chapter Seven, which created spaces for discussion and negotiation. The groups' operation of participatory democracy did not work often enough in harmony with the structures of representative democracy. The groups were potential vehicles for participatory democracy, ideally sitting alongside complementary models of local democracy and local leadership.

6 The legitimacy of community groups was questioned by many other bodies and often misunderstood

Only a self-selecting minority got actively involved in community self-help organising, anywhere between 1% and 21% of the national population, with the lower levels of activity found in poor neighbourhoods, as we examined in Chapter Eight. The small numbers involved led to the legitimacy of community action, groups and volunteers being extremely controversial for the groups and across the UK. There was no common understanding of what being representative might mean in practice. The basis for the legitimacy of community groups was commonly misunderstood in a free-for-all barrage of criticism from other community groups, local authorities, social landlords, other mainstream service providers, academic commentators, policy makers and other residents. The central charge was that community groups were not truly 'representative' in either an electoral or statistical sense.

It was the case that the groups had to negotiate complex and ambiguous relationships with their constituencies, with their own users, and the wider community, as we saw in Chapter Seven. Active organisers had passive support from the wider community.

We argued in Chapter Seven that electoral representativeness was inappropriate for the relationships between groups and the wider population in many situations of participatory democracy. This was not least because it pitted community volunteers against local elected members in an unhelpful way. We argued that other methods of getting 'representativeness', such as ensuring statistical representativeness, were the responsibility of the organisations doing the consulting, rather than the groups – the consultees. There are situations which are better informed by people with direct grass-roots experience rather than by a statistical sample. 'From the horse's mouth' is a powerful and convincing way to get a message over. 'Representatives' offering powerful personal experiences to illuminate policy decisions could be sought out and nurtured. We contended that this was the responsibility of mainstream organisations wanting to be informed by users, consumers or residents, and not the groups' responsibility.

In Chapter Seven we sketched out alternative grounds for judging the groups' legitimacy. Despite sometimes ambivalent and conflictual relationships with the wider community, the positive signs of backing for the groups were also very much in evidence. The groups used common sense indicators to gauge how the wider population felt about their work. The weakest form of this was an absence of criticism.

There were two sets of measures of the accountability and legitimacy of the groups. The first was about the groups' direct or informal relationships with other people in their neighbourhoods: services the groups provided; informal advice; help with fundraising; lack of vandalism or criticism; and consultation. The second set of measures was about the groups' relationships with external bodies or externally imposed criteria: they were open to scrutiny and the groups had positive approaches to promoting diversity.

Where groups were organising activities and services, attendance at activities and usage of services should be the primary measures of the groups' appropriateness to perform these tasks. Where the group was lobbying on behalf of other residents, their legitimacy was based on their organising role. The groups' community self-help activities were demonstrable forms of proof that they had some legitimacy and standing in the wider community. Reasonable usage of facilities or attendance at events was a good 'ready reckoner' of the groups' credibility and organisational ability. The groups were worth listening to because they had relationships with the wider community through their activities. Building these relationships was the responsibility of the groups.

The ways that the groups engaged with their wider communities suited their small size, their informal nature and their modest and practical goals. Establishing informal activities was a way of establishing links, demonstrating credibility and gaining experience of implementation. Methods of accountability varied within the community sector by size of organisation. Modest-sized groups, like the ones in the study, made up over half of the voluntary sector. Their accountability could be summed up as 'accountability through tea and toast'. Larger, more complex organisations faced the challenge of becoming too distant from the community. Accountability for these organisations needs to be adapted to suit.

The groups were keen to be externally scrutinised and recognised as part of their desire to be seen as performing a legitimate function. In Chapter Seven we found that the groups had welcomed all 'races' and cultures in their work where it was immediately relevant.

7 Community organising is strong, yet fragile

The groups in the study showed their many strengths. Where successful, they had a philosophy of collaboration and cooperative problem solving, rather than 'old-school them-and-us' confrontation. They emphasised the need for a clear organisational vision, strong leadership, inclusivity and a proactive outlook, as we saw in Chapter Six. They followed blueprints for 'high performance organisations' as outlined by many management 'gurus', despite not having read this literature.

These were voluntary groups of individuals held together by their own motivation, shared vision and common sense of purpose rather than primarily through formal structures or the framework of paid employment. As described in Chapter Six, where successful, the groups developed their shared vision through discussion and they negotiated differences, despite many internal battles. They tried to treat all members equally and to help members develop. They created organisational systems from scratch to order their work, prevent fraudulent behaviour and enhance a team-working environment. They prided themselves on being forward and outward-looking, with strong cost-saving entrepreneurship. The examples we gave of their work in Chapter Four show that they had the organisational strength to deliver and do things they had never done before.

At the same time, the groups were fragile in many ways, seen in the evidence in Chapters Six and Eight of weaknesses, lack of experience and confidence, and other barriers. Internal difficulties included the fact that members were self-selecting and brought whatever skills they happened to have, which resulted in skills gaps. Even though the organisers had many skills and abilities, they themselves identified weaknesses such as handling paperwork. The groups had to have a strong bond to work together. But in any organisation there are rows, power struggles and disputes over who is in charge. Where roles are allocated by agreement there is always potential for conflict over leadership roles. There were also questions about how to ensure delivery without being able to tell volunteers what to do, unlike managers of paid staff in other organisations.

In a few cases the groups suffered from high turnover of members, sometimes made worse by domineering leaders. The lack of other people coming forward to shoulder some of the burdens, coupled with obstacles from outside agencies, could result in frustration, stress and burnout of volunteers. Funding problems were not just about a lack of available funding, but nevertheless groups wrestled with financial sustainability. In Chapter Six the groups could be seen doing fundraising for the costs of basic organising, such as refreshments, photocopying and venue costs. Some of their activities were self-funding, like social events. But the groups lacked funding for some aspects of their work, such as subsidising ongoing activities for people on low incomes, or for improvements to communal spaces, as seen in Chapter Eight.

We explored segmentation within the community and voluntary sector. Income generation is extremely concentrated, with 2% of the voluntary sector generating two thirds of the total sector income in 2003/04 (NCVO, 2006a). As we understood from Chapters Two and Eight, at least half of the voluntary and community sector is made up of small groups like those in the study. Our own failed experiment, revealed in Chapter Eight, designed to 'speed up' some of the groups' progress also signalled that groups go at their own pace, in their own direction. All of this argues against an instrumental view of the community sector based on what policy makers and lobbyists would like the sector to do, rather than what it does actually do. It argues for a recognition of what the groups offer based on how things are in reality for this massive part of the sector. As depicted in Chapter Four, the groups did many amazing things, but not necessarily to the level of contract service delivery.

So, based on the barriers and obstacles to the groups' work from Chapter Eight, what we know about size and scale of organisations from Chapter Two, the informal way they work from Chapter Six, the scope and limits of what they do in Chapter Four, the internal issues and weaknesses from Chapter Six, and lack of desire in many cases to expand from other research (Chapman et al, 2006), we get some strong clues about what could be appropriate roles for the sector. We argued again in Chapter Eight that there was a danger that what community self-help at this informal scale could offer would be lost.

One factor that undermined the groups was their lack of official status, recognition, credit or reward, both from within the community and from outside bodies. An illustration of this was the groups' positive reactions to the research visit, which they saw as validation of their existence. The majority of the volunteers did not have high levels of formal education, or other commonly used bases for personal credibility. The groups sat outside formal structures; many were formed to directly counter them. They were unusual in the local context; not many people were doing similar things. Their work often felt like a thankless task, as we saw in Chapter Eight. Successful groups in the study had won external backing to overcome their feelings of isolation and being on the margins of larger-scale regeneration work.

One solution touted as a reward for volunteering was payment for volunteers' contributions. We showed in Chapter Eight that the issue of payment for volunteers was still highly controversial, possibly counterproductive and unpalatable to many community volunteers. The benefits of volunteering as seen by the community volunteers in the study and volunteers in other research focused on fun and friendship rather than financial reward, although the fun people derived from unpaid community work was often neglected in explanations of why people volunteered. Recognition in non-monetary ways was important to the groups. The Gatsby Project held an annual celebration party to congratulate the groups on their successes, commiserate and support any blockages, and bring groups together to overcome feelings of isolation.

As discussed above community volunteers were inappropriately criticised for being unrepresentative. Community asset ownership, service delivery and budget control options for residents being floated in government policy all resulted in a need for and competition over a small pool of active residents. It seems unfair and ironic that authorities and agencies carp on about a lack of citizen involvement while being unwelcoming to those that do bother to turn up. One pejorative term for the minority of active volunteers is 'the usual suspects'. This is illustrative of the lack of recognition and championing of community volunteers we have pointed to. Our work suggests that an alternative way of describing these people is 'gold dust'.

Community organising is boosted by community development supports

New volunteers were put in a situation of doing something they had never done before, and even organisations with a track record were disadvantaged by lack of experience when it came to new activities. Doing something new and unknown even for skilled or experienced people is a challenge. The groups described their initial nervousness and lack of confidence. Over and above that, the projects they undertook required new technical knowledge, for example, what would a good business plan look like? What were the laws on child protection? When was the best time to plant the garden? How much would it cost to refurbish a building? How did the local authority work? What were current government policies and funding streams?

As detailed in Chapter Eight, nearly all of the groups interviewed and three fifths of the wider pool of groups surveyed had had some form of external community development support in addition to the Gatsby Project. However, not all of the help they received was of an adequate standard, and levels and sources of help were extremely dependent on locality. The landscape of community development that we saw, sometimes called the community infrastructure (Skinner, 1997), showed patchy and uneven levels and quality of provision, as outlined in Chapter Eight.

However, we note that it is unclear whether significant new activity to underpin the community infrastructure is producing results, or targeting appropriate groups and activities. Policy may be targeting resources on a small segment of the community sector rather than the majority. Our work suggests that policy aims are overly ambitious for the majority of the sector who may not benefit from community capacity building.

Our own findings from the Gatsby Training and Small Grant Project programmes were that demand for information, inspiration, skills and networking was higher than for grant funding from small informal groups. We found that one-off investment of small amounts helped groups with specific activities, but they wanted and needed longer-term ongoing help in addition. Our work at the national level complemented community capacity building work at a local or regional level, it added something different, but it was diminished when forced to substitute for a lack of local input.

Conclusion and recommendations – a community-building framework

In this chapter we placed the work briefly in the historical context of the continual renegotiation of relationships between the state and society. We offered definitions of 'community' and 'social exclusion' that help us understand why residents felt their community activity was making a valuable contribution towards improving deprived neighbourhoods, and the lot of the people that lived there.

We then put forward seven lessons based on the Gatsby research, arguing that:

- problems of achieving neighbourhood renewal and social inclusion are about more than poverty, and economic success cannot compensate for neighbourhood disorder;
- neighbourhoods and communities matter to people;
- self-help in all forms is at the base of community building, both individual and collective forms of self-help;

- in particular, community self-help solutions are positive human responses to difficult situations by the minority that produce benefits for the majority;
- community self-help in poor communities provides triple benefits in improving mainstream services, in generating neighbourhood renewal and reviving democracy, and these benefits are not widely enough championed in this complex set of tasks;
- the legitimacy of community groups engaged in community self-help was questioned by many other bodies, and often misunderstood;
- community action is strong, yet fragile, and is boosted by community development supports.

The Gatsby Project started with the 'million dollar' question – what would you do if you had, say, one million pounds to help combat social exclusion in needy communities? The results of our work demonstrate that investing in community self-help can unlock people's desire and potential to solve community problems, and that their DIY community action has a critical role to play in community building.

The fabric of neighbourhood life is woven from small deeds, informal neighbourhood contact, local activity and local services. Having people in precarious communities to keep these almost invisible channels open is central to the wider community. The work done by the community groups in the study often went unnoticed, and was often poorly recognised. This is not just because of its small scale, but also because it could be hand to mouth, poorly presented, or even unrecognisable to bigger organisations. This does not take away from the intrinsic value or community action and the community benefit it gave. If anything, it helps to explain the strong desire that people feel to organise themselves at a level below that of official structures, no matter how low or lowly. It is at this level that the most nebulous and yet most lasting of our social life-support systems operates – that catch-all of local well-being: community. The Gatsby groups help to explain why it is important, and possible, to validate the efforts that people make to help themselves.

Based on what we have argued so far in this chapter, our conclusion is to put forward a framework for community building. This framework could enhance the scope for self-help for individuals and groups across the board. In the framework community building is a broad set of actions, rather than a narrow one. It includes improving places and services, enhancing civic responsibility, strengthening social relationships, increasing community involvement, as well as (but not limited to) facilitating community self-help and the work of community groups.

Community-building framework

1 Good quality services and the management of neighbourhoods

Social inclusion is about giving people access to good quality environments and services, as well as social supports. Viable communities, as seen by residents, are additionally about maintaining standards of behaviour and informal social controls. Because of this, the first priority for a community-building framework is to deliver good quality neighbourhood services and to manage neighbourhoods to reduce the impact of neighbourhood problems. Any policy that affects the configuration of neighbourhoods – what they look like, how they are run, what services they have and who lives there – will have knock-on impacts on the viability of that community. This is community building, in the sense of improving places and the services supplied to places.

How could this facilitate self-help? We saw in Chapter Five that if institutions and mainstream service providers did more then people could be spurred to do more. Quality services and places can offer a sympathetic environment for people to exercise their own agency and help themselves as individuals and families without having to fight against disorganised neighbourhood conditions that work against people making the best that they can of their lives. As we have seen, people in well-managed, orderly, better-off areas are more likely to be civically engaged.

2 Civic engagement, democratic renewal and local accountability

Despite the many positive trends and results in improved public service delivery discussed in Chapter Three, there is still some way to go to get all local authorities and service providers to be truly responsive to their clients:

> 'The neighbourhood management idea for me personally is about how to get big organisations that have forgotten the importance of the customer or the citizen to be more responsive. The voice of the citizen in reality is the weakest. So if we want to respond [to service delivery problems] how do we increase the voice of the citizen.' (Joe Montgomery, Director General, Tackling Disadvantage Group, DCLG, speaking at the Community Action and Neighbourhood Management Think Tank, Trafford Hall, Chester, 20 May 2003)

We saw in Chapter Eight that the majority of citizens do not get actively involved. Therefore, more effective mechanisms are needed to hold authorities and public services accountable to the majority. We need smarter ways to allow the 98% who do not get actively involved to exercise some control or influence over decisions that affect their lives.

Therefore, the second strand for a community-building policy is to engage as many residents as possible in decisions that affect local neighbourhoods and hold services accountable.

3 Stable communities, strong communities

Community engagement is about more than communities being involved with agencies. It is also about the community engaging with itself. Social networks and social responsibilities are the third strand of the community-building framework. This is about building communities in the sense of increasing civic responsibility and strengthening social relationships. We have argued in this book for a renegotiation of the relationship between the state and the individual to allow people more responsibility for their behaviour and lives. Strengthening civic responsibility could prevent people 'helping' themselves in ways damaging to others. Strengthening relationships allows people to help each other out informally through mutual aid.

4 Community self-help

The fourth and final strand of the community-building framework is about informal community-run groups and projects, such as the groups in the study. This strand involves the community engaging with itself and with agencies, through the intermediary of micro-community organisations. The minority who do get involved in community self-help – the 'gold dust' – could be facilitated to achieve the most they can and provide benefits for the wider community.

Recommendations for community building

Finally, we present our recommendations for a community-building strategy, based on the framework for community building.

1 Good quality services and the management of neighbourhoods

The residents in the study were angry at past and present failures in service delivery to low-income neighbourhoods. The prospects for improving service delivery and the management of neighbourhoods in disadvantaged areas look better, but there are still serious gaps and challenges.

Seeing and feeling change: the legacy of poor quality service delivery exerts a powerful effect on people's perceptions of improvement in the work of local authorities in particular, and possibilities of positive change. A perception that things are not getting better, against a long history of public sector underperformance, can undermine the scope for self-help. For example, people weighing up whether to improve their own home in small ways may factor into their decision how the neighbourhood is improving, or not. People can feel overwhelmed and demotivated in their personal lives by poor quality surroundings they feel nobody is in charge of (Mumford and Power, 2003).

> **Recommendations**
>
> - Local government, service providers and social landlords should make sure residents in low-income neighbourhoods see and feel that services are improving, rather than focusing just on internal performance targets. Public bodies need to do psychological as well as physical regeneration.
> - Small visible neighbourhood improvements – quick wins – can help create a sense of change and should be more widely used. Frontline staff are critical to communicating with residents, and could be better harnessed.

Local systems for public service improvement and innovation: recently public service improvement has been driven by regulation from central government. Service users and residents have tended to be left out of performance management and improvement systems, as have frontline staff. With central government easing off on regulation, one idea is to hand over the baton to local people to keep local authorities and others on track. The idea is that if local authorities genuinely listen to local people then this will ensure quality services and good management of neighbourhoods. There are many ideas about how this might be done, for example in the 2006 local government White Paper (DCLG, 2006), but the way forward is still far from clear.

The challenges include figuring out how decision making can be devolved to frontline staff to enable them to design and implement day-to-day innovations and be problem solvers. How can organisational leaderships generate ideas for improvement from the grass roots, and how can ideas from frontline staff and service users be properly captured? How can change and innovation driven by corporate centres link to neighbourhood decision-making structures and residents' views? How can residents be more involved in developing innovative solutions as well as identifying areas for improvement?

> **Recommendations**
>
> - Public agencies must tackle the challenges of involving residents in developing locally driven systems and structures that keep service providers accountable and improving. Central government can encourage this to happen through policy.
> - Neighbourhood structures with devolved decision making are a crucial part of local accountability and devolution could go much further than current forms.
> - Local review systems should maximise innovative thinking by offering space for residents and frontline staff to solve problems in ways that have not happened so far.

Changing behaviour: behaviour change is sometimes called co-production of public services (Parker and Gallagher, 2007). Co-production simply means citizens playing their part to produce desired outcomes such as a safe, healthy, educated and happy population. It is complex and difficult to change the behaviour of individuals and families, which was illustrated by some of the brave attempts to do this by a few of the community groups in the study. This is doubly true for public bodies with different sorts of relationships with residents and service users. There is a task to be done by local and central government to frame the context for altered individual, family and community responses. To date work on behaviour change by public services has been patchy and even contradictory. Some public services feel nervous talking about behaviour change because they see it as telling people what to do. We see it differently. We have discussed the same thing in this book using the concept of people's agency, or their ability to engage in self-help. In the context of the framework for community building, promoting behaviour change is about enhancing the scope for self-help for individuals by encouraging people to take more control over their lives in a positive way.

Recommendations

- Public agencies need to understand more about how people can change their behaviour and lifestyle to encourage people to take more control over their lives in a positive way. Public bodies should not be frightened of grasping the nettle on this agenda.
- Both residents' groups and public bodies, including local government, could facilitate behaviour change if more sophisticated approaches to persuading people are used.

2 Civic engagement, democratic renewal and local accountability

The engagement of citizens is taking off in importance for the renewal and strengthening of democracy at a fundamental level. Things look very different now than they did for the community groups in the past, when influencing decisions often meant placards and petitions and angry shouting. Now complaints are invited, and comments welcomed in specially designed accessible systems. However, there are still many issues to resolve before we can truly say that there is effective democratic renewal and local accountability. There is a clear gap between our raised expectations for citizen engagement and influence, and the reality.

Appreciating active volunteers: practitioners who are consulting residents are very often concerned that their consultees are representative, that there is widespread involvement, and that involvement can be sustained. Resident activists like those in the study felt exposed, vulnerable to criticism and overcommitted where there was not widespread community involvement. Residents and agencies face a joint problem. Therefore, ensuring good quality community involvement is a shared concern for both resident representatives and services alike. This offers a potentially strong shared agenda on which to do things differently. Accepting and valuing those who are willing to put themselves forward on whatever basis is the first step. We should thank people for taking responsibility for what they feel passionate about as part of our effort to promote self-help.

Recommendations

- Everyone committed to community engagement should appreciate the value of the small number of active volunteers that do come forward, seeing 'the usual suspects' instead as 'gold dust'.
- Organisations should use appropriate criteria (for example as outlined in this book in Box 7.2 (p 177)) to assess the legitimacy of existing members of neighbourhood groups. Individuals who are not members of organisations should be welcomed as offering useful first-hand experiences, and as people who speak on their own behalf for our illumination.
- Active volunteers could be supported so the 'gold dust' does not get tarnished, for example through celebrations, training and awards.

New definitions of accountability: new understandings of accountability and legitimacy would mean respecting the mandates of all stakeholders – residents, local politicians, professionals and national politicians. This could allow all parties to contribute and problem solve. Recognising different forms of local accountability would also allow each group to exercise their capacity for self-help – the core goal of the framework.

Recommendations

- Public bodies – local and national – need to take responsibility for making sure that involvement processes are representative of different people's views. Other bodies should stop asking community volunteers to prove their 'representativeness'.
- Agencies should develop a more sophisticated understanding of different forms of accountability and legitimacy. Agencies must respect the claims of all the different groups (for example, as outlined in this book in Table 7.3 (pp 194–5) if all parties are to contribute to making neighbourhoods better.

Having more two-way conversations, finding 'smart' forms of engagement: consultation is a relatively passive form of one-way involvement and does not mean an increase in active and effective citizen influence or genuine dialogue. Deliberative engagement – or deliberation – is participation that involves a dialogue, that is, a two-way conversation; it involves educating each other as to the facts, the background, the possibilities and the constraints. It is a process that happens over a period of time.

The essential problem is that the ways we currently do deliberation tend to limit the number of people who get involved. We demand a very high level of commitment from people, meaning only a few end up doing it. So far we have recommended valuing those who come forward and improving the range of people who are brought forward in small numbers into involvement structures. The next step is to increase the actual numbers involved and influencing decisions.

Recommendations

- Public bodies should find new ways to dramatically increase the numbers of people involved in two-way conversations to make decisions.
- We need to have a better understanding of who the 98% are who do not volunteer, what would most appeal to them and where they are best reached.
- We need to try out many new forms of deliberative engagement to see what works.

Starting where people are at: co-option of the involvement agenda by public bodies is without doubt a good thing, as decision making is opened up and made more transparent. However, one danger is that co-option has at times negatively transformed opportunities for engagement into leaden-footed bureaucratic exercises that display a typical or classic bureaucratic obsession with their own interests rather than what people are really bothered about. In some places consultation and involvement are almost too popular, with some local authorities running over 100 different individual consultation exercises simultaneously. In the midst of this level of activity, residents continue to feel that they do not get listened to. One crude reason for this is that consultation is sometimes done badly, is based around public bodies' needs, and does not relate to people's real concerns.

Recommendations

- Anyone doing engagement should start where people are at, and relate to residents' priorities not those of organisations.
- Consultation and engagement should be better linked to action, and residents should be told what has happened as a result of their involvement.

3 Stable communities, strong communities

We have shown that community matters to people across income groups in the UK. This continues to be true despite many widespread changes to the way that society operates and communicates (Kitchen et al, 2006a, 2006b). However, there are still outstanding challenges to strengthen and stabilise communities. More people want a strong community feeling than have one. Levels of community strength are lower in less well-off places than better-off places. Areas traditionally seen as socially fragmented and individualistic like suburban neighbourhoods are more together than in deprived neighbourhoods. Levels of trust and togetherness are undermined by anti-social behaviour. It is hard to see how people can be forced to be friends by public bodies and landlords.

Bolstering trust and tackling anti-social behaviour in less well-off places: people's sense of belonging to their neighbourhood is similar regardless of income (Kitchen et al, 2006b). But places where people have more contact with each other are places where people trust each other less (Pennant, 2005). While this may be an example of 'what you don't know doesn't hurt you', it is also a rather sad statistic that hints at problems of informal social control in less well-off places.

One of the issues undermining levels of trust and togetherness in disadvantaged places is high levels of concern about anti-social behaviour. Other research has shown that people's obvious commitment to their neighbourhood and friendly contact with neighbours is not enough by itself to change their behaviour to protect that neighbourhood (Wilson, 1987; Sampson, 2004). The underlying conditions of law and order and management of neighbourhoods need to be in place before people can make their contribution to tackling anti-social behaviour. 'Civic absence', that is, lack of attention by services, no visible presence on the estate, awkward conditions for communicating with authorities and poor response times, appears to diminish the neighbourly response to incivilities (Richardson, 2006).

Recommendations

- Public agencies can help lower-income communities trust each other more, feel less beleaguered, and do more to tackle anti-social behaviour by being more visible and more responsive.
- Public bodies and landlords could put in place more effective ways for residents to support agencies by reporting anti-social behaviour.

Creating more community spirit: there are gaps between how much community people have, and how much they would like. In these cases, the challenge is to find ways to increase a sense of community and also social networks. It is not easy to socially engineer these things. Our community groups' attempts to forge bonds through communal participation in social activities, to link people in, to form mutual aid networks, to increase associational memberships and to set models of behaviour, are just part of the picture. It is more than likely that people will continue to form their own informal networks and small associations as they always have done in a more organic way. It can be hard to see how central government, local authorities or other agencies can force people to be friends or to get on with each other. But there is interest in trying to do this. There are many possibilities for ways that organisations can nurture the development of social networks.

It is telling that social networks and strong communities are very often at the margins of public agencies' activities, but some of the issues that professionals understand have a direct and serious impact on their work, for example in the case of anti-social behaviour. If we are to take the stability or strength of communities seriously, then we need to look at the unintended consequences of policies where they could damage social networks. For example, should priority be given to families of existing residents to live nearby? How can housing redevelopment be managed to protect existing social networks?

Recommendations

- Residents, authorities and landlords could offer new ways to create a stronger sense of community spirit where people want more. This might include schemes for creating friendship networks and meeting points in communal spaces.
- Celebrations and social events are potentially useful tools that local public agencies can use to help people rub along together better. They should not be dismissed as marginal activities.
- Researchers and others with an interest in community building need to persuade others of the benefits of social networks. Public and voluntary bodies need to take responsibility for building social networks as a core activity.
- Residents, politicians and professionals living and working in neighbourhoods need to have more discussion about the unintended consequences of policies where they damage the stability or strength of communities. We need to find ways of people 'getting on' without 'getting out'.

4 Community self-help

For many years the voluntary and community sectors argued for recognition of their role and activity by governments and others. Unfortunately, the heightened profile for community and voluntary groups in policy has had some unwelcome and inappropriate strings attached. Offers to take on delivery of public services on a bigger scale fit uncomfortably with how and why the community sector operates. It is not a surprise that central government and political parties have an instrumental agenda attached to its support for the sectors. But it is crucial that the 'gold dust' of community organisers doing bread-and-butter work should not be lost in a rush to offer voluntary and community organisations a bigger role as deliverers of public services.

But for those that do want to take on a bigger role, there could be an acceleration of capacity. Changing public sector procurement systems is the flipside of the coin. There is recognition of the need to change the way that councils and others procure, or buy in, services. The way that public bodies currently tender out services for others to deliver is not sympathetic to the voluntary and community sector.

Accelerating local capacity to deliver public services: how do we increase third sector capacity to take on public service contracts? One approach that has been tried, and has failed, is to try to shoehorn existing organisations in particular areas into the right mould. Our own brief attempts within the bigger Gatsby Project to jump-start small groups into playing a much broader role did not fulfil our hopes. We fatally ignored the reality of the groups we were working with. There is what we call a 'linear fallacy' in thinking about the growth of community organisations, which is that small organisations will move in a straight line from small to big, from one activity to more strategic activities. The idea that expansion will occur naturally is not correct for many groups. Small organisations may remain small organisations, just doing what they want to do.

An alternative complementary model is the 'accelerator' model. Here, established community-based and led third sector organisations would set up, or become involved in, projects away from their home base. This could happen on a similar basis to private sector franchising operations. For the local community sector to welcome in 'outsiders', this approach would need to be firmly based on consensus and local control to ensure local capacity was also built up.

There is still a long way to go as local authorities and other public bodies start the long and complex job of reassessing and redesigning their systems. Some current attempts to open up procurement to the third sector seem well intentioned but restrictive, and likely to result in a narrowing of opportunities, not a widening. There are counter-pressures on local government as public spending constraints get tougher.

Recommendations

- Local government should adapt public sector procurement systems to encourage bids from the third sector, and measure whether this has taken place.
- The 'linear fallacy' needs to be challenged.
- Central and local government should use an 'accelerator' model to grow local social enterprises to deliver public services, where existing social enterprises franchise operations away from their home base. This should replace the current approach of shoehorning existing organisations in particular areas into the right mould.

Offering more support for small community groups: the groups in the study may have been entrepreneurial but they, and many other voluntary organisations, were neither ready, capable nor willing to take on the role of delivering public services under contract. The case for more support for small community organisations for their basic day-to-day non-income-generating community activity is clear. The organisations in the study found ongoing funding for basic running costs extremely hard to get. However, it is very unclear whose responsibility it is to provide backing for small-scale community activity.

Grants from charitable trusts are a mainstay for community organisations and those providing support for the sector. However, charitable trusts should not be left holding the ring for what is essentially an open-ended commitment to this vital community-building work. We now urgently need to agree a way forward about how bread-and-butter community work is supported and funded. The way forward cannot leave charitable trusts to pick up the tab, nor be the sole responsibility of national or local government.

Recommendations

- All stakeholders – central government, local government, charitable trusts – should take responsibility for offering small grants and other forms of support for small community groups. This must include basic running costs for bread-and-butter community work.

Providing a wider range of forms of support, and bringing people together nationally: if support is offered by central government, local government and/or charitable trusts, what form should that support take? One argument is that community groups need more grants. We are not arguing against more small and large grant schemes for community projects, but there are two riders to this argument: cash needs to be given in the right way for small organisations, but cash alone is not sufficient. The work found that capacity building is as important as cash resources for embryonic community organisations.

Residential training, like that in the Gatsby Project, complements local support through providing unique opportunities for inspiration, confidence boosting, network building, practical ideas gathering and team building for community groups. The importance of confidence boosting and recognition is vital. Residential training helps to make the often 'thankless task' of community volunteers more rewarding and productive.

A national programme gives a sense of a nationwide groundswell of active people united in common purpose. Participants told us how much they liked meeting other people 'in the same boat' because this helped overcome their feelings of isolation. They felt validated and re-motivated in what they were trying to do through feeling part of something bigger. The core idea of a national centre dedicated to training and support for community organisers and others working in low-income neighbourhoods was unique, and raises the game of community action more generally.

National support services are moving towards being virtual and internet-based. While this is all to the good, the risk is that the benefits of face-to-face national programmes will be lost.

However, residential training courses are just one form of community development support. Going away to learn is not for everyone – training is not always what is needed. Many groups found it difficult to access the type of community development supports that they ideally needed – residential training should be used as a complementary resource to local and other specialist help. Other forms of capacity building could include local training, help with premises and equipment, shadowing, study visits, mentoring, consultancy help, local ongoing community development work, paid project staff, tailored advice and information.

> **Recommendations**
> - Access to funding for start-up groups is helped by the funder and the applicants having a face-to-face, developmental relationship.
> - Between all of the supporters of community activity there should be a wide range of forms of support. More forms of capacity building need to be offered that cater for organisations of different sizes.
> - Support should include bringing people together face-to-face across the country in national programmes that reward volunteers, share experience, generate new ideas, create a groundswell and help people feel validated and re-motivated.

Summary of recommendations

Good quality services and the management of neighbourhoods

Seeing and feeling change

- Local government, service providers and social landlords should make sure residents in low-income neighbourhoods see and feel that services are improving, rather than focusing just on internal performance targets. Public bodies need to do psychological as well as physical regeneration.
- Small visible neighbourhood improvements – quick wins – can help create a sense of change and should be more widely used. Frontline staff are critical to communicating with residents, and could be better harnessed.

Local systems for public service improvement and innovation

- Public agencies must tackle the challenges of involving residents in developing locally driven systems and structures that keep service providers accountable and improving. Central government can encourage this to happen through policy.
- Neighbourhood structures with devolved decision making are a crucial part of local accountability and devolution could go much further than current forms.
- Local review systems should maximise innovative thinking by offering space for residents and frontline staff to solve problems in ways that have not happened so far.

Changing behaviour

- Public agencies need to understand more about how people can change their behaviour and lifestyle to encourage people to take more control over their lives in a positive way. Public bodies should not be frightened of grasping the nettle on this agenda.

- Both residents' groups and public bodies, including local government, could facilitate behaviour change if more sophisticated approaches to persuading people were used.

Civic engagement, democratic renewal and local accountability

Appreciating active volunteers

- Everyone committed to community engagement should appreciate the value of the small number of active volunteers that do come forward, seeing 'the usual suspects' instead as 'gold dust'.
- Organisations should use appropriate criteria (for example, as outlined in this book in Box 7.2 (p 177) to assess the legitimacy of existing members of neighbourhood groups. Individuals who are not members of organisations should be welcomed as offering useful first-hand experiences, and as people who speak on their own behalf for our illumination.
- Active volunteers could be supported so the 'gold dust' does not get tarnished, for example through celebrations, training and awards.

New definitions of accountability

- Public bodies – local and national – need to take responsibility for making sure that involvement processes are representative of different people's views. Other bodies should stop asking community volunteers to prove their 'representativeness'.
- Agencies should develop a more sophisticated understanding of different forms of accountability and legitimacy. Agencies must respect the claims of all the different groups (for example as outlined in this book in Table 7.3 (pp 194–5) if all parties are to contribute to making neighbourhoods better.

Having more two-way conversations, finding 'smart' forms of engagement

- Public bodies should find new ways to dramatically increase the numbers of people involved in two-way conversations to make decisions.
- We need to have a better understanding of who the 98% are who do not volunteer, what would most appeal to them and where they are best reached.
- We need to try out many new forms of deliberative engagement to see what works.

Starting where people are at

- Anyone doing engagement should start where people are at, and relate to residents' priorities not those of organisations.

- Consultation and engagement should be better linked to action, and residents should be told what has happened as a result of their involvement.

Stable communities, strong communities

Bolstering trust and tackling anti-social behaviour in less well-off places

- Public agencies can help lower-income communities trust each other more, feel less beleaguered, and do more to tackle anti-social behaviour by being more visible and more responsive.
- Public bodies and landlords could put in place more effective ways for residents to support agencies by reporting anti-social behaviour.

Creating more community spirit

- Residents, authorities and landlords could offer new ways to create a stronger sense of community spirit where people want more. This might include schemes for creating friendship networks and meeting points in communal spaces.
- Celebrations and social events are potentially useful tools that local public agencies can use to help people rub along together better. They should not be dismissed as marginal activities.
- Researchers and others with an interest in community building need to persuade others of the benefits of social networks. Public and voluntary bodies need to take responsibility for building social networks as a core activity.
- Residents, politicians and professionals living and working in neighbourhoods need to have more discussion about the unintended consequences of policies where they damage the stability or strength of communities. We need to find ways of people 'getting on' without 'getting out'.

Community self-help

Accelerating local capacity to deliver public services

- Local government should adapt public sector procurement systems to encourage bids from the third sector, and measure whether this has taken place.
- The 'linear fallacy' needs to be challenged.
- Central and local government should use an 'accelerator' model to grow local social enterprises to deliver public services, where existing social enterprises franchise operations away from their home base. This should replace the current approach of shoehorning existing organisations in particular areas into the right mould.

Offering more support for small community groups

- All stakeholders – central government, local government, charitable trusts – should take responsibility for offering small grants and other forms of support for small community groups. This must include basic running costs for bread-and-butter community work.

Providing a wider range of forms of support, and bringing people together nationally

- Access to funding for start-up groups is helped by the funder and the applicants having a face-to-face, developmental relationship.
- Between all of the supporters of community activity there should be a wide range of forms of support. More forms of capacity building need to be offered that cater for organisations of different sizes.
- Support should include bringing people together face-to-face across the country in national programmes that reward volunteers, share experience, generate new ideas, create a groundswell and help people feel validated and re-motivated.

The Gatsby Project: further details

Training courses

The residential training courses covered practical 'How To' subjects, such as how to work with young people, how to improve environments, and how to run community facilities (see Table A1). The training was interactive, and open to residents and community volunteers across the UK. It had a strong focus on doable ideas, hands-on learning and action planning. The training was advertised widely through local authorities, community development networks and networks of community organisations. Each course ran for two or three days, facilitated by specialist trainers from the field. There were 20-25 training places on each course. A handful of community volunteers from the same community group usually came together. There were up to 12 different groups from different neighbourhoods on each course, which meant that participants could share experiences and learn from each other. Bursaries to cover the cost of the course and accommodation were provided for unfunded groups.

In the first five-year period, there were (on average) 18 training courses a year, involving up to 400 people from over 100 different community organisations. In total, over five years, 1,800 community volunteers from over 700 different small community groups attended 93 Gatsby courses. They came from a wide range of areas of England, Scotland and Wales. Two thirds were women, and a quarter were under 35 years old. Most (75%) were from areas of social housing and 8% were from minority ethnic groups. Many of the 700 groups attended more than one course; 82% of participants received bursaries.

Small grant fund

Participants who attended training could apply for grants ranging from £50 to £5,000 towards a wide range of projects related to the training. After the groups completed a grant application form, there was a face-to-face grant assessment visit for all applications. The small grant fund supported projects like community centres, youth activities, community gardens, cafes, parents and toddlers groups, after-school clubs, fishing trips and advice sessions (see Table A2). The grant programme started in January 1997, 10 months after the trial training courses began. In the four years between January 1997 and the end of December 2000, 125 grant applications were processed, 90 of which were successful.

Table A1: Training courses, March 1996 to end February 2001

Themes	No. of courses	Course topics	Grant awards generated
Crime	22	• Community action to prevent crime • Crime and young people • Getting the Crime and Disorder Act working • Tackling drugs together • Mediation skills	15
Community enterprise	13	• Setting up community enterprises • Setting up LETS • Setting up community cafes • Setting up food cooperatives • Setting up resident services organisations • Local economic initiatives	13
Generic skills	13	• Entrepreneurial management skills • Voluntary committee skills • Business planning • Bookkeeping • Training for trainers • Publicity and presentation skills • Action planning skills • First aid	7
Environment	11	• Setting up community gardens • Growing ideas for your table • Developing recycling • Energy efficiency • Rescuing land and buildings	11
Fundraising skills	8	• Fundraising skills • Applying to the National Lotteries Charities Board • Money from trusts	10

One in five of the groups that attended training applied for a small grant. We gave 23 grants a year on average, close to the original target. While the maximum grant was £5,000, the average request was well under, at £3,500, and the average grant award was £2,800. Just over a quarter of the grant requests were for the maximum amount, and 16 awards were made for the full amount. There was an average time lag of seven months between groups attending training and applying for a grant. Half of the groups had been operating for over five years when they applied for a grant, but most of the specific project activity we supported was new.

Table A2 shows that the training courses generated related projects but the projects that came out of the courses were wide-ranging, for example the

Table A2: Examples of grant awards, March 1996 to end February 2001, by training theme

Training theme	Grant awards	Types of project	
Crime	15	Educational work with excluded pupils Advice and training centre Youth leisure and sports activities Neighbourhood Watch scheme	Children's play facility Older residents' housing Adult education group Play scheme Youth drop-in Youth cyber-cafe
Community enterprise	13	Community cafes Study visit (to cafe) Resident services organisation	Tenant management organisation Food cooperative LETS
Generic skills	7	Community house Mental health support group Minority ethnic involvement in regeneration Youth activities	Social activities for older residents Health support group Lunch club
Environment	11	Asian women's 'backyard' project Area-wide recycling project Community gardens Community buildings	Community allotment Cycling project Environmental workshops Outdoor space IT training rooms
Fundraising skills	10	Youth cafe and drop-in Cycling project Credit union Community garden Chinese lunch club	Welfare rights project IT training project Community centre Music studio Advice centre
Community facilities and events	11	Community centres Community garden Youth activities Tool bank After-school club	Youth house IT training project Multi-cultural buildings Family centre
Estate image	8	Vocational education and arts project Community house Youth club	Community forum and small grant fund Community newspaper

Training theme	Grant awards	Types of project	
Family and children	6	Parenting classes After-school club	Majorettes club Crèche
Youth	8	Youth fishing club Work with excluded pupils Educational arts work	A residents' association Young women's group Homework club
Housing plus	3	Set-up of a residents' association Cycling club	Social activities for older residents

community facilities courses sparked grant applications for projects to improve the physical environment such as a tool bank, a project to help educate young people through an after-school club and a youth house offering youth activities. Table A3 shows the grant-funded projects categorised by type of project, which shows that the biggest single category was projects relating to young people.

Types of community group

Forty-six of the 90 projects were delivered by groups set up between 1996 and 2000, the same period as the project was running. Another 28 of the grants were given to groups that had been set up a few years before the project started, between 1991 and 1995. Ten of the grants were to organisations that had been

Table A3: Types of grant-funded project in the study

Type of project	No. of projects	Rank
Youth projects	23	1
Multi-use community buildings	11	=2
Community enterprise	11	=2
Physical environment	8	4
Environmental	5	=5
Work with families	5	=5
Tenant involvement	5	=5
Publicity/information	5	=5
Children	4	=9
IT/adult learning	4	=9
Social events	4	=9
Advice	3	12
Crime prevention	2	13
Total	**90**	

set up between 1980 and 1990, up to 16 years before the project started. Three grants were to long-standing groups created before 1980.

Using average annual turnover as a crude indicator of size, 81% of the groups had annual turnovers of under £5,000: 34% under £1,000 and 47% between £1,000 and £5,000 (excluding the Gatsby grant).

In total, half the 82 groups were predominantly made up of people who were not working, mostly under retirement age: 10 were made up of mostly retired people and 17 leaders of the groups were people of retirement age. These older residents brought with them a background of useful practical and organisational skills. Nine of the 17 group leaders over the age of 65 had previously worked in blue-collar jobs, in particular as skilled manual workers. Fourteen of the groups (17%) were predominantly made up of volunteers who were in paid employment outside their voluntary work. These people performed their voluntary commitments on top of their paid work. Of these groups with volunteers in paid work, half were in fields of work loosely related to their voluntary activity, and half were in completely unrelated jobs. Sixteen (20%) of the groups' leaders were in paid work outside their voluntary work, such as nurses, school supervisors and cleaners. Another eight of the groups were made up of people in paid employment on the project, seven of which were all composed of ex-volunteers.

References

6, Perri (2004) 'Can government influence our friendships? The range and limits of tools for trying to shape solidarities', in C. Phillipson, G. Allan and D. Morgan (eds) *Social networks and social exclusion: Sociological and policy issues*, Aldershot and London: Ashgate, pp 180-204.

Aldbourne Associates (2001) *Implementing Best Value in housing and tenant participation compacts – The first year*, London: Office of the Deputy Prime Minister.

Aldridge, S. and Halpern, D. with Fitzpatrick, S. (2002) *Social capital: A discussion paper*, London: Cabinet Office.

ALG (Association of London Government) and GLE (Greater London Enterprises) (2003) *LSPs and neighbourhood renewal in London: The story so far ...*, London: ALG.

Almond, G.A. and Verba, S. (eds) (1963) *Civic culture: Political attitudes and democracy in five nations*, Princeton, NJ: Princeton University Press.

Amin, A. (2002) 'Ethnicity and the multicultural city: living with diversity', *Environment and Planning A*, vol 34, pp 959-80.

Anastacio, J., Hart, L., Keith, M., Mayo, M., Kowarzik, U. and Gidley, B. (2000) *Reflecting realities: Participants' perspectives on integrated communities and sustainable development*, Bristol: The Policy Press.

Ashworth, C. (2000) 'Changing cultures and shared ownership', *Local Economy*, vol 15, no 3, pp 256-61.

Aspden, J. and Birch, D. (2005) *New localism – Citizen engagement, neighbourhoods and public services: Evidence from local government*, London: Office of the Deputy Prime Minister.

Atkinson, A.B. (1998) 'Social exclusion, poverty and unemployment', in A.B. Atkinson and J. Hills (eds) *Exclusion, employment and opportunity*, CASEPaper 4, London: London School of Economics and Political Science.

Attwood, C., Singh, G., Prime, D., Creasey, R. et al (2003) *2001 Home Office Citizenship Survey: People, families and communities*, London: Home Office.

Audit Commission and IDeA (Improvement and Development Agency) Performance Management Measurement and Information (PMMI) Project (2005) *Interim findings from research into performance management in well-performing local authorities*, London: IDeA.

Audit Commission and The Housing Corporation (2004) *Housing: Improving services through resident involvement*, London: Audit Commission.

Babb, P. (2005) *Measurement of social capital in the UK*, London: Office for National Statistics.

Barber, M. (2003) 'Progress in public services', Presentation at Prime Minister's Press Conference, 10 Downing Street, London, 30 July.

Barber, M (2004) 'Progress in public services', Presentation at Prime Minister's Press Conference, 10 Downing Street, London, 22 July.

Barnes, M. (2005) *Power, participation and political renewal*, Swindon: ESRC.

Barnes, M., Stoker, G. and Whiteley, P. (2003a) *Developing civil renewal: Some lessons from research*, ESRC Seminar Series, Swindon: ESRC.

Barnes, M., Newman, J., Knops, A. and Sullivan, H. (2003b) 'Constituting the "public" in public participation', *Public Administration*, vol 81, no 2, pp 379-99.

Barr, A. and Taylor, P. (2007) *Better community engagement: A framework for learning*, Glasgow: Scottish Community Development Centre.

Barry, B. (2002) 'Social exclusion, social isolation and the distribution of income', in J. Hills, J. Le Grand and D. Piachaud (eds) *Understanding social exclusion*, Oxford: Oxford University Press.

Bastow, S., Beck, H., Dunleavy, P. and Richardson, E. (2007) 'The role of individual incentives within strategies promoting civil renewal', in T. Brannan, P. John and G. Stoker (eds) *Re-energising citizenship: Strategies for civil renewal*, Basingstoke: Macmillan.

Beck, H. and Richardson, E. (2004) *LSE evaluation of the Trafford Hall Making Things Happen Capacity Building Programme 1999–2003*, CASEReport 26, London: London School of Economics and Political Science.

Beck, H., Richardson, E. and Sefton, T.A.J. (2005) *Report of the Eaga Partnership Charitable Trust roundtable event: Setting a research agenda: Fuel poverty, communication and access*, London: London School of Economics and Political Science.

Beckford, J., Dougal, A., Millward, E. and Reid, B. (2003) *Encouraging participation: A toolkit for tenants and social landlords*, Coventry/York: Chartered Institute of Housing in assocaition with Joseph Rowntree Foundation.

Bennett, F. with Roberts, M. (2004) *From input to influence: Participatory approaches to research and inquiry into poverty*, York: Joseph Rowntree Foundation.

Bines, W., Kemp, P., Pleace, N. and Radley, C. (1993): *Managing social housing*, London: HMSO.

Birchall, R.J. and Simmons, R.A. (2002) *A theoretical model of what motivates public service users to participate*, Swindon: ESRC.

Blakey, H. (2004) *Usual suspects or community leaders – What's the difference?*, Bradford and Leeds: University of Bradford and Yorkshire and the Humber Regional Forum.

Blair, T. (2002) 'New Labour and community', *Renewal*, vol 10, no 2, pp 9-14.

Brett, E.A. (2003) 'Participation and accountability in development management', *Journal of Development Studies*, vol 40, no 2, pp 1-29.

Bridge, G. (2002) *The neighbourhood and social networks*, CNR Paper 4, Glasgow: ESRC Centre for Neighbourhood Research.

Bromley, C., Stratford, N. and Rao, N. (2000) *Revisiting public perceptions of local government: A decade of change?*, London: Office of the Deputy Prime Minister.

Burchardt, T., Le Grand, J. and Piachaud, D. (2002) 'Degrees of exclusion: developing a dynamic, multidimensional measure', in J. Hills, J. Le Grand and D. Piachaud (eds) *Understanding social exclusion*, Oxford: Oxford University Press.

Burrows, R. (1997) *Contemporary patterns of residential mobility in relation to social housing in England*, York: Centre for Housing Policy.

Burton, P. (2003) *Community involvement in neighbourhood regeneration: Stairway to heaven or road to nowhere?*, CNR Paper 13, Glasgow: ESRC Centre for Neighbourhood Research.

Burton, P. (2004) 'Power to the people? How to judge public participation', *Local Economy*, vol 19, no 3, pp 193-8.

Burton, P., Goodlad, R., Croft, J., Abbott, J., Hastings, A., Macdonald, G. and Slater, T. (2004) *What works in community involvement in area-based initiatives: A systematic review of the literature*, Home Office Online Report 53/04, London: Home Office.

Bynner, J. et al (2002) *Young people's changing routes to independence*, York: Joseph Rowntree Foundation.

CABESpace (Commission for Architecture and the Built Environment) (2005) *Start with the park: Creating sustainable urban green spaces in areas of housing growth and renewal*, London: CABE.

Cabinet Office (1999) *Modernising government*, London: The Stationery Office.

Cabinet Office (2002) *Private action, public benefit: A review of charities and the wider not-for-profit sector*, London: Cabinet Office.

CACI Ltd (2001) *ACORN: The complete consumer classification*, London: CACI.

CACI Ltd (2004) *ACORN user guide*, London: CACI.

Cairncross, E., Clapham, D. and Goodlad, R. (1997) *Housing management, consumers and citizens*, London: Routledge.

Cairns, B., Harris, M. and Hutchison, R. (2006) *Servants of the community or agents of government? The role of community-based organisations and their contribution to public services delivery and civil renewal*, London: Institute for Voluntary Action Research.

Centre for Civil Society (2005) *Report on activities 2002-2005*, London: London School of Economics and Political Science.

Chanan, G. (2004) *Community sector anatomy*, London: Community Development Foundation.

Chanan, G., West, A., with Garratt, C. and Humm, J. (1999) *Regeneration and sustainable communities*, London: Community Development Foundation.

Chapman, T., Brown, J., Crow, R. and Ward, J. (2006) *Facing the future: A study of the impact of a changing funding environment on the voluntary and community sector in the North East of England*, Middlesbrough: University of Teesside.

Chivite-Matthews, N.I. and Teal, J. (2001) *1998 British Social Attitudes Survey: Secondary data analysis of the local government module*, London: Department of the Environment, Transport and the Regions.

Clarson, D. (2005) Presentation to Renewal Academy course, 24 November, Luton.

Cochrane, A. (2003) 'The new urban policy: towards empowerment or incorporation', in R. Imrie and M. Raco (eds) *Urban renaissance? New Labour, community and urban policy*, Bristol: The Policy Press.

Cole, I. and Reeve, K. (2001) *Housing and physical environment domain: A review of the evidence base*, New Deal For Communities National Evaluation Scoping Phase Research Report, Sheffield: Sheffield Hallam University.

Cole, I., Hickman, P. and Reid, B. (1999) *Accounting for the uncountable: Tenant participation in housing modernisation*, Coventry: Chartered Institute of Housing.

Community Matters (2002) *The visible difference*, London: Community Matters.

Cooke, B. and Kothari, U. (eds) (2001) *Participation: The new tyranny?*, London: Zed Books.

Coulthard, M., Walker, A. and Morgan, A. (2002) *People's perceptions of their neighbourhood and community involvement: Results of the social capital module of the General Household Survey 2000*, London: The Stationery Office.

Cowell, R., Downe, J., Leach, S. and Bovaird, T. (2005) *Meta-evaluation of the local government modernisation agenda: Progress report on public confidence in local government*, London: Office of the Deputy Prime Minister.

Davis Smith, J. (1998) *National Survey of Volunteering*, London: Institute for Volunteering Research.

DCLG (Department for Communities and Local Government) (2006) *Strong and prosperous communities – The local government White Paper*, Norwich: The Stationery Office.

Dean, J. and Hastings, A. (2000) *Challenging images: Housing estates, stigma and regeneration*, Bristol: The Policy Press.

Devine, F. (2003) *A qualitative study of democracy and participation in Britain*, Swindon: ESRC.

DETR (Department of the Environment, Transport and the Regions) (1998) *Modernising local government*, London: The Stationery Office.

Docherty, I., Goodlad, R. and Paddison, R. (2001) 'Civic culture, community and citizen participation in contrasting neighbourhoods', *Urban Studies*, vol 38, issue 12, pp 2225-50.

DTI (Department for Trade and Industry) (2002) *Social enterprise: A strategy for success*, London: DTI.

DTI (2003) *Public procurement: A toolkit for social enterprise*, London: DTI.

DTLR (Department for Transport, Local Government and the Regions) (2001) *Public attitudes to directly elected mayors*, London: DTLR.

Duffy, B. (2000) *Satisfaction and expectations: Attitudes to public services in deprived areas*, CASEPaper 45, London: London School of Economics and Political Science.

Duncan, P. and Thomas, S. (2000) *Neighbourhood regeneration: Resourcing community involvement*, Bristol: The Policy Press.

Edomi, V. (2004) *Communication department structures and their impact on CPA scores*, London: IDeA.

Ekins, P. (2003) *An introduction to the ESRC New Opportunities Programme: Environment and human behaviour*, Swindon: ESRC.

Elias, N. and Scotson, J.L. (1965) *The established and the outsiders. A sociological enquiry into community problems*, London: Frank Cass & Co.

Electoral Commission (2006) *Turnout: Factsheet*, London: Electoral Commission.

ESRC (Economic and Social Research Council) (2007) *Localism and local governance*, Swindon: ESRC.

Ferguson, R.F. and Dickens W.T. (1999) 'Introduction', in R.F. Ferguson and W.T. Dickens (eds) *Urban problems and community development*, Washington, DC: Brookings Institution Press.

Foster, A. (2000) *Putting your house in order: Evaluating tenant satisfaction with improvements to social housing*, London: HM Treasury.

Freire, P. (1972) *Pedagogy of the oppressed*, Harmondsworth: Penguin.

Gains, F. (2006) *New council constitutions: A summary of the ELG research findings*, Norwich: The Stationery Office.

Gardner, H.E. (1995) *Leading minds: An anatomy of leadership*, New York, NY: Basic Books.

Garmston, R.J. and Wellman, B. (1999) *The adaptive school: A sourcebook for developing collaborative groups*, Norwood, MA: Christopher Gordon Publishers.

Gibson, T. (1996) *The power in our hands*, Oxford: Jon Carpenter Publishing.

Giddens, A. (1984) *The constitution of society: Outline of the theory of structuration*, Cambridge: Polity Press.

Giddens, A. (1993) *New rules of sociological method*, Cambridge: Polity Press.

Gilbert, T.F. (1978) *Human competence: Engineering worthy performance*, New York, NY: McGraw-Hill.

Glen, A., Henderson, P., Humm, J., Meszaros, H. and Gaffney, M. (2004) *Survey of community development workers in the UK: A report on paid and unpaid community workers*, London: Community Development Foundation.

Goodlad, R., Burton, P. and Croft, J. (2005) 'Effectiveness at what? The processes and impact of community involvement in area-based initiatives', *Environment and Planning C: Government and Policy*, vol 23, no 6, pp 923-38.

Grant, C., Pirotta, M., Ames, A. and Page, B. (2002) *The business case for communications – Why investing in good communication makes sense*, London: Office of the Deputy Prime Minister.

Grayson, J. (ed M. Walker) (1996) *Opening the window: Revealing the hidden history of tenants organisations*, Barnsley and Manchester: Northern College and TPAS.

Grootaert, C. (1998) *Social capital – The missing link?*, Social Capital Initiative Working Paper No 3, Washington, DC: The World Bank.

Hall, P.A. (1999) 'Social capital in Britain', *British Journal of Political Science*, vol 29, pp 417-61.

Halpern, D., Bates, C., Beales, G. and Heathfield, A. (2004) *Personal responsibility and changing behaviour: The state of knowledge and its implications for public policy*, London: Cabinet Office.

Hampton, K. and Wellman, B. (2003) 'Neighboring in Netville: how the internet supports community and social capital in a wired suburb', *City & Community*, vol 2, no 4, pp 277-311.

Harris, K. (2006) "'Do you live on 'ere?" Neighbouring and respect', in K. Harris (ed) *Respect in the neighbourhood*, Lyme Regis: Russell House Publishing.

Hart, L. (2005) *To have and to hold: The DTA guide to asset development for community and social enterprises*, London: DTA.

Hastings, A., McArthur, A. and McGregor, A. (1996) *Less than equal? Community organisations and estate regeneration partnerships*, Bristol: The Policy Press.

Henderson, P. (2005) *Including the excluded: From practice to policy in European community development*, Bristol: The Policy Press.

Henkel, H. and Stirrat, R. (2001) 'Participation as spiritual duty; empowerment as secular subjection', in B. Cooke and U. Kothari (eds) *Participation: The new tyranny?*, London: Zed Books.

Hills, J. (2004) *Inequality and the state*, Oxford: Oxford University Press.

Hirschman, A.O. (1970) *Exit, voice, and loyalty: Responses to decline in firms, organizations, and states*, Cambridge, MA: Harvard University Press.

HM Treasury (2002) *The role of the voluntary and community sector in service delivery: A cross cutting review*, London: HM Treasury.

HM Treasury (2004) *Exploring the role of the third sector in public service delivery and reform: A discussion document*, London: HM Treasury.

HM Treasury et al (2001) *Choosing the right FABRIC: A framework for performance information*, London: HM Treasury.

Home Office (1999) *Report of the Policy Action Team on community self-help*, London: Home Office.

Home Office (2003) *Home Office Citizenship Survey: People, families and communities*, Home Office Research Study 289, London: Home Office.

Home Office (2004a) *ChangeUp: Capacity building and infrastructure framework for the voluntary and community sector*, London: Home Office.

Home Office (2004b) *Firm foundations – The government's framework for community capacity building*, London: Home Office.

Home Office (2005a) *Together we can: Action plan part 1*, London: Home Office.

Home Office (2005b) *Home Office targets: Autumn performance report*, London: The Stationery Office.

Home Office (2006) *Respect action plan*, London: Home Office.

Home Office and Office of Government Commerce (2004) *Think smart … think voluntary sector! Good practice guidance on procurement of services from the voluntary and community sector*, London: Home Office and Office of Government Commerce.

Horton, S. and Hughes, R. (2000) *Checks and balances health check: Getting an effective organisation*, Liverpool: A Sense of Place.

Housing Corporation, The (1999/2000) *Study of tenant participation in RSLs*, Working Paper 5, London: The Housing Corporation.

Housing Corporation, The (2001) *Building on success – Three-year corporate strategy 2001-2004*, London: The Housing Corporation.

Housing Corporation, The (2003) *A charter for housing association applicants and residents*, London: The Housing Corporation.

Howarth, C., Kenway, P., Palmer, G. and Street, C. (1998) *Monitoring poverty and social exclusion: Labour's inheritance*, York: Joseph Rowntree Foundation.

ICM (2004) *Public attitudes to public services*, London: ICM.

Imrie, R. and Raco, M. (eds) (2003) *Urban renaissance? New Labour, community and urban policy*, Bristol: The Policy Press.

Independent Sector (1999) *Giving and volunteering in the United States*, Washington, DC: Independent Sector, http://www.independentsector.org/gandv/s_impo. htm

Johnston, M. and Jowell, R. (2002) 'How robust is British civil society?', in A. Park et al (eds) *British Social Attitudes: Public policy, social ties* (18th report), London: Sage Publications, pp 175-96.

JRF (Joseph Rowntree Foundation) (1999) *Voluntary sector organisations' experiences of funding*, Findings 149, York: JRF.

JRF (2003) *The relationship between social landlords and tenants' organisations*, Findings 643, York: JRF.

Katz, J.E., Rice, R.E. and Aspden, P. (2001) 'The internet, 1995-2000: access, civic involvement, and social interaction', *The American Behavioral Scientist*, vol 45, no 3, pp 5-419.

Katzenbach, J.R. and Smith, D.K. (1993) *The wisdom of teams: Creating the high-performance organization*, Boston, MA: Harvard Business School Press.

Kearns, A. (2003) 'Social capital, regeneration and urban policy', in R. Imrie and M. Raco (eds) *Urban renaissance? New Labour, community and urban policy*, Bristol: The Policy Press.

Kempson, E. (1996) *Life on a low income*, York: Joseph Rowntree Foundation.

Khan, H. and Muir, R. (2006) *Sticking together: Social capital and local government*, London: IPPR and London Borough of Camden.

Kitchen, S., Michaelson, J. and Wood, N. (2006b) *2005 Citizenship Survey: Community cohesion topic report*, London: Department for Communities and Local Government.

Kitchen, S., Michaelson, J., Wood, N. and John, P. (2006a) *2005 Citizenship Survey: Active communities topic report*, London: Department for Communities and Local Government.

Kolb. D.A. and Fry, R. (1976) 'Toward an applied theory of experiential learning', in C.L. Cooper (ed) *Theories of group process*, London: John Wiley.

Kumar, S. and Nunan, K. (2002) *A lighter touch: An evaluation of the governance project*, York: Joseph Rowntree Foundation.

Lawler, E.E. (1986) *High-involvement management*, San Francisco, CA: Jossey-Bass.

Layard, R. (2005) *Happiness: Lessons from a new science*, London: Allen Lane.

Lee, P. and Murie, A. (1997) *Poverty, housing tenure and social exclusion*, Bristol: The Policy Press.

LGA (Local Government Association) (2001a) *Role of councillors in neighbourhood management: LGA discussion paper*, London: LGA.

LGA (2001b) *Follow the leaders: A survey of local authority approaches to community leadership*, London: LGA.

Lowery, D., DeHoog, R.H. and Lyons, W.E. (1992) 'Citizenship in the empowered locality: an elaboration, a critique, and a partial test', *Urban Affairs Quarterly*, vol 28, no 1, pp 69-103.

Lowndes, V. and Wilson, D. (2001) 'Social capital and local governance: exploring the institutional design variable', *Political Studies*, vol 49, pp 629-47.

Lowndes, V., Pratchett, L. and Stoker, G. (2001) 'Trends in public participation: Part 1 – Government perspectives', *Public Administration*, vol 79, no 1, pp 205-22.

Lupton, R. (2003) *Poverty Street: The dynamics of neighbourhood decline and renewal*, Bristol: The Policy Press.

Lupton, R. and Power, A. (2002) 'Social exclusion and neighbourhoods', in J. Hills, J. Le Grand and D. Piachaud (eds) *Understanding social exclusion*, Oxford: Oxford University Press.

Lyons, W.E. and Lowery, D. (1986) 'The organization of political space and citizen responses to dissatisfaction in urban communities: an integrative model', *Journal of Politics*, vol 48, no 2, pp 321-46.

McInroy, N. and MacDonald, S. (2005) *From community garden to Westminster: Active citizenship and the role of public space*, Manchester: Centre for Local Economic Strategies.

Manion, T. (2002) Seminar on management issues by the chief executive of Irwell Valley Housing Association at the London School of Economics and Political Science, London, 8 November.

Marriot, P. (1998) *Are we doing it right? An organisational health-check for management committees of community buildings*, London: Community Matters.

Martin, S. and Bovaird, T. (2005) *Meta-evaluation of the local government modernisation agenda: Progress report on service improvement in local government*, London: Office of the Deputy Prime Minister.

Marx, K. (ed J. O'Malley, trs by A. Jolin and J. O'Malley) (1970) *Marx's critique of Hegel's philosophy of right (1843)*, Cambridge: Cambridge University Press.

Mayo, M. and Rooke, A. (2006) *Active learning for active citizenship: An evaluation report*, London: Together We Can.

Miliband, D. (2006) 'Empowerment and the deal for devolution', Keynote speech to NLGN Annual Conference, 18 January.

Mohrman, S.A., Cohen, S.G. and Mohrman, A.M. Jr (1995) *Designing team-based organizations: New forms for knowledge work*, San Francisco, CA: Jossey-Bass.

MORI (2002) *The rising prominence of liveability or are we condemned to a life of grime?*, London: MORI.

Morrison, Z. (2003) 'Cultural justice and addressing "social exclusion": a case study of a single regeneration budget project in Blackbird Leys', in R. Imrie and M. Raco (eds) *Urban renaissance? New Labour, community and urban policy*, Bristol: The Policy Press.

Mumford, K. and Power, A. (2003) *East Enders: Family and community in East London*, Bristol: The Policy Press.

NAO (National Audit Office) (2001) *Joining up to improve public services*, Report by the Comptroller and Auditor General, HC 383 Session 2001-02, 7 December, London: The Stationery Office.

NAO (2004) *Getting citizens involved: Community participation in neighbourhood renewal*, Report by the Comptroller and Auditor General, HC 1070 Session 2003-04, 25 October, London: The Stationery Office.

NCVO (National Council for Voluntary Organisations) (2006a) *The UK voluntary sector almanac 2006: The state of the sector*, London: NCVO.

NCVO (2006b) *Response to the HM Treasury / Cabinet Office Review of the Future Role of the Third Sector in Social and Economic Regeneration September 2006*, London: NCVO.

ODPM (Office of the Deputy Prime Minister) (1999) *Cross-cutting issues affecting local government*, London: ODPM.

ODPM (2000) *Housing research summary*, Evaluation of National Tenants' Training Programme No 135, London: ODPM.

ODPM (2002a) *Housing Statistics 2002* Norwich: The Stationery Office.

ODPM (2002b) *Survey of English housing provisional results: 2001-02*, Housing Statistics Summary, No 13, London: The Stationery Office.

ODPM (2002c) *Living places: Cleaner, safer, greener*, London: ODPM.

ODPM (2004a) *Making it happen: The northern way*, London: ODPM.

ODPM (2004b) *Best Value User Satisfaction Surveys 2003 / 04: General survey initial topline report*, London: ODPM.

ODPM (2005a) *Improving delivery of mainstream services in deprived areas – The role of community involvement*, Research Report 16, London: ODPM.

ODPM (2005b) *National Framework for tenant participation compacts*, London: ODPM.

ODPM and Home Office (2005) *Citizen engagement and public services: Why neighbourhoods matter*, London: ODPM.

OPM (Office for Public Management) (1999) *Models of resident controlled housing*, London: The Housing Corporation.

Page, B. (2004) 'Delivering nationally or locally?', Presentation at the Institute of Political and Economic Governance Conference, 'Public Services under Labour – a symposium and mid-term review', University of Manchester, 22 January.

Page, B. (2005) 'How can we make local community involvement work?', Presentation slides, London: MORI.

Parker, S. and Gallagher, N. (eds) (2007) *The collaborative state: How working together can transform public services*, London: Demos.

Parkin, F. (1979) *Marxism and class theory: A bourgeois critique*, Cambridge: Tavistock.

Parry, G., Moyser, G. and Day, N. (1992) *Political participation and democracy in Britain*, Cambridge: Cambridge University Press.

PAULO (2003) *National occupational standards for community development work*, Grantham: PAULO.

Pawson, H., Kearns, A. and Morgan, J. (1997) *Managing voids and difficult-to-let property: Literature review*, London: The Housing Corporation.

Pearce, J. (2003) *Social enterprise in Anytown*, London: Calouste Gulbenkian Foundation.

Pennant, R. (2005) *Diversity, trust and community participation in England: Findings 253*, London: Home Office.

Peters, B.G. and van Nispen, F.K.M. (eds) (1998) *Public policy instruments: Evaluating the tools of public administration*, Cheltenham: Edward Elgar.

Peters, T. (1989) *Thriving on chaos: Handbook for a management revolution*, London: Pan.

Policy Commission on Public Services (2004) *Making public services personal*, London: National Consumer Council.

Policy Research Initiative (2005) *Social capital as a public policy tool: Project report*, Canada: Government of Canada.

Portes, A. and Landolt, P. (1996) 'Unsolved mysteries: the Tocqueville Files II: the downside of social capital', *The American Prospect*, vol 7, no 26, 1 May-1 June.

Power, A. (1987) *Property before people: The management of twentieth century council housing*, London: Allen & Unwin.

Power, A. (1997) *Estates on the edge: The social consequences of mass housing in northern Europe*, Basingstoke: Macmillan.

Power, A. (2004) *Neighbourhood management and the future of urban areas*, CASEPaper 77, London: London School of Economics and Political Science.

Power, A. and Mumford, K. (1999) *The slow death of great cities? Urban abandonment or urban renaissance*, York: Joseph Rowntree Foundation.

Power, A. and Richardson, E. (1996) *Housing plus: An agenda for social landlords*, London: LSE Housing.

Power, A. and Richardson, E. (2001) *Stimulating community self-help: A report on Gatsby Training and Grant Programme 1996-2001*, London: LSE Housing.

Power, A. and Tunstall, R. (1995) *Swimming against the tide: Polarisation or progress on 20 unpopular council estates, 1980-1995*, York: Joseph Rowntree Foundation.

Prime, D., Zimnmereck, M. and Zurawan, A. (2002) *Active communities: Initial findings from the 2001 Home Office Citizenship Survey*, London: The Stationery Office.

Purdue, D., Razzaque, K., Hambleton, R. and Stewart, M. (2000) *Community leadership in area regeneration*, Bristol: The Policy Press.

Putnam, R.D. (2000) *Bowling alone: The collapse and revival of American community*, New York, NY: Simon & Schuster.

Radcliffe, P. et al (2001) *Breaking down the barriers: Improving Asian access to social rented housing*, Coventry: Chartered Institute of Housing.

Rallings, C. and Thrasher, M. (2002) *NDC elections: A study in community engagement*, London: Office of the Deputy Prime Minister.

Rao, N. and Young, K. (1995) 'Faith in local democracy', in D. Ahrendt, L. Brook, J. Curtice, R. Jowell and A. Park (eds) *British Social Attitudes: The 12th report*, Aldershot: Dartmouth Publishing.

Rao, N. and Young, K. (1999) 'Revitalising local democracy', in R. Jowell, J. Curtice, A. Park and K. Thomson (eds) *British Social Attitudes: The 16th report: Who shares New Labour values*, Aldershot: Ashgate Publishing.

Reid, B. and Hickman, P. (2002) 'Are housing organisations becoming learning organisations? Some lessons from the management of tenant participation', *Housing Studies*, vol 17, no 6, pp 895-918.

Reason, J. and Hayes, R. (2004) *Voluntary but not amateur: A guide to the law for voluntary organisations and community groups*, London: London Voluntary Service Council.

Richardson, E. (2004) *Summary report of a think tank on low demand for housing*, CASEReport 22, London: London School of Economics and Political Science.

Richardson, E. (2005a) 'Social and political participation and inclusion', in J. Hills and K. Stewart (eds) *A more equal society? New Labour, poverty, inequality and exclusion*, Bristol: The Policy Press.

Richardson, E. (2005b) 'User engagement in public services: policy and implementation', *Benefits*, vol 13, no 3, pp 189-97.

Richardson, E. (2006) 'Incentives and motivations for neighbourliness', in K. Harris (ed) *Respect in the neighbourhood: Does neighbourliness matter?*, Lyme Regis: Russell House Publishing.

Richardson, E. and Hills, J. (2000) *Views of the National Strategy for Neighbourhood Renewal*, CASEReport 11, London: London School of Economics and Political Science.

Richardson, E. and Le Grand, J. (2002) 'Outsider and insider expertise: the response of residents of deprived neighbourhoods to an academic definition of social exclusion', *Social Policy and Administration*, September, vol 36, no 5, pp 496-515.

Richardson, E. and Mumford, K. (2002) 'Community, neighbourhood and social infrastructure', in J. Hills, J. Le Grand and D. Piachaud (eds) *Understanding social exclusion*, Oxford: Oxford University Press.

Richardson, E. and Sefton, A.J.T. (2003) 'Assessing small community groups: what makes them tick', *Community, Work and Family*, vol 8, no 1, pp 69-92.

Roberts, J.M. and Devine, F. (2004) 'Some everyday experiences of voluntarism: social capital, pleasure, and the contingency of participation', *Social Politics*, vol 11, no 2, pp 280-96.

Rogers, B. and Robinson, E. (2004) *The benefits of community engagement: A review of the evidence*, London: Home Office.

Rossi, P.H. (1999) 'Evaluating community development programs', in R.F. Ferguson and W.T. Dickens (eds) *Urban problems and community development*, Washington, DC: Brookings Institution Press.

Ruston, D. (2001) *Social capital matrix of surveys*, London: Office for National Statistics.

Sampson, R.J. (1988) 'Local friendship ties and community attachment in mass society: a multilevel systemic model', *American Sociological Review*, vol 53, no 5, pp 766-9.

Sampson, R.J. (1999) 'What "community" supplies', in R.F. Ferguson and W.T. Dickens (eds) *Urban problems and community development*, Washington, DC: Brookings Institution Press.

Sampson, R.J. (2004) 'Neighborhood and community: collective efficacy and community safety', *New Economy*, vol 11, pp 106-13.

Schneider, A.L. and Ingram, H.M. (1997) *Policy design for democracy*, Lawrence, KA: University Press of Kansas.

Scott, S., Currie, H., Dean, J. and Kintrea, K. (2001) *Good practice in housing management: Case studies, conclusions and recommendations, Edinburgh:* Scottish Executive Central Research Unit.

Sefton, T., Byford, S., McDaid, D., Hills, J. and Knapp, M. (2002) *Making the most of it: Economic evaluation in the social welfare field*, York: York Publishing Services.

SEU (Social Exclusion Unit) (1999) *Bridging the gap: New opportunities for 16-18 year olds not in education, employment or training*, London: SEU.

SEU (2001) *A new commitment to neighbourhood renewal: National strategy action plan*, London: Cabinet Office.

Shaw, K. and Davidson, G. (2002) 'Community elections for regeneration partnerships: a new deal for local democracy?', *Local Government Studies*, vol 28, no 2, pp 8-15.

Sherif, M. (1970) *Group conflict and co-operation: Their social psychology*, London: Routledge and Kegan Paul.

Silverlock, L. (2000) *Tackling crime on estates – Community training manual*, Swindon: Crime Concern.

SJPG (Social Justice Policy Group) (2006) *Denying the vulnerable a second chance: Third Sector Working Group 'State of the nation' report*, London: SJPG.

Skidmore, P., Bound, K. and Lownsbrough, H. (2006) *Participation: Who benefits? Community participation in governance and social capital*, York: Joseph Rowntree Foundation.

Skinner, S. (1997) *Building community strengths: A resource book for capacity building*, London: Community Development Foundation.

SOCQUIT (2004) *Report of literature and data review, including conceptual framework and implications for IST*, The Netherlands: D6 SOCQUIT Consortium.

Stack, J. (1992) *The great game of business*, New York, NY: Currency Doubleday.

Stewart, M. and Taylor, M. (1995) *Empowerment and estate regeneration: A critical review*, Bristol: The Policy Press.

Stoker, G. (2005) *New localism, participation and networked community governance* Manchester: University of Manchester.

Sullivan, H., Smith, M., Root, A. and Moran, D. (2001) *Area committees and neighbourhood management: Increasing democratic participation and social inclusion*, York: Joseph Rowntree Foundation.

Taper, T. (2001) 'Citizen engagement', Paper given to the NHF Annual Conference, 'Transformations – Leading Change', 19 September.

Taylor, M. (2000) 'Communities in the lead: power, organisational capacity and social capital', *Urban Studies*, vol 37, no 5-6, pp 1019-35.

Taylor, M. (2005a) *Willing partners? Voluntary and community associations in the democratic process*, Swindon: ESRC.

Taylor, M. (2005b) 'Councillors and community advocates', Policy and Expert Workshop on Citizen Participation and Neighbourhoods at the Office of the Deputy Prime Minister, 23 May. Unpublished notes and presentation slides

Taylor, P. (2006) *Who are the capacity builders? A study of provision for strengthening the role of local communities. Summary report*, London: Community Development Foundation.

Thake, S. (1995) *Staying the course: The role and structures of community regeneration organisations*, York: York Publishing Services, for Joseph Rowntree Foundation.

Titmuss, R.M. (1970) *The gift relationship: From human blood to social policy*, Glasgow: HarperCollins.

Tocqueville, A. de and Mansfield, H.C. (eds) (2002) *Democracy in America*, Chicago, IL: University of Chicago Press.

Tunstall, R. (2000) 'The potential of participation in social policy and administration: The case of tenant management organisations in English council housing', PhD thesis, London: Department of Social Policy, London School of Economics and Political Science.

Ward, M. and Watson, S. (1997) *Here to stay: A public policy framework for community based regeneration*, London: Development Trusts Association.

Warde, A et al. (2003) 'Trends in social capital: membership of associations in Great Britain, 1991-98,' *British Journal of Political Science,* vol 33, pp 515-534.

Watson, D. (1994) *Putting back the pride: A case study of a power sharing approach to tenant participation*, Liverpool: Association of Technical Aid Centres.

Weber, M. ([1922] 1978) *Economy and society*, Berkeley, CA: University of California Press.

White, G. et al (2006) *Exemplars of neighbourhood governance*, London: Department for Communities and Local Government.

Williams, K. and Green, S. (2001) *Literature review of public space and local environments for the cross cutting review*, Oxford: Oxford Brookes University.

Wilson, R. (2005) *The true costs of public participation*, London: Involve.

Wilson, W.J. (1987) *The truly disadvantaged*, Chicago, IL: University of Chicago Press.

Young, M. and Lemos, G. (1997) *The communities we have lost and can regain*, London: Lemos and Crane.

Young, S. (2006) *Accelerator model*, Unpublished paper.

Young Foundation, The (2005) *Seeing the wood for the trees: The evolving landscape for neighbourhood arrangements*, London: The Young Foundation.

Index